IN SUNSHIN[

The family story of Danny Boy

Anthony Mann

ISBN: 978-1-300-77501-0

Copyright © 2013 Anthony Mann

All rights reserved, including the right to reproduce this book, or portions thereof in any form. No part of this text may be reproduced, transmitted, downloaded, decompiled, reverse engineered, or stored, in any form or introduced into any information storage and retrieval system, in any form or by any means, whether electronic or mechanical without the express written permission of the author.

www.publishnation.co.uk

Cover design by Scott Gaunt

Dedication

For Alec, Ethel, Betty and Marjory,
A family that might have been

Acknowledgments

I would like to thank the many members of the Weatherly family who have generously contributed photographs and useful information, so that I have been able to piece together the story of our family. Peggy Churchill and her brother Fred Weatherly gave me vital information at the outset; they were both interested in the family and I am just sad that they are no longer here to read this account. My thanks go to Jane Phillips, Margaret Bowater, Lilia Weatherly, Fiona Dostal, Trevor Churchill and Philip Weatherly. Special thanks are due to Pat Jeffreys who gave me her time, knowledge and hospitality.

I am grateful to Ann Hoffman, formerly of the Ouray Historical Society, for her hospitality and assistance and to the archivist at the University of Colorado library in Boulder for the time he gave me. Michael and Sarah Brown provided the vital connection to Durango and thence to Ouray for me. Professor Jane Ridley with her expertise in biography mentored me as I was preparing to write this research up, so that the facts are I hope appropriately organised into a narrative. Discussions with David Turner and Peter Montagnon always encouraged me when my enthusiasm was flagging.

Sources

Jane Ridley said that it was an advantage to be researching professional people of the Victorian and Edwardian periods. Their milestones tend to be documented. It was the case for Fred and his family. These were starting points for searches in national, local and professional newspapers. Fred Weatherly was sufficiently well known for him to get a mention in the autobiographies by other people of his world – music, the stage and the law. Mercifully they are indexed, so it's not necessary to plough through each of them. Internet searches turn up information on arcane topics, such as the principles of silver fox farming.

The more intimate stories of the family members have been gleaned from the letters by Herbert and Luke Weatherly to their brother Eddie and the copious writing left behind by Jess. Fred's own book of memoirs provides the structure of his life and details of his musical and legal achievements but is highly selective in the information it provides about his family life (Piano and Gown: Fred Weatherly KC, GP Putnam's Sons: 1926). Two books,obtained via the historical society, set the scene for me so that I could understand silver mining and what life was like in San Juan Mountains for those engaged in this activity. .

Chapter contents

1	Introduction
2	Opening
2	Danny Boy
3	Research Process
4	The Weatherly Family Tree
5	Fred - Oxford and London until 1910
6	Alec - career and death in 1910
7	Eddie and Jess - San Francisco and Ouray to 1911
8	Birth of Danny Boy 1910-1915
9	Herbert and Ethel - America 1915-1925
10	Fred - Bath 1915-1929
11	Eddie and Jess - Ouray 1913-1939
12	Ethel and daughters - America and England 1925-1940
13	Marjory - England 1930-1989
14	Closure – Fred - plagiarist and womaniser? Who was the real author of Danny Boy?
15	Closure - The Family Secret

1. INTRODUCTION

Fred Weatherly –an official photo.

My mother was the granddaughter of Fred Weatherly, author of the words of Danny Boy. She inherited the copyright of his works from his widow in 1941. The royalty income made a huge difference to our family life in the post-war years and to mine especially, as it paid for my education. Ungratefully perhaps, I didn't take any interest in Fred Weatherly or his songs when I was growing up – they were as far away from the music of the1960s as they could be. My mother on the other hand was proud of her grandfather, to whom she had been close as she was brought up in his house because of the early death of her father, Fred's only son.

Only recently has it become recognised again that this Englishman wrote the words of what everyone thinks to be a quintessentially traditional Irish song. Weatherly never visited Ireland; yet he managed to write words for an Irish melody, the Londonderry Air, that superseded all other versions and captured Irish hearts all over the world after its publication in 1913 to become one of the best selling songs of the twentieth century. How he managed this feat has always been a mystery, but I hope this book will throw light on that. I was shocked and saddened by the story that I discovered in archived family letters, not made public until now.

Fred Weatherly was no mean song writer – he published over 1500 during his life time, of which Danny Boy, Roses of Picardy and Holy City have been the most enduring. He is forgotten now but, at the time of his death in 1929, he was a household name because of his songs but also because of a late career as a broadcaster. A resident of Bath, he was a barrister by profession, gaining as much pleasure from his practice of law as from his writing. For a gentleman of the professional class of the period, he led a complicated and irregular personal life, details of which will emerge as I give the background to Danny Boy.

I inherited my mother's copy of Fred's memoirs, 'Piano and Gown', published in 1926, and some photos of him and of his family. While she often talked of her grandfather, she was always vague as to who everyone else was in these family photos and what happened to them. I was told little about her father who had died when she was three or about her mother. She had barely seen any of her several first cousins since childhood, telling me that she never liked them. In fact the only relative from her family I regularly met was a more distant cousin, Peggy, who had two sons of about my age but the Weatherly family was never discussed when we met. My father's family was my family.

I was thus not at all informed about or involved with Fred Weatherly and his family when my mother died in 1989, leaving me the copyright of his works. There were 30 bound volumes of his published songs, which, with many unpublished verses and opera libretti that he had written, I donated to the British Music Library.

Photos, cuttings and articles about him and others in the family I stored away. My mother's personal photos were mainly taken after her marriage but there were a couple of albums of box snaps that dated from earlier in her life. In them, many of the photos had only half remaining, showing either my mother or someone who I imagined was her mother, my grandmother. The other half of the photo had been crudely torn out. Without knowing who anybody was in the remaining photos and assuming my mother was in the process of destroying the albums, I chucked them out without thinking further. That was it, so far as my mother's family was concerned.

I was wrong. There has been a revival of interest in Danny Boy and, as part of that, in Fred Weatherly and the circumstances in which he wrote the words of the song. I was thankful that I had kept my mother's material about him. I could therefore provide some hitherto unseen photos of him for a TV programme which appeared in 1998. I was later interviewed myself for radio and TV about Danny Boy. To prepare, I read up all I could from 'Piano and Gown' and went through the newspaper cuttings that I had, adding for the interviews some snippets that I remember my mother telling me about her grandfather's character. It was during the last of these, for a TV programme produced by BBC NI that I was struck by the enthusiasm of the producer and the interviewer for the story of the song, but also by how little I actually knew. I couldn't answer quite obvious supplementary questions that followed on from Fred's brief account in his memoirs about the origin of Danny Boy, such as "Why did his son die young?" and "Who was this sister-in-law in America who sent Fred the music of Londonderry Air?" I had to ask not to be asked them in the live broadcast. The surprise at my lack of interest in finding out more about Fred and the context of Danny Boy decided me that, when I could, I would do some family research.

Coming back from the interview in Belfast, it struck me objectively for the first time how little my mother had ever told me about her parents, her childhood, about growing up in her grandfather's house and her life before marriage. For instance, she would have been living with her grandfather when Danny Boy was published - she never mentioned that, but then I never asked her either.

I began the research in 2003, little knowing that this quest for knowledge about Danny Boy would lead to information that turned upside down long held assumptions that I had made about a traumatic period in my own childhood and that would enable me to gain a new understanding and sympathy for my own mother and father.

2. OPENING

Over 300,000 soldiers were demobilised in the first two months of 1946. Most were returning from four or five years of war service overseas to a country that they must have found hard to recognise - it was poor, dotted with bombsites, short of housing and with food, alcohol and clothes rationing. Interrupted marriages had to be resumed and fathers had to get to know their children again or meet them for the first time. One of these returning soldiers was my father who had been posted to India and Burma in 1941, leaving my mother and me to spend the war in a rented house next to that of his family outside Skegness on the coast of Lincolnshire. We all went to Boston station to meet his train. There was my father, of whom at the age of five I had no memory, a small thin man in uniform whose peaked officers' hat seemed far too big for him. He had had a hard time at the end in Burma and had lost much weight.

It was not a happy homecoming. My father had to find a job, so we immediately left Skegness for Nottingham where he had spent his life before and after marriage until the war broke out. He joined his old firm but at a much lower level than that he had left five years earlier and rented a house in a gloomy suburb, which my mother hated after the light and space of a seaside house. I was not at all prepared for a father's presence in my life. As far as I was concerned he had taken me away from the house by the sea, from my aunt and grandmother and now in this new house was taking up my mother's attention. When he tried to get to know me by doing fatherly things - taking me out, bathing me, reading stories - I would resist and cry for my mother. My mother usually gave in, which can't have endeared me - or her - to him. I regularly asked him or my mother or aunt when he was going back to India, referring to him as that horrid man. It must have been intolerable for a man struggling to find his feet again and not in the best of health after the war.

Two months later in May my mother disappeared from my life. She had a nervous breakdown (which I deduced later) and, after two months in a local nursing home where I was taken to see her once, spent eighteen months in a clinic in Wales. I never saw her during that time, was told nothing other than 'she had to get well' but never what the matter was. My father arranged for me to spend the rest of the local day school summer term living with some friends of his who had a son at the same school; at the end of which I returned to my aunt and grandmother in Skegness. My grandmother was now becoming ill, so that autumn I began, aged 5, as a boarder in a prep school. I was terrified of the place, shrieked and had to be pulled off my aunt's skirt when she left me there.

These events of 1946 had a fundamental effect on me. I developed as an anxious child; afraid to step out of line for fear that my mother might leave me again. I linked my mother's absence to my father's return just before she went missing to me, thinking he must have done something to cause it; a belief that made me keep my distance from him all my childhood. My mother was never truly well for many years after return to us at Christmas time 1947. I believed it was my duty to look after her and would worry even when away at school. My mother's ill health and my reaction to it were undoubtedly influential in my choice of medicine as a career and psychiatry as a speciality. As I began my training, I realised that my mother must have had a severe depression in 1946 and that this condition had never fully resolved for many years, as she was often weepy, anxious and ill with various non-specific physical symptoms. I could also think about the cause of her illness rather more objectively -the stresses of the privations of the post-war years, making a life in Nottingham where she had no roots, having to live with a husband who had been changed by his war experiences -might have been important precipitants. A marriage that seemed to be cold, routine and distant helped to maintain it. However, I could also by then see that, being someone with persistent anxiety and depressive symptoms, she must have been difficult for my father to live with and felt for the first time some sympathy for him and could see why he might have withdrawn from her. It hit home when I read the clinical observation that a child, often a son, could be made an antidepressant by his depressed mother by being given responsibility to care for her and cheer her up.

My personality traits of conscientiousness and eagerness to please, combined with adequate brainpower, meant that my medical career progressed well. However I became aware by my late twenties that despite plaudits during my developing career as a psychiatrist, I wasn't able to get beyond friendships, of which I had many, to more intimate relationships. My friends were all pairing off. I saw myself ending up alone once my mother had died - as I saw it even more my duty to look after her, once she became a widow. I eventually turned to psychoanalysis, easy to fix up as a young psychiatrist. This process over four years undoubtedly helped me to find me and thus take a new, independent direction both professionally and sexually. I gained detachment from my mother and began to mourn my father, which I hadn't done at the time he died when I was twenty. The events of 1946 as I recounted them featured often both in the conscious and unconscious (dreams) material that was analysed. Now thirty years later, I have found that the account, and my interpretation of my parents' actions in 1946 that I returned to so often in the analysis, which were the memories of my five year old self, were mistaken. I had had nothing to contradict those assumptions until the discoveries about my mother and her family during these last few years of Danny Boy research provided me with a whole new explanation of what happened then. The psychoanalysis had helped me to detach from sad feelings about being abandoned that had been present since childhood but never of course could explain why it happened to me, because I never heard my parents' account. Any questioning of why I had too been put in boarding school at the age of 5 made my mother immediately upset and my father angry.

I have sometimes encouraged a patient to prepare a biography of a dead parent with whom they still have unresolved anger from childhood and which is thus too late to resolve face to face. The account should be objective, recording the childhood of the parent, ambitions, frustrations and life stresses, and written by an adult about another adult. The parent's apparent neglect or persecution of the child has usually an explanation when put into the context of the parent's life at the time. Seeing that the parent was contending with his or her own difficulties helps the adult patient to understand and the hurt child inside to let go. Telling my mother's story and seeing how she had been adversely affected by what happened to her own mother has had this liberating effect on me.

The main purpose of the research, the quest for knowledge of Danny Boy, was to find the story of the man behind the words and the circumstances of his writing them. From information in family letters archived in America since1936, I can report a new and moving story about the song's creation, which doesn't show Fred Weatherly in the best light. The next chapter gives the story of Danny Boy as it is told now, before my new findings are incorporated. Then, before I begin the story of Fred Weatherly and his family, I have described something about the process of learning family research and the pleasure from one of the positive results - meeting family that I never knew even existed.

From time to time during the storytelling, I will interrupt to comment on what is happening. Sometimes I will be the family member-researcher making links between then and now, noting several coincidences with my own life which have been startling. Second, I will be commenting as a psychiatrist. One of the discoveries has been that members of this family were affected by mental illness, information hidden from me, even when I declared my hand and became a psychiatrist. These illnesses had effects on others in the family and guided the fate of many of the next generation. In some cases, I have enough detail about symptoms to make a diagnosis and can compare treatments available then and with what would be offered now.

3. THE STORY OF DANNY BOY

Oh, Danny Boy, the pipes, the pipes are calling
From glen to glen, and down the mountainside.
The summer's gone, and all the roses falling.
It's you, It's you must go and I must bide.
But come ye back, when summer's in the meadow,
Or when the valley's hushed and white with snow,
It's I'll be here in sunshine or in shadow.
Oh Danny Boy, Oh Danny Boy, I love you so.

But if you come and all the flowers are dying
If I am dead, as dead I well may be,
Ye'll come and find the place where I am lying,
And kneel and say an Ave there for me,
And I shall hear, though soft you tread above me,
And all my grave will warmer, sweeter be,
For you will bend and tell me that you love me,
And I shall sleep in peace until you come to me!

Boosey and Hawkes published Danny Boy in 1913. The marriage of a haunting Irish melody the Londonderry Air, and words by the country's successful lyricist of the day, Fredrick Weatherly, proved to be rapidly popular. A recording of the song by Ernestine Schumann Heink in 1918, an American of German origin who was one of the most famous sopranos of the day, helped knowledge of Danny Boy to spread through the English speaking world. Fred Weatherly himself encouraged the young soprano Elsie Griffin (1895-1989), whose voice he admired, to make it her song. Indeed her obituary stated that she helped to make this song among the most popular of the century.

Fred Weatherly conceived Danny Boy as a song about a woman mourning a man who has gone away. However as the song was also being taken up by male singers and, to avoid any sensitivity about a man singing about another man, Weatherly proposed 'a male version' in 1918 substituting 'Eily Dear' for Danny Boy. Another potential embarrassment came from the vulgarity of repeating Londonderry Air (London derriere), so the music was often titled an 'Air from County Derry'. Neither of these pruderies lasted long. The skill of his words is such that they convey strong emotion without it being tied to a specific situation; singer and listener can imagine whomever they wish. These words of loss and reunion after death had though special resonance with Irish people and, as they were set to well known Irish air, they adopted Danny Boy. The song had special relevance at a time of mass migration from Ireland, when families were being split apart with those left behind believing that they would never again see those who had left and vice versa. Unrest against British rule was continuing in Ireland itself at the time of its publication. The words also spoke to those grieving the loss of a family member, who had died for the cause of Independence. But, the Unionist side also sang it, the pipes calling being thought to refer to the recruiting music for the British Army. Weatherly wrote in 1926 in his reminiscences 'Piano and Gown' p.279:

'However Danny Boy is accepted as an accomplished fact and is sung all over the world by Sinn Feiners and Ulsterman alike, by English as well as Irish, in America as well as the Homeland. It will be seen that there is nothing of the rebel song in it and no note of bloodshed.'

'The accepted fact' makes reference to a dismissal of Danny Boy at the time of its publication by Alfred Percival Graves, noted Irish scholar and poet, who had already written two sets of words to the melody – 'Erin's Apple Blossom' and 'Emer's Farewell'. Danny Boy had immediately superseded these in popularity. Weatherly had written to Graves saying that beautiful as Graves' words were they didn't quite fit the melody and that there was room for another version. That went down badly and their friendship was over.

Gradually Danny Boy became owned by the Irish at home and overseas, particularly in the USA where it was and is seen as part of the traditional repertoire of songs, sung on family occasions, reunions and funerals. Presumably the rubric 'traditional Irish air' always used to describe the melody was thought to cover the words as well for, after Weatherly's death in1929, his contribution was forgotten; despite his widow and descendents obtaining the royalties from the public performances of the song. Inevitably, people who loved the song would speculate about who was Danny, where he was leaving for and who was singing to him. Some thought Weatherly wrote it about his own son who had gone away to fight in the First World War. Others thought that it was about a young man emigrating to America, others about a man who had joined the Nationalists to liberate Ireland from the British .The 'Eily Dear' version was never needed as people seemed comfortable that the words were suitable for a father to sing to his son or brother to brother as well as mother to son or wife to husband or female lover to a man.

A third verse much more warlike in nature appeared and was sometimes sung as part of Danny Boy:
But should I live, and should you die for Ireland
Let not your dying thoughts be all of me
But breathe a prayer to God for our dear sireland,
That He will hear, and He will set her free.
And I will I take your place and pike, my dearest,
And strike a blow, though weak that blow may be,
To help the cause to which your heart was nearest,
And you will rest in peace until I come for thee.

This verse was finally shown not to be authentic in 2001 when a letter written by Fred to an admirer, who had congratulated him on Danny Boy, was sold at auction. In this letter, he wrote out what he called the second and final verse of the song, which was not the warlike verse. The letter was estimated at £50 but in competitive bidding was sold at £950.

Danny Boy letter, reproduced with kind permission of Philip Weatherly.

During the years after the Second World War, Danny Boy was recorded over one hundred times and included in the albums of such stars as Judy Garland, Frank Sinatra, Jackie Wilson and Elvis Presley; the latter saying that it was one of his favourite songs. It was sung at his funeral. It is unlikely that anyone making or hearing these recordings in America at this time would have known or even believed that the words of this Irish song were written by an Englishman. From the late 1980s, the song became increasingly recognised in Ireland as one that appealed to people from the North and South, thus bringing them together. Barry McGuigan, the bantamweight boxer, was steadfastly non-sectarian during his career. Born in the republic and a Catholic, married to a Protestant, he represented both Northern Ireland and Ireland at the Commonwealth Games in Edmonton and at the Moscow Olympics respectively. His supporters at the fights were drawn equally from both sides of the border. His father Pat, a well-known tenor, would lead the singing of Danny Boy before his son came on so that the entire crowd could join in. John Hume, the leader of the Northern Irish Social and Liberal Democratic Party was another enthusiast of the song. A key player in the peace process in Ireland for more than twenty years, he used the song to bring the opposing politicians together and, having a good voice, he would lead the singing. Indeed he believed that Danny Boy could become a symbol one day of a united Ireland, even its national anthem. Such an occasion was on St Patrick's Day in the White House in 2000 when President and Mrs Clinton joined him in singing Danny Boy along with the then Taoiseach, Bertie Ahern, David Trimble and other politicians. President Clinton was challenged to prove that he knew the words and did. The Clintons sang the song again with a huge crowd in front of the Town Hall in Dundalk on his last visit to Ireland as President in December 2000.

Maybe because of this publicity, the last ten years has seen a new interest in the origin and the meaning of the song. The Londonderry Air itself has been researched. The most scholarly account is by Brian Audley, then of the University of Ulster, published in the Journal of the Royal Musical Association in 2000. There are several inconsistent accounts of the Air's origin as there is no documentation; most information comes from family stories, passed through several generations. The Air was first published in 1855 by George Petrie who was the first President of the Society for the Preservation and Publication of the Melodies of Ireland, whose purpose was to collect, classify and publish Irish music and songs. People were invited to send into Dublin copies of any material they had. When Petrie published the tune, it was called 'An Anonymous Air' and was a piano arrangement. The person who sent it in was Jane Ross of Limavady, a member of a family interested in collecting Irish folk music. One story is that she heard the Air being played on a fiddle outside her house on the main street of the town by an itinerant fiddler, asking him to keep playing until she had correctly memorised it. Another story is that she heard her brother whistle the tune, asked him where he heard it and travelled to a mountain cabin where she heard a very old man playing. This man told her that his father's father had got it from a harpist. The collection of the tune by Jane Ross was thought to be in 1853.

Before that date, the story of the music is imprecise and perhaps fanciful. The original composer of the Air is unknown, but it may have been a blind harpist Rory Dall O'Cahan living in the early seventeenth century. The tune may then have been promulgated during the eighteenth century by a long living blind itinerant harpist Denis O'Hampsey who did pass the tune on to a young musician Edward Bunting who was collecting Irish harp music in the 1790s. O'Hampsey died at the age of 112 in 1807, so couldn't have been the person who played to Jane Ross while she annotated. That honour may belong to yet another blind musician, a fiddler Jimmy McCurry. Bunting's papers were lost to view until they were discovered in a music shop in 1910, so the version published by Petrie became that recognised.

A question arose as to whether the tune was in fact that old, as its structure wasn't in keeping with a traditional Irish folk form. An article in the Times in January1935 lists these discrepancies, the most important being that the Air is in four-four time rather than three-four that fits to most Gaelic verse form. A hypothesis published by an Ann Gilchrist in 1934 is cited, which suggested that Jane Ross wrote the tune down wrongly, but in the process of doing this, had evolved the tune to a new beauty. The article concludes that folk music owes its character to the operation of trial and error and is moulded by the oral tradition but rarely can 'sheer mistakes have achieved so striking a result'. However in 1979, Hugh Shields published his findings from the Bunting papers now in the library of Trinity College Dublin. Among them he found a tune called 'A Young Man's Dream', which was very close to the version noted by Jane Ross. According to this finding, the tune wasn't a wrongly transcribed Irish folk song but one with a different root.

Charles Stanford, Frank Bridge and Percy Grainger made orchestral arrangements of the Air and several sets of words were put to it. The earliest is thought to be 'The Confession of Devorgilla', with the first lines - 'O shrive me father - haste, haste and shrive me'. Alfred Percival Graves' attempts, 'Erin's Apple Blossom' and 'Emer's Farewell to Cucullain', and Kathleen Tynan's 'The Irish Love Song' were all published but never became the run away success that was to be Danny Boy's fate.

Fred Weatherly has begun to be resurrected as part of this new interest. The BBC broadcast two radio programmes; 'Up from Somerset' and 'The Man of a Thousand Songs' in the 1980s. This told his life story based upon his memoirs 'Piano and Gown'. A TV programme (1995), entitled 'Sunshine and Shadow' was devoted to the song itself, with numerous artists, including Eric Clapton, Marianne Faithful and Van Morrison singing or playing their version of it. Jim Hunter, another Ulster expert on the song, was the narrator, describing the history of the Air. He then moved on to Fred Weatherly, reading the account from Fred's memoirs of how the words met the music:

'In 1912 a sister-in-law sent me the 'The Londonderry Air'. I had never heard the melody or even heard of it. By some strange oversight Moore had never put words to it, and at the time I received the MS, I did not know that anyone else had done so. It so happened that I had written in March of 1910 a song called 'Danny Boy', and re-written it in 1911. By lucky chance it only required a few alterations to make it fit that beautiful melody.'('Piano and Gown' p 278).

Hunter comments that 1910 was the year that Weatherly lost his father, a West Country doctor and his only son, an actor, within three months of each other and maybe that these deaths coloured the verses that he first wrote in 1910. He also reported that Fred's brother, Edward,had emigrated to the United States, to Colorado, where he married a Margaret Anastasia Enright, whom he postulates as being the sister-in-law who sent the manuscript of the music to Fred. There were many Irish migrants in Colorado working in the gold and silver mines and he felt that Margaret Weatherly would have heard the Air being played by them. This programme was widely aired in the USA and the accompanying DVD a good seller. A TV programme produced by BBC Northern Ireland of Irish ballads sung by Brian Kennedy, in which I was intervened, led to more information on Fred Weatherly becoming disseminated.

It was thus now becoming public again that Danny Boy was not a traditional Irish song but the words were written by an Englishman. In the main, this did not affect the Irish-American community's affection for the song. It has been traditionally sung at funeral wakes, but many families have also wanted it included in the funeral mass itself. These requests were becoming sufficiently common that the singing of Danny Boy has been formally banned by the church authorities at masses in the Catholic diocese of Rhode Island and formally discouraged in the archdioceses of New York and Boston. However this ruling has caused outrage in some quarters; Danny Boy has been particularly taken as their own by members of the fire and police services, many of whom are Irish-American. It was sung at many of the firemen's funerals after 9/11.

Following 'Sunshine and Shadow', some critical comments appeared in the American press, such as this in the Milwaukee Sentinel: 'No Danny Boy: Out of haze of ambiguity emerges one clear fact; the song's about as Irish as the Queen of England'. Others wrote that the song was depressing and/or schmaltzy and should not be seen as an Irish ballad. In March 2008, covering St Patrick's Day, the owner of Foley's bar and restaurant, near the Empire State Building, banned the singing of Danny Boy for the whole month in his premises on the grounds that it is overplayed, depressing and not even Irish. He explained to the newspapers: 'On karaoke nights, everybody thinks, whatever race, creed or colour, that, after 3 pints of Guinness, you're entitled to get up there and butcher the song'. His action was sufficiently shocking for the owner to be profiled in newspapers around the world and to be asked for interviews by Associated Press, television and radio stations. In opposition to him, a bar in Michigan arranged Danny Boy to be sung over 1000 times in 3 days around St Patrick's Day. As a result of this criticism, when the ban was over, the owner of Foley's bar arranged for an Irish tenor to come to sing Danny Boy to show that business was back to usual. Danny Boy remains embedded in the Irish-American community and the recognition of the English Fred Weatherly as author hasn't affected this.

4. THE RESEARCH PROCESS

In this chapter I have tried to recreate the process of discovery of this family, but I fear I cannot recapture how exciting it was to trace an unknown cousin who could provide me with new family photographs and stories. Each seemed to know a fragment about the Weatherlys and assembling these enabled me to build up quite a comprehensive story.

The family group, Hillside porch ca 1880. Left to Right- Fred with Minnie seated, Alec in sailor suit and two daughters Gertrude, Cecil seated, Eddie, Dr Weatherly. Mrs W seated, Elsie, Alfred, Herbert, Lionel and Maude seated with daughters.

First I put together what I knew. I had Fred's memoirs, cuttings, details of his funeral in Bath Abbey and obituaries to tell me about his life, but there are only a few references to his family in them. This group taken outside his parent's house in Portishead was thus very important, being all I had about Fred's immediate relatives. My mother's information about them was as follows:

Fred is on the left holding his head. He was born in 1848, my mother thought he was in his thirties in the photo, thus dating this photo to the 1880s. His wife Minnie is seated; she, according to my mother, had to be put away when, in her 50s, she became very strange. My mother never knew her, for a friend of Fred's called Maude Francfort moved into his house in Bath to look after Fred and help raise my mother. The boy with the sailor outfit is Alec, my mother's father, who died when she was 3; his sisters Muriel and Christine are with him. Aunt Muriel turned out to be a very dominant woman who had a big hand in my mother's upbringing but to whom she never felt close. The younger sister was known as Aunt Bee and was a much gentler character but lived under her sister's thumb. Fred's parents are in the middle; his father was the General Practitioner in Portishead where this photograph is taken; his wife is seated in front. My mother would comment that she looked worn out having all those children – there were thirteen pregnancies in all. Next to Dr Weatherly is Eddie who, according to my mother, went to South America to mine for sapphires and was always asking Fred for money. The boy in the Eton collar is the youngest, Tommy, who went sheep farming in New Zealand. The parson was Alfred, who became Rector of Weeley in Essex. He married late to a much younger woman and had four children, one of whom was Peggy, the only cousin we met. Peggy was in fact first cousin to my mother's father but was a few years younger than my mother. The two women and the half hidden man were never given names as she could not remember who they were. The man on the right is Lionel, whom she called the ugly one, was a nerve specialist but my mother knew nothing of his wife and children. There was another brother called Herbert apparently who bred silver foxes in New York State.

This was, looking back, a very inaccurate account of an interesting family group, surprising as she grew up in Fred's house, where she would have heard him talk about his family and must have met some of them. This account was never elaborated on from when I first saw the photograph. I had assumed that Lionel was a neurologist, so was very surprised to see his name in an article in the British Journal of Psychiatry in1990 about the development of community psychiatry, listed as one of the pioneers of this movement to care for mentally ill patients outside asyla and in their own homes as far as possible. There was a book by him in our Institute library, 'A Plea for the Insane', published in 1919.It contained his arguments for the need for early diagnosis and the importance of the family doctor in this respect. He wrote about the damaging effect of institutional care. Both these views were prescient of attitude and policy changes about fifty years later. His obituary in 1940 in the BMJ indicted that he was a distinguished man in his field, President of the medico- psychological section of the BMA in1934 and co-founder of the London Medical Society. As a sideline he was a magician, using this expertise to debunk the contemporaneous fashion for séances and spiritualism, writing a book with Henry Maskelyne, the most famous magician of the day, on the subject. After finding all this out, I was surprised that my mother never told me about him, particularly when I had taken up psychiatry. But then, in contrast to my medical training, she had asked no questions about where and what I was doing as a psychiatrist, which I read as disappointment that I had chosen a subject that to her generation was disreputable. Later I found that there was a whole lot in her experience that would have coloured her view about the speciality.

She told me even less about her own father and mother. Her father Alec had left Oxford where he was studying law to go on the stage. There was a falling out with Fred as a consequence. He died in 1910 in his thirties; she had a copy of a funeral card with a photograph. What happened in his career in between she claimed she didn't know but I sensed that her father was something of a black sheep. Her mother was called Ethel, which my mother invariably said was a silly name, the maiden name was Balcombe and her father was a solicitor in Sussex. Her mother died shortly after my parents got married. I did often push for more information about Ethel, particularly when my mother let out that she had gone to visit her in Richmond, Virginia in 1929. She was out there when Grandfather Fred died. I thought this trip sounded very interesting, but my mother claimed that she couldn't remember why her mother was in America so there was nothing else she could tell me about her, that it was all a long time ago.

My mother was brought up by Fred in Bath with Maude Francfourt running the house; her best friend with whom she went to day school was Maude's great niece, Miriam Ford with whom she kept up all her life. I got to know Miriam quite well - she was convinced that Fred had married her great-aunt but my mother was adamant that he didn't. Otherwise my mother was thrown into the charge of her Aunt Muriel who had married well and had a large house in Clifton outside Bristol. She had 6 children, who were my mother's first cousins. The time spent at her aunt's house left a lasting, negative legacy as my mother had little good to say about her aunt who frightened her and she had nothing to do with her cousins once she had grown up, claiming that she always felt excluded and patronised by them. Maude became bed-bound and a nurse companion, Miriam, moved in to help. After Maude's death, Fred married Miriam, a much younger woman, as his second wife. My mother got on well with Miriam who became my godmother but she died when I was a baby.

As with the photograph, this is very sketchy. In truth, I had little idea of my mother's life before marriage – not through want of enquiry on my part. I now realise that vagueness and evasions were deliberate to keep her secrets.

My next step was to contact the cousin Peggy whom I knew. She was by now in her late eighties. Peggy had been immensely fond of my mother as she made plain to me when talking to her some fourteen years after my mother had died. I pumped her for what she knew of Fred, my mother's parents and childhood, and the fate of the others in the family photo who would be her uncles and aunts. Peggy told me about Fred visiting her family in Weeley Rectory and of going to stay with Lionel, the psychiatrist, in Bournemouth. Because my mother was seven years older than she, the two of them did not become friends until the 1930s when they both had grown up. Peggy never visited Bath when my mother was a child there. Thus she could tell me nothing about my grandfather Alec but did say that his wife Ethel had been an actress. Fred apparently did not approve of Ethel and, on a visit to Weeley, told Peggy's mother that he found Ethel common, didn't want her to bring up my mother and so 'sent her packing' to America to housekeep for his fox farmer brother. Peggy had no details of Ethel's stay there but confirmed that my mother did go for a visit but it was after her return that the two became friends. Then she dropped a bombshell. She referred in passing to Marjory (my mother) and Betty. I asked, "Who was Betty?" Silence. Then 'I've let the cat out of the bag; I promised your mother that I never would. How will I ever face her?' My first reaction was that Peggy was muddling us up with another family as I replied that my mother didn't have a sister. But she did. Betty was my mother's older sister who had become mentally ill on the trip to America with my mother, causing my mother and grandmother Ethel to return home together with her. There was a big scandal for the family because Betty caused a disturbance on the sea journey home by running round the ship's dining room naked. On arrival, Betty was admitted straight into hospital, Peggy thought in Virginia Water. She didn't leave hospital. Peggy never met Betty before the American visit and never saw her in hospital afterwards. She thought Betty had been a wild child and very much dominated my mother, her younger sister. Neither Ethel nor my mother ever wanted to talk about her when Peggy visited them regularly during the 1930's, so Peggy knew nothing about her illness. When it came to my mother marrying in 1938, my father apparently was not to know about Betty, so she and Miriam Ford were sworn to secrecy, being the only of her friends that he met. My father only found out when Betty died sometime after the war and official papers arrived at the house for my mother who was next of kin. He apparently was furious with my mother for not telling him and told her that she was mad to have done such a thing. However my mother was adamant that I should never know, so the secrecy now included my father as well as the other two. I could get nothing more about Betty from Peggy who had become distressed about breaking her word. All I could do was to thank her and tell her that she had done the right thing.

I was pole-axed by this information. I racked my brains to see if there was any occasion when my mother had actually told me that she was an only child. I couldn't remember her exactly saying that, so it must have been that because no aunts or uncles were ever mentioned on my mother's side, alive or dead, I assumed there weren't any. How on earth had she managed to keep this secret from me all these years? My father's family didn't know, nor did any of her friends in Nottingham for it would have leaked out to me after her death. One way she had managed was never to talk about her family or early life or if pushed providing only scant information. On one occasion I remember her shutting me up by telling me that it was none of my business. We never saw any of her family, other than Peggy, so there was no other possible leak. Then I remembered the torn photographs in the albums that I had thrown out. She must have torn out Betty from photographs with either my mother or grandmother in America. There were a couple of letters from Fred to her among the papers my mother left that had a piece torn out – were these references to Betty? I scoured all the other material. Then I found, in the report of Fred's funeral in Bath Abbey ,a long list in small print of about a hundred names of the people who had sent flowers. Listed were Ethel, Betty and Marjory, who must have arranged for a wreath to be sent while they were in the States. My mother had missed this, as did I when I had glanced through the list before. It was my first factual evidence of Betty's existence, confirming Peggy's story.

The psychiatrist in me kicked in. What would have been wrong with Betty - likely to be psychosis given her out of control behaviour on the boat, followed by institutionalisation for the rest of her life? I had a lead to follow - Virginia Water Hospital; maybe they might still have case notes? To avoid stigma, Ethel and my mother must have decided to airbrush Betty out of their daily lives, even if they privately went to visit her in hospital. When my mother came to marriage, their anxiety must have been high, given the unusual step of swearing two close friends to secrecy. The 1930s were still in the time when families with mental illness among its members were regarded as tainted and a risk to marry into - for the children of the marriage might be affected. It must have thus been an unsavoury piece of news when I told her I was taking up psychiatry and her lack of interest in my career from that point might be explained. I just wonder if she could have seen my career choice as a perverse retribution for what she had done. She must have felt considerable guilt at denying Betty's existence in the family. I was now hooked into this research and determined to find out as much about Betty as I could and their trip to America.

I next telephoned Peggy's younger brother Fred, known as Petey in the family. I had only met him once before because he had lived for most of his life in Penang. He also remembered Fred visiting his family and gave me a character sketch; Fred had helped pay for his schooling. He told me that there was another Weatherly brother, Luke, who lived in San Francisco who used to send him comics from there, of which he was very appreciative. He never met Luke. Herbert the fox farmer had arrived drunk to stay at his father's rectory and had a terrible row with his father that he could hear from his bedroom upstairs. He had no knowledge of the Bath set up, of the women there or of my mother growing up and had no idea that my mother had a sister - Peggy kept her word even in her family.

I made an error in not going to see Peggy and Petey instead of talking on the phone. A professional researcher would have gone immediately with recorder and interviewed them systematically, going through all the family members in turn. I should have asked to be shown all the Weatherly material they had and noted their comments and/or interpretations of it. They both had known Fred in person, crucial witnesses but in their eighties. Both have died since. I am sure I could have learnt much more from them, but it was early days for me and I didn't know the ropes.

Petey copied to me several newspaper cuttings about Fred. There were two about others. One was a report of the drowning at Bournemouth in 1935 of Edith Somerset, daughter of Lionel Weatherly. She had walked into the sea in winter fully clothed – didn't sound like an accident. The other was the December 7 1934 obituary of Edward Weatherly of Ouray, Colorado, married to Margaret Enright. It was this obituary that was quoted in the 1997 film; Petey having sent the cutting in to the producer. This obituary perhaps was my starting point to find out about the American sister-in-law Fred cites as sending him the manuscript of the music. The obituary came from the Durango Herald and Ouray Plaindealer. It begins in style:

"E C Weatherly answers the call of death. E C Weatherly, doctor, editor, mining authority and outstanding citizen of Ouray died at his home at 10'clock. Had he lived until next June he would have been 80."

This was the one my mother had identified in the family photo as mining sapphires in South America - confusion or obfuscation, I wondered. I had to look up Ouray and Durango in an atlas finding them in the San Juan Mountains in South-western Colorado, looking as though they were several thousand feet up. I tried to make contact with the Durango paper to see if they had more material on the Weatherlys but I received no response from e-mails or phone messages.

A coincidence now occurred. At dinner with some American friends, the conversation turned to visits to the US; Michael and Sarah our hosts describing their upcoming trip to the West Coast, which would include a visit to Durango to see family. On explaining my interest in the place and the difficulties with the Durango Herald, Sarah said that I was in luck because her cousin was the current owner of the paper.

Contact with the owner led to an introduction to the Ouray Historical Society and its chairman, Ann Hoffman. I was launched. Ann told me that she had heard, but hadn't yet verified, that a collection of papers of the Weatherlys was in the Archives of the University of Colorado at Boulder. I immediately checked and the archivist there confirmed that there was indeed a collection - 31 boxes, lodged in 1936 but not catalogued until 1964. He sent the catalogue to me. Five boxes were of personal papers, letters and photographs; the rest contained papers on silver production, mining economics and lists of mining claims. In the front, Margaret Weatherly was described by the cataloguer as a poet and visionary.

This couple were now intriguing and a visit to Colorado necessary. The boxes, I was to discover, turned out to contain numerous letters written during the 1920s from Herbert and Luke Weatherly to Eddie in which they discuss not only their own lives but the family in England and the doings of my mother and Betty in America. Herbert was a man of strong opinions with a mordant view of the motives of other; his letters are a good read. He gives a graphic account of the onset of Betty's mental illness. Eddie's wife, Margaret, wrote profusely - verses, draft letters that seemingly weren't sent and long introspective pieces. Among her notes, I found her account of the creation of Danny Boy, confirming that she was indeed the sister-in-law to whom Fred had referred, but did not confirm his account in Piano and Gown of how the words met the music. It was these contemporaneous letters that have both brought this generation of Weatherlys to life and enabled me to tell a new story of Danny Boy.

Internet searches on Fred Weatherly, Danny Boy, Roses of Picardy and Holy City produced thousands of web pages in response. Most were about recordings of the songs and speculative pieces about their meaning. One concerned 'Holy City' and inferred that Fred was a mason, furthermore linking him to Jack the Ripper through Michael Maybrick, whose nom de plume was Stephen Adams the composer of the music of many of Fred's songs. With the Weatherly family notice board - a facility for those seeking information about people called Weatherly - I had another piece of luck. There was a note from a lady in New Zealand saying that her cousin was the great-niece of Fred Weatherly and that she, the cousin, would like to hear from any other relatives. I was thus put in touch with Margaret who is the granddaughter of Tommy, the boy in the Eton collar in the photograph. His real name was Cecil Octavius Weatherly (the eighth son). He didn't go to New Zealand as my mother said but his only son Jim did, sent by his parents at the age of 18 to make a living there. Jim had done well in farming, married happily and had five children including Margaret. Margaret herself was a psychotherapist in Auckland. She copied to me the family photos that she had of her parents and grandparents, of Luke Weatherly (missing from the family photo) and of Freda Weatherly, daughter of Herbert in front of the fox farm in New York. She also sent photos of a couple whom she had labelled as Dr and Mrs Weatherly, parents of Cecil. The trouble was that they weren't the same couple as in the family photo with all the children, which Margaret had never seen. This had to be sorted out. I later worked out that they were of Mrs Weatherly's brother and his wife, the Fords of Bristol.

Margaret made an important introduction for me to Pat whom she had met on trips to England while exploring Portishead. Pat, a keen genealogist, belonged to another stream of the Weatherly family being descended through one of Dr Weatherly's brothers. She had already collected much information about the family through the Family Record Office, census data and searches in the Ealing area where the Weatherly family were living until the mid nineteenth century. She had traced back to a Ralf Weatherly in 1564. All this she generously shared with me providing copies of some birth and death certificates relating to my bit of the family. One of these showed that my grandfather, Alec, had married twice divorcing his first wife to marry my grandmother Ethel who was aged 20.

I owe a lot to Pat who taught me the basics of family research. It was necessary to search out more birth marriage and death certificates and wills; with her guidance I spent productive and enjoyable times in the Family Record Office then in Islington and in Holborn searching for wills. Together we went through local newspaper archives in Bath and then in Weston looking at those papers that covered Portishead. Both were laborious tasks; the Bath papers were on microfiche upon which it is impossible to concentrate for long and the Portishead papers were the original broadsheets, which, because of their fragility, had to be turned slowly page-by-page. Pat generously gave her time to help me trawl through them. Another coincidence emerged through this new friendship. Her husband Anthony is a lawyer and photographer; his father was in charge of the pathology laboratories at Ruthin Castle in North Wales, then the clinic where my mother became a patient in 1946. He would have taken blood specimens from her!

I now had some information on all Fred's brothers, save Arthur. I knew that Luke was not one of the six featuring in the family photo. The half hidden one in the family photo could be Herbert, the fox farmer, or Arthur.The latter, I discovered, was yet another doctor who became a missionary, working and dying young in Bengal. His widow and four children returned to Portishead where the local papers reported her going to events with Minnie Weatherly, Fred's discarded wife. Their son Christopher joined the Indian army also dying young when in service. He had one son John whom Pat had managed to trace through his school records. His wife was called Lilia; they had immigrated to Tasmania. He was another doctor.An internet search for John and Lilia Weatherly turned up Lilia who was a noted rosarian in Australia, a breeder of new strains. I got into touch with her to discover that John who had died recently was in fact a psychiatrist with responsibility for the administration of services for the mentally ill around Hobart.

I had a few years ago been invited to Hobart where I had given a lecture at the hospital where John was based. He was probably in the audience, but he couldn't have guessed any link to him because I'm not called Weatherly. It was another coincidence though. I have absolutely no idea if my mother knew of these relatives that I was turning up - I assume not.

I had another trip to Australia coming up, so visited Lilia outside Hobart. She showed me her family photographs including one of

Arthur, which indicated that the half hidden brother was not he but Herbert. Luke and Arthur were the missing brothers. In her house, Lilia had two pieces of antique oak furniture which came she said from the Weatherly house in Portishead. One was a carved oak chair. I then produced the family photo which I had copied to give her and we discovered that it was the chair that Minnie was sitting on in it, taken some 120 years ago. Lilia filled me in as far as she could on the children of Arthur's three daughters. I chased up her leads to discover three general practitioners and a heart surgeon among them.

My search for Lionel's descendants was less successful. The report of Edith Somerset's death said that her husband had been the son of Lord Henry Somerset of the Beaufort family. I found Edith and her husband listed with children and grandchildren in Burke's peerage. Eventually, I spoke on the phone to one of these grandchildren who was thus Lionel's great-granddaughter. Edith's death was a scandal in the family, never discussed when she was growing up, so she had no sense of belonging to the Weatherly family, had no current information and was not keen to be contacted again. I did find out from her that Edith and husband ran a nursing home in Hastings, which was inherited by my informant's parents. It was sold with all records and papers in the 1960s. There was nothing of Lionel's in her possession.

I was hopeful my mother's aunt Muriel's grandchildren, my second cousins, might be a source of information about my immediate family. In fact when I met Jane, I discovered that she had never heard mention of Alec, Muriel's brother, when she was a child. So far as she was concerned Christine was her grandmother's only relative.She had been told as a child that there was another side of the family where the royalties went. Having met Peggy and her brother, she knew about my mother and me, but it sounded that the distance between my mother and her cousins was maintained reciprocally.

At the family records office, I found Betty's birth and death certificates, the former indicated that she was born four months after Alec's second marriage - was this the source of the estrangement between father and son? Betty died in Camberwell in 1946. Another shock as she was in a psychiatric hospital, I assumed she must have been in the Maudsley, located in that borough, where I had trained and worked. This would have been too much. However the full death certificate revealed that she died in Camberwell House, a private hospital round the corner from the Maudsley, which closed in the late 1950s.

I was coming to admire my mother's sang-froid. As well as becoming a psychiatrist, I had made my career in Camberwell - Betty must have seemed to be haunting her. I was keen to trace Betty's body - her burial or cremation must have been difficult for my mother to arrange from Nottingham in the face of my father's hostility. I traced her to Alperton Cemetery, Wembley where she is buried with my grandmother.

Ringing around cemeteries asking to look at records to see if a certain person was buried there is time consuming and irritating. No one will check for you, so it means a visit in person fitting in with restricted access hours. On my fourth attempt, a kind person working in Brent took pity on me saying that it would take me months and leave it to her. A few hours later, she rang back to say 'Bingo!' She had found the grave in Wembley where Betty was buried with her mother. I found the visit there very moving, particularly when I was shown a blank piece of land. Apparently the cross on it had collapsed and, because my mother hadn't replied to letters about the situation, the authorities had the grave cleared. I had to pay to 'take over' the grave before I could have a small tablet with Ethel and Betty's names installed there.

While I was in the middle of all this, Gilles Gousset of the Picardy Historical Society contacted me. He was researching 'Roses of Picardy' in advance of a celebration in his region for the centenary of the Entente Cordiale. A new rose – 'The Rose of Picardy' - was to be baptised and hence his wish to write the story of that song. I could by then fill him in about Fred Weatherly and wrote a piece about him for the programme for the ceremony, attended by the Duchess of Gloucester in the gardens of the Abbe de Valloire. He in turnprovided me with something remarkable, a short film of Fred Weatherly he had discovered in the Pathe film archive - somewhere I had not thought to look. This film is silent, made in Fred's garden in Bath and lasts three minutes. It was made to celebrate his 80th birthday in 1928 and would have been shown as an additional news item between main features in the cinema. I hoped to pull off a double by contacting the BBC to see if any recording of Fred's broadcasts during the 1920s were still extant. They weren't but they sent me copies of the Radio Times showing dates and contents of the broadcasts.

To write the story of this family, I have had to inform myself about William Gladstone, the aesthetic movement at Oxford, freemasonry, the musical life in 1880s London, the Victorian theatre, in particular the life of Ellen Terry, the US dollar and the silver standard, silver mining in the San Juan mountains, silver fox farming, as well as mental hospitals and psychiatric treatments of the day. This is a testament to the varied and interesting lives of this family.

5. FAMILY TREE

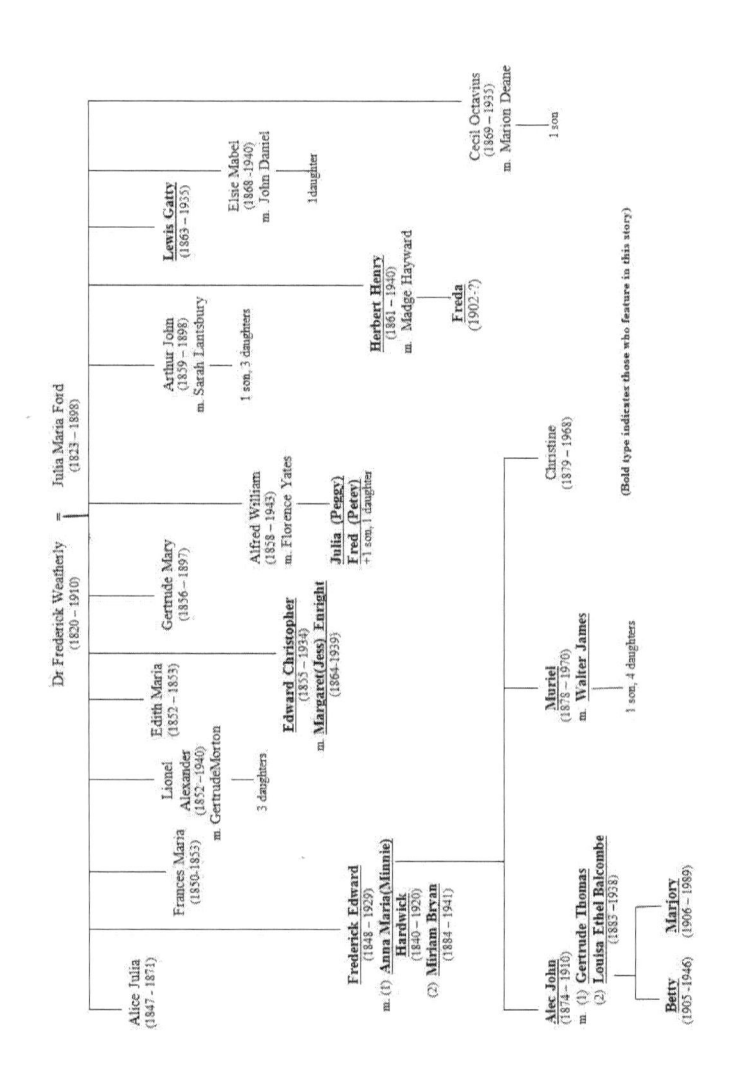

Dr Frederick Weatherly = Julia Maria Ford
(1820 – 1910)   (1823 – 1898)

- Alice Julia (1847 – 1871)
- Frances Maria (1850-1853)
- Edith Maria (1852 – 1853)
- Lionel Alexander (1852 – 1940) m. Gertrude Morton
  - 3 daughters
- Gertrude Mary (1856 – 1897)
- **Edward Christopher** (1855 – 1934) m. **Margaret (Jess) Enright** (1864-1939)
  - Alfred William (1858 – 1943) m. Florence Yates
    - **Julia (Peggy)**
    - **Fred (Peter)**
    - +1 son, 1 daughter
  - Arthur John (1859 – 1898) m. Sarah Lauusbury
    - 1 son, 3 daughters
  - **Lewis Gatty** (1863 – 1935)
  - Elsie Mabel (1868 – 1940) m. John Daniel
    - 1 daughter
  - **Herbert Henry** (1861 – 1940) m. Madge Hayward
    - **Freda** (1902-?)
  - Cecil Octavius (1869 – 1935) m. Marion Deane
    - 1 son

Frederick Edward (1848 – 1929)
m. (1) Anna Maria (Minnie) Hardwick (1840 – 1920)
(2) **Miriam Bryan** (1884 – 1941)

- Christine (1879 – 1968)
- Muriel (1878 – 1970) m. Walter James
  - 1 son, 4 daughters
- Alec John (1874 – 1910)
  m. (1) Gertrude Thomas
  (2) Louisa Ethel Balcombe (1885 – 1938)
  - Betty (1905 -1946)
  - Marjory (1906 -1999)

(Bold type indicates those who feature in this story)

The fate of the other children of Dr and Mrs Weatherly was largely an unsuccessful one -particularly the five daughters. Two died in infancy. Alice, said to have inherited her mother's musical talent, was Fred's favourite and died aged 24, while Gertrude remained a spinster living with her parents. She is in the family photograph between Fred and Eddie. She was an accomplished linguist and did charitable works in Portishead. Elsie, also in the photo, married John Daniels; they had one child who died when a baby. John Daniels claimed to be an inventor but made a living repairing clocks and musical instruments. Unfortunately he was alcoholic. John and Elsie also tried it in America in 1910 but soon returned to England. Fred supported Elsie financially until his death.

Alfred became a respected parson, being Rector of Weeley in Essex for most of his life. Arthur became a medical missionary dying relatively young in India. Luke emigrated to the USA, settling in San Francisco, where he had a cigar selling franchise, Cecil (Tommy) became a lawyer then an unsuccessful businessman - Fred helped pay for the education of both Alfred's and Cecil's children.

The descendents who provided information were:
a. Jane, Fred's great-granddaughter
b. Lionel's great-granddaughter
c. Trevor and Philip, Alfred's grandsons
d. Lilia, Arthur's granddaughter in law, Tasmania
e. Margaret, Cecil's granddaughter, New Zealand

6. FRED WEATHERLY

Fred Weatherly (1847-1929) has largely been forgotten today. Yet at the end of his life he was one of the best known men in England through his writing of a myriad of songs that captured the affection of the middle classes and later his regular BBC broadcasts. He is said to have been the most prolific lyricist of all times - over 3000 songs written and 1500 published. He was called the Grand Old Man of Song and even the People's Laureate.

Fred's book of reminiscences, 'Piano and Gown', tells of his life but its focus is on song writing and his successes as a barrister. This book is the obvious start point to understanding him, as he is central to the family story that follows. What does it tell us about him as a man? Reading the reminiscences, one gains the impression of a good-natured man, who saw the law as his primary identity but who was pleased with the success of his songs, while downplaying any talent required to write them. He came across many famous people as friends or acquaintances and he enjoys telling the reader about them. Contemporary newspaper articles and his obituaries invariably refer to his good humour, blithe spirit or love of humanity. The good humour extended in late life to becoming a compulsive teller of humorous stories. His daughter Muriel would keep her children, when they were young, away from him in order to shield them from what could be lewd jokes. There is an account of his telling stories to his fellow travellers in the railway carriage all through the journey from Bath to London.

Family relationships are barely mentioned in this book apart from the happiness he gained through his second marriage to Miriam Weatherly towards the end of his life. He was in fact a much more complex man than might be supposed from his book; his responses to members of his family range from the generous to the grudgingly supportive to the callous. He was the senior and most successful member of his sibship. His brothers and sisters looked up to him -

metaphorically speaking - as Fred was very short - and turned to him for financial help. He was generous to nephews, paying for their education if their fathers couldn't.He was a stickler for etiquette and professed a strong Anglican faith, yet he could want in charity and didn't observe a most necessary social convention of the day - sticking by his wife, at least in public.

Fred was indeed short, about 5 feet 1 inch in height. He would not be so conspicuous because of his height then as he might be today as the average male height was 4 inches less - around 5ft 5 one hundred years ago. Photographs from midlife onwards show him as a natty dresser - suit, wing collar, bow tie, spats and polished shoes. He was moustached all his life. In all outdoor photographs including those taken in his garden, he is wearing a bowler hat - perhaps to give extra height? He refers to his smallness only on two occasions in his memoirs – the advantages of being able to wriggle through small spaces in a crowd when a boy and being a cox at Oxford. At school his nickname was Button. His friend, the pianist and novelist Alice Mangold (Mrs Louis Diehl), describes her first impression of him in the 1880s in her memoirs,

Fred aged ca 60 in Bath.

'True story of my life', published in 1908:
"His fine, broad-craniumed head, his face with a certain rapt meditative look reminded me forcibly of a celebrated youthful painting of the author of the Angel of the House, Coventry Patmore."

She doesn't mention his size but then he was seated at the time behind the scenes at St James's Hall with all the performers who were to sing or play at a concert there.accounts of him written after his death invariably however refer to him as a little man or wanting in stature. There is a vignette of him in Sir John Squire's memoir 'Solo and Duet' (1946). Fred was an extra guest at a cricketing house party in Devon. Fred was then nearly 80 and on this occasion initially reticent in the company of a much younger and noisy crowd.This 'chubby little rodent of a man' became 'a happy man' after being asked to sing one of his songs, 'Nancy Lee'. He repeated this twice. Interestingly Squire commented later that this 'charming old man is fading from memory'. In fact his small size provided no apparent handicap to his professional or personal life and he never expressed any negative comments about it.

Small men are said to compensate by assertiveness and a wish to control -'a Napoleon Complex'. His memoirs don't read as written by a person who thought himself some kind of genius; they are self deprecatory at times and he assesses his success as due to good fortune. Perhaps he would have dominated at say the dinner table through his persistent jollity, penchant for jokes, anecdotes and reminiscences, which, unchecked, must have been fatiguing for those around. For younger members of his family he could be intimidating. My mother late in life when looking at a photo of him that she hadn't seen before exclaimed 'That's grandpapa, the dear darling man', but she also said to me that he could be like a headmaster at times. She recalled him dressing down staff in a hotel restaurant who had served him roast meat carved the wrong way, against the grain rather than with it. He sent the plate back. When Fred took her to the seaside at Weston-super-Mare, he insisted that she pronounced it super marais (received Latin) rather than the usual maire. He would also correct the train staff's pronunciation of the place .His nephew Petey remembered, when he was a small boy, sending his uncle Fred a thank you letter for a pair of gloves sent for Christmas. The letter was returned with spelling mistakes corrected and an accompanying note for his father, Fred's brother Alfred, complaining about the illiteracy. These stories make him sound pedantic today, but one hundred years ago such details would be seen as important to have right if you are part of the educated class.

Portishead:

Fred was the oldest son of a Portishead doctor, Fredrick Weatherly. He was one of 13. Fred referred to his father as a poor country doctor, who seemed very staid, solemn and masterful. He would have been an example of Victorian manliness - brusque and direct in manner, very hard working and thus not sharing in domestic activity in the house, self reliant and with a strong sense of morality. His father lived to be 90, so father and son grew old together, but

Dr and Mrs Weatherly ca 1890 Hillside, Portishead.

Fred wrote that his father had never been young, for he himself could always recall his youth. In contrast, he described his mother as 'a born artist, full to the fingertips of music and poetry, a born raconteuse whose voice alone compelled one to listen'- and - 'it is her soul and her spirit speaking in whatever songs I have made'. This conjunction of a distant formal male, the paterfamilias, poles apart from a soft idealised female parent figure in which all feminine, domestic and artistic virtues are assembled was usual for the upper middle classes of the period. However in Fred's case there was a third parent figure in the household - the 'patient' who lived with the family, a man under Dr Frederick's care for 37 years. He, Owen Blayney Cole, was for the Weatherly children the 'wonderful magician, Father Christmas, Santa Claus, Hans Anderson and Scheherazade all rolled into one'.

A rich portrait of Dr Frederick comes from an interview with him aged 85 published in the Clevedon Mercury newspaper in 1905. By then he was known as the Grand Old Man of North Somerset. Dr Fredrick Weatherly was born into a yeoman, land owning family in Ealing. After qualifying at St Bartholomew's Hospital in London, he set up practice in Portishead just before his marriage in 1846. Portishead was then a small fishing port along the coast from Bristol and for the next fifty years he acted as doctor and surgeon to the small town and surrounding countryside. He was a familiar sight on the road in horse drawn gig - a large man with a pock-marked nose and known for his hot temper. He was said to be loved and trusted by all his patients. He was a great believer in vaccination and would bully mothers reluctant to have their child so treated by telling them that the child would have 'a nose like mine' unless done. Asked by the reporter what his hobby was, he replied, 'none, except work,' and 'simplicity, living as near as possible on sixpence a day and earning it'. In fact he had an extensive collection of Elizabethan oak furniture and of china.

He gave up medicine and for the last twenty years of his life became a local public servant – member of Somerset County

Council, Chairman of the local Board of Guardians, Commissioner of Taxes and Justice of the Peace. The journalist tactfully says that a chat with Dr Weatherly is an education in itself, which his memory in old age is still clear and he can take his hearers back four score years. One early memory was of being in Kew Gardens and seeing the young princess Victoria with two of her 'wicked' uncles - Cumberland and Cambridge - jumping over seats to entertain her. Closing the interview, Doctor Frederick said, "Living a quiet life, I have been thrown amongst some extraordinary people." His son Fred also earned the appellation of Grand Old Man and shared his father's pleasure at being acquainted with famous people and recalling these contacts in old age.

This rather formidable man married Julia Maria Ford, three years his junior, in 1846. The Fords were a wealthy Bristol merchant family, many becoming Tory politicians, her brother becoming Mayor of Bristol. Their town house was King Street Hall, the

Hillside House Portishead.

country seat Wraxall Court near Portishead. The Mercury journalist records a picture of Mrs Weatherly, similar to that given by Fred in his memoirs, which he said was shared by all – 'a lady of estimable qualities, great tenderness as a wife and mother, sought after for advice by all classes and conditions of people, the advice readily given and sure to prove helpful'.

Dr and Mrs Weatherly set up house at 7 Wood Hill in Portishead and began breeding; their first child Alice was born in 1847 followed by Fred in 1848. Eleven others followed. The Weatherlys built their own house just down the road in 1855 to accommodate their growing family. This is Hillside, described by the reporter as, 'a charming house in its own grounds with splendid view of the Bristol Channel, it was constructed according to the homely and quiet ideas of its owner'.

Not really true! There was a gathering of Weatherly descendants in Portishead in 2003 to unveil a plaque commemorating Fred's birthplace at 7 Wood Hill. We visited Hillside, a huge, grey stone and rather plain Victorian pile - not my idea of homely and quiet - but with the said grounds and view of the channel. It does not fit with the poor country doctor life style that Fred claimed of his father and that his father seemed keen to promote. The writer of the 1905 article seemed of this opinion too as he wrote ,before describing Hillside, that Dr Frederick must have received 'some slight reward' for his work over the years. The house has been, since then, an institution and been divided up. The current owners are in the process of restoring it to its 1855 original. They kindly showed us all round and had recently uncovered an escutcheon over the front door saying FJW1855 (Fred and Julia) which we could explain to them.

Thirteen children were born between 1847 and 1866, 8 boys and 5 girls. This was a large family even in those days when 6 or 7 children would have been usual. The boys were well-educated – local nursery school, Hereford Cathedral School and then 7 went up to Oxford, usually with a scholarship. As Fred states, it was an enormous achievement for a poor country doctor. The brothers that went into the professions did well; while the brothers who went into business failed. Each of the latter followed moneymaking schemes, but shared an obstinate inability to see when things were going wrong and stop.

One of the oddities of a large sibship, such as Fred's, is that Cecil the youngest, was only six years older than his nephew, Fred's son Alec, while 18 years younger than his eldest brother Fred. This imbalance carries on today for Cecil s grandchildren are younger than Fred's great-grandchildren. Alfred, the parson, married late in life a much younger woman. Two of their children, Peggy and Petey, who survived until recently, were first cousins to my mother's father, yet several years younger than my mother.

There was great competition between the growing boys for their mother's attention. Fred was constantly asking her whether, as the oldest son, he was her special one. He recalls that, as she got older, his mother became stouter and less able to run about as she had done for him looking for pen, paper, book or whatever her younger children wanted. She had had her first child at 24 and her thirteenth delivery was when she was 44; it's perhaps remarkable that she could run around at all. Alice, the older sister to whom Fred was devoted – 'a gentle and motherly soul' - died at 21. The remainder of his siblings, he wrote, are hard to recall as children, but, despite their separation during life, 'it is the memory of the mother that we worshipped and of the father of whom we are so proud that keeps us one family still.' Indeed the brothers living in America used to make a point of corresponding on the anniversaries of their mother's death, August 15.

The surprising extra to this household was his father's patient – Owen Blayney Cole, who came to live with them in 1848 and stayed until his death in 1886. Of Irish origin the Blayneys were landowners in Monaghan. Cole is described in the censuses as deputy lieutenant for the county and is recorded in the Court columns of the Times as sitting in the Irish Council in Dublin in 1841, representing that county. He married Lady Fanny Monck, third daughter of the Earl of Rathdowne - the Orange Earl. They had two children - a son,

Blayney Owen Cole, and two daughters, one of whom married her first cousin Viscount Monck later to become Governor of Canada. Cole was a friend of W.E Gladstone at Christchurch, Oxford, being another of the twelve members of the Gaskell essay club at the time and remained one of the few people apart from Mrs Gladstone, with whom Gladstone exchanged some intimate, personal correspondence. Fred describes the letters arriving in Gladstone's own hand even at the busiest times of his career and with envelopes personally addressed. An example of their closeness comes from a letter in 1835 when Gladstone, recently out of office, was attracted to Caroline Farquhar – later to become his wife. His anxiety about these physical feelings seem to have driven him to write to his friend, Owen Cole to seek support for a cautionary aphorism. "Physical beauty is a real good so long as respect paid to it was never alternate to that due to moral and mental beauty." Cole didn't go along with this. "Who is that crippled, crooked, squinty, pockmarked lady who has taught you to prefer moral to natural beauty? I cannot say and, since you don't provide a name, I will not guess at it. Whoever it is, I am certain that with such well regulated feelings as described in your letter, she cannot fail at being a happy woman when united with you." He had the confidence to tease a highflying young ex (at the time) government minister.

Fred quotes an 1848 letter when Cole was newly resident in his family house. Gladstone exhorts Cole, "in the name of our God and Saviour" to bear up."Blessed are the dead that die in the Lord for they rest from their labours. But we must not seek to grasp that blessedness before our time." Fred says that Gladstone was referring to Cole's illness and despondency.

It's not stated how Mr. Cole came to the Weatherlys. There is never a suggestion of a social or family connection, though he was living in Clifton shortly before. The boarding out of mentally ill individuals in private professional houses, a Victorian movement of which Lionel Weatherly was later a leading proponent, had started. It was referred to as solitary care in private dwellings and was meant for the wealthier classes in the early stage of a disorder to avoid admission to an asylum. The theory behind this approach was that the regularity of life in a Victorian household with good diet and prescribed exercise would restore the balance of the disturbed individual. It was a professional, financial arrangement and under the inspection of the Board of Lunacy.

Writing in 1931 about his career as a psychiatrist, Lionel describes his lifetime experience of caring for the mentally ill in his home. "In 1876 I married. My wife and I soon after our marriage were dining in Clifton with my teacher in medicine, Edward Long Fox, and he asked if we would care to take a resident patient. We decided to do so, and through this case, the daughter of a well-known man in Parliament, I got to know some of the leading alienists of that day, and very soon had many early cases of mental disease located in suitable families living near me. Later my own home became a provincial licensed house. I may here interpolate an interesting fact. Some three years ago we celebrated our golden wedding, and we were able to say that during our fifty years of married life we had never sat down to a meal other than breakfast without having with us mental or nervous patients. I pride myself in the belief that this is a unique experience. Prior to my taking up my residence at Bailbrook House I had been in correspondence with Dr. John Bucknill (afterwards Sir John), author with Daniel Hack Tuke of that well-known textbook, Psychological Medicine. I had found how we mutually agreed regarding the treatment of many early cases of mental disease in private dwelling."

It sounds that Owen Cole had depression or melancholia as it would have then been called. He must have made a suicide attempt, judging by Gladstone's exhortation in the letter to Dr Weatherly about not seeking the Lord's blessedness before one's time; such an event must have occasioned his transfer to residential care with the Weatherlys. They kept him on permanent suicidal caution, as Fred wrote that, in all the thirty-seven years, his parents never left Cole at the same time for a single night. Though Cole recovered from his depression, he remained living with the family of which he had become an integral part.

His son Blayney Owen Cole introduced in the Cornhill magazine of September1924 hitherto unpublished letters from Gladstone to his father. In the article, he wrote that his father having been a close friend of Gladstone at Oxford led for many years the life of a recluse, while Gladstone developed into a great statesman. The Cornhill letters dated from the 1830s when both were young men, and there's no information in them on what went wrong with Cole a decade later that took him to Portishead. In the British Library manuscript section, there are over thirty letters from Cole to Gladstone but they do not refer to the reason for moving in with the Weatherlys. His address just changes to Hillside without comment. Cole mentions severe neuralgia and a fear of going blind on one occasion. Fred does not mention Lady Fanny or Cole's children when writing about his long residence with the Weatherlys. However Lady Fanny was godmother to one of Fred's sisters who died in infancy. From his own correspondence, Cole makes it plain that he saw his children regularly.

Owen Cole seems to have evolved from patient into revered and loved friend of the family and a teacher for the children. Fred said that Cole had the guts to follow Gladstone's advice, presumably bearing up or not seeking the Lord too soon. Cole was a polyglot, speaking six languages and would read Virgil, Homer, Tasso, Cervantes and Goethe in the original languages. He would read their works to the children translating as he went along. Fred later said that it was from his lips that he heard so many wonderful words rather than the printed page. Cole would tell them of English and Irish history. He wrote his own verse, publishing about ten books of romantic and narrative poetry and some carols during his time in Portishead. The poetry he sent to Gladstone for comment could be in French, German and Latin as well as English. A specific interest seems to have been the Icelandic sagas which Cole, to use his own word, versified.

Lionel's account of Cole is similar to Fred's. "This patient (of my father) was a well-known man who often made my brothers' mind and my own happy by the stories he would tell us from Gil Blas, Don

Quixote, Baron Munchausen or The Arabian Nights. His eccentricities not only amused me but created in me a new interest. He had been a school companion of Thackeray at Charterhouse, a personal friend of Gladstone at Christ Church - a friendship that lasted all his life - and he had travelled through Italy with Sir Walter Scott. And who was the man who came to visit this interesting personality? None other than Samuel Warren, one time Master in Lunacy, and the author of those books that will always live - 'Ten Thousand a Year', and 'The Diary of a Late Physician'."

Fred puts his song writing down to hearing 'Old King Cole' (as Cole liked to be called by the children) sing some verses and accompanying himself on the guitar. It was a musical household. Eddie Weatherly writes nostalgically about his memories of England, when an old man in the States, "We are in the Hall at home and Father and Mother and all of us children together and Old King Cole, father's patient has come down to the Hall, and he has his daughter Nina with him. She has just come over from Ireland and is going to sing to us -the little girl with great blue Irish eyes and the far away look in them. She's going to sing 'The Wearing of the Green' and we, who know nothing of the tragedy of Ireland, listen thrilled because there are tears in her voice and the sorrow in those eyes of hers."

The Gladstone connection broadened to include all the family, though there is no account of him actually visiting the Weatherly house. Each boy received a personal postcard from Gladstone if they achieved a prize at school or passed into University, so Cole must have kept him up to date about the doings of the family. In 1886, Cole became very ill, so Dr Fredrick wrote to Gladstone to inform him. Gladstone wrote back. 'I have never forgotten him and trust I never shall.' He asked that the hymn 'Hark my soul, it is the Lord' be drawn to Cole's attention and enclosed a copy. Finally, in the letter, to Dr Frederick, 'You, who have watched over him through these long years and are now a solace at his deathbed, may you have your reward.' Cole died in his room in the presence of the Weatherly parents. His room was left as it was until the house was sold in 1910.

Fred in old age looks back with great gratitude for all that Owen Cole taught him. Owen Cole certainly had a big influence on Fred's development, not least writing and publishing poetry and carols. Fred called his mother with his muse, but Cole contributed as well, allowing Fred to associate artistic accomplishment with maleness. Cole and his family, from Eddie's story, contributed to musical events in the house. Without Cole's role model, Fred would have left that side of himself behind as belonging to women at home, his mother and sisters being the accomplished musicians and linguists, to follow a more traditional masculine Victorian lifestyle. Eddie reacted emotionally to the Irish song he heard - he later was to marry an Irish American woman. Cole and his family were Irish, thus giving Fred an early contact with that culture, perhaps relevant for the future author of Danny Boy.

Another effect of Owen Cole's presence in the house must have had on Fred and his brothers and sisters is that of having to observe mental illness at first hand. Presumably their parents would have explained what Cole was doing in the house. Their long term and dutiful care of 'the patient' would have set their children an example and should have given them an understanding of such problems, which would be rare for young people of this period. For Lionel, this experience was positive, leading to his career choice, but less obviously so for Fred, judging by his actions when he had to contend with his wife's mental illness.

There is a return of interest in placing certain patients with mental illness in families who are paid to look after them. No more than three patients are now allowed by law to be looked after in one household. The important feature of a successful placement that helps a patient to rehabilitate and thus move on to independent living is that the patient is integrated into the family activities rather than being made to be separate in the house. Sharing meals is an important marker of integration. Children in the house are seen as a plus: they are more accepting than adults and the patient can have a role as a friend or informal teacher depending on the skills of the patient.

Even under today's rules this would be seen as a successful placement. Owen Cole must have had very positive feedback from the pleasure of the Weatherly children at his company -very good for someone with a tendency to depression. He certainly contributed to their lives. However 36 years under the care of Dr Weatherly probably wasn't necessary for clinical need - he stayed for reasons of friendship. Financial support for such an arrangement today would be discontinued once it could be shown that the patient could live independently. I have a book signed by OB Cole as a present to Alfred and Arthur Weatherly.

School

At the age of 11, Fred went to board at Hereford Cathedral School – it is not explained why he and all his brothers were sent there. It was neither local nor would be regarded in the top rank of public schools of the day. A school attached to Hereford Cathedral has existed since the eighth century but the foundation of the current school was in the fourteenth. He was taken there by his mother, who hated leaving him. Fred recalls Hereford as the time when he began his love for music by attending the Cathedral services and the local philharmonic society concerts, writing that he seized every opportunity to experience music. Under the tutelage of the Headmaster, whom Fred thought an Oxford don manqué, he extended his knowledge of the classical literature. He also used to go to the local assize courts claiming that his fascination with the law stemmed from listening to the cross-examinations there. In his last year at Hereford he began writing verses and won the school poetry prize. Verse-writing and the law, the two enthusiasms that were to characterise determined Fred's life were thus already apparent by the time he finished school.

Dr Frederick was a presence in Fred's life until Fred was 62 and must have remained a model of Victorian paternalistic moral authority for him. Sons were expected to grow into this mould, so many public schools fostered the virtues of self reliance, physical rather than intellectual or artistic prowess and emotional continence (stiff upper lip). Wives were for hearth and home rather than intellectual companionship, which would be found with business colleagues or in gentlemen's clubs. Music and poetry would be left behind as part of domestic pleasure and not feature in the day-to-day life of the professions or business. Fred escaped that restraint probably through the influence of Owen Cole in Hillside who counterbalanced his father but also from the fact that Hereford was a choir school that allowed a boy with ability to pursue an artistic path. Fred never said what his father thought of his verses - paternal pride in his fame or dismissive of it as a waste of time that should be better spent in the serious pursuit of a profession.Fred seemed aware that, from school age, there was in him a tension between an artistic, amused, curious self and a father-like self, which needed a serious career like the law. However it was the former that made Fred, on going to Oxford, eager to learn more about literature and music.

Fred's mother died in 1898, the old man living on until 1910, dying aged 90. For his last twelve years, Arthur Weatherly's widow Lizzie moved into Hillside to look after him. He cast a long shadow on all his sons; the younger ones who settled in America to prove themselves wrote that they only wished that their activities could be approved by him.

Oxford – undergraduate

Fred came into residence at Brasenose College in 1867, having sat for and obtained an exhibition earlier that year. He was awed to have a sitting room and bedroom of his own. "My own furniture, my own pictures and my own piano (eventful piano!). To be able to order my breakfast, my lunch in my rooms, alone or with friends, it all seemed so strange to me then."Brasenose was then a successful rowing college with nine members in the university eleven. Thus Fred was very proud as a freshman to be asked on his arrival to report to the College barge to steer a trial crew. He was later unwittingly to change the course of rowing history.

His tutor was the renowned Walter Pater, then a fellow of Brasenose, distinguished art historian, author and a founder of the aesthetic movement.Assignation to him was a 'rare piece of good fortune'. Fred's enthusiasm to learn more about the arts seemed to have got through to Pater. After a lecture in Pater's rooms, Fred stopped to admire a painting by Ingres. Pater asked him if he loved pictures. Fred's response led to regular private sessions with Pater before or after lectures in which Pater would tell him about Italian art. He heard about the woman with the wonderful smile (la Giaconda). Pater described her as 'set in a marble chair on the circle of fantastic rocks; her head upon which ends of the world are come. She is older than the rocks upon which she sits. Like the vampire, she has been dead many times and learnt the secret of the grave'. This interpretation of the painting was published in Pater's monograph on Leonardo da Vinci some years later – Fred liked to think he heard it first. When he looked at paintings later in his life, snatched moments of talk with Pater came back like 'the sweet memories of his mother's stories and songs'.

Pater was gay. When a student at Queen's, he was said to have had an affair with Ingram Bywater (later Regius Professor of Greek.). While a Fellow and tutor at Brasenose, he had affairs with William Money Hardinge called 'the bugger of Balliol' and later a poet and novelist and with the artist Simeon Solomon. Correspondence between Pater and Hardinge became public, causing Hardinge to be rusticated in 1874. Pater was blocked by the Master of Balliol from a promised proctorship and did not proceed to apply for the Professorship of fine art. He resigned his Brasenose tutorship in 1880 and retired to live with his sisters in Norham Gardens.Falconer Madan, librarian of the Bodleian, wrote to Fred after the publication of Fred's memoirs to explain that Pater was eased out of his tutorship because he was 'literary not educational and had no idea of helping a stupid man'. By the time of the resignation, Pater's genius, in Fred's words, was well known and Pater gave himself up to literature but Madan commented to Fred that Pater must have felt much the diminution of income, for he was quite poor.

Fred was obviously aware of Pater's sexual interests, though the scandal attached to him was after Fred's time at Brasenose. Describing Pater, he used typical giveaways. "Beautifully dressed, he was a dandy with a touch of the ascetic, spoke with a gentle voice, polite as a woman."His rooms were different to other fellows' rooms. "The panelled walls were painted a pale apple green. The floor was stained and varnished and covered with oriental rugs." Apart from the painting by Ingres hanging in the rooms, there was one by Simeon Solomon, whom Fred hoped "no one confuses with Solomon Solomon RA."

Later, when tutoring in Oxford during the 1870s, Fred would bump into Pater, who would give Fred a 'shy little wave and smile'. Sometimes he asked what Fred was writing. " Don't forget," Pater said to him on one occasion, "it is just as necessary to be scholarly and sincere in the simplest song as in the great epic and a simple song may be just as artistic as the greatest epic." Fred visited Pater and his sisters in Norham Gardens. The latter 'wore dresses of weird style and wondrous colours'. Morris papers were on the walls and the whole house and its occupants were in 'strange and pleasant contrast to the Victorian homes of the Oxford of those days'.

Pater was a leader of the Aesthetic movement along with Rossetti, Burnes-Jones and William Morris. The core of this movement was pursuit of beauty, in itself pure and noble. This value system, also cited as 'art for arts sake,' brought conflict with religious values of the day and denunciation in pulpits. The group later contained those known as sensualists, producing works celebrating overtly or covertly male beauty. The difficulties that Pater had with the Oxford establishment was because of the apparent decadence, implying homoeroticism, of his writing and of his association with the lives of his two lovers, Simeon Solomon (arrested for importuning) and William Money Hardinge (rusticated because of his overt homosexuality). Oscar Wilde, also a student of Pater in the 1870s was in Fred's mind the leader in this move from aestheticism to sensualism. Fred stoutly defended what he regarded as the good side of aestheticism e.g. the works of William Morris and emphatically dissociated his mentor Pater from 'those aesthetes who were but a decadent type, first as poseurs and afterwards as an unwholesome gang of sensualists'. The downfall of Oscar Wilde came as, he wrote, 'a wholesome check' and 'suggesting that there was anything in common between Pater and Oscar Wilde was most unfair and I believe pained him (Pater) very much.' Fred gained a great deal from Walter Pater as he had done from Owen Cole at home; they noted and encouraged his enthusiasm for the arts.

Both, in Fred's own words, were gentle men. Pater was gay as Fred suggests in his descriptions. What about Fred himself in this respect? Asking Fred to stay behind to look at pictures could have been an opening, not an unknown gambit for dons towards students through the years - though the Weatherlys are not a good looking bunch and Fred was tiny. Interestingly one writer speculates on his internet website that Fred may have had an affair with Michael Maybrick who, under the name of Stephen Adams, collaborated as the composer on many songs, the Holy City being the most famous. This story comes from a Maybrick family descendant. Maybrick remained a bachelor to the age of 49 then married unhappily but ended up as a famous mayor of Ryde in the Isle of Wight. In 1913, the year of Maybrick's death, Fred writes movingly of a last meeting in Bath between them. Fred had written the words for a song 'Friend O Mine' specifically for Maybrick and sent it to him before the visit to Bath. Maybrick ended the visit early without speaking of the song. Fred writes, "I shall always believe that it touched him too deeply to enable him to set it to music or even speak of it. But I like to think that the words went to his heart as they came from mine."

Last lines of 'Friends of Mine'
Look with your dear old eyes in mine,
Give a handshake true;
Whatever fate our souls await,
Let me be there - with you!

This is not homoerotic writing, but perhaps conveys something more intense than just a friendship. Fred most probably would have tolerated deep attachments between men (as he expressed with Maybrick) and the idea that in that attachment an older man could impart knowledge to the younger (Pater to him). But as an old man writing his memoirs, he clearly condemned the crossing of a line to any physical expression of such affection (Wilde).

Fred continued coxing for the College boat and in 1868 made his first appearance at the Henley Regatta. Brasenose had had a special boat built for a coxswainless four, a rowing crew as yet unknown in England. They were to enter this four for the Ladies Plate at Henley after four college men had practised hard. It was accepted by the Stewards and caused considerable interest among the rowing fraternity. At the last minute, the stewards passed a special rule that no boat shall start without a cox - a rule that the Brasenose coach decided could be circumvented by starting the race with a cox and dropping him immediately. Fred was sent for by wire to come immediately from Portishead. It was only when he joined the crew at the Red Lion in Henley that he was told what he had to do -jump off the boat into the river as soon as the race started, which would 'only' be fifteen feet deep at that part of the river. Fred then announced that he could not swim. Not allowed to be deterred; he was taught a few strokes and then spent the rest of the day practising the jump from a chair in his hotel bedroom. Next day, he jumped from his perch on the boat as soon as the word 'Go' was shouted to begin the race. Unfortunately he jumped straight into tangled water lily stems at the bottom of the river, didn't surface and had to be pulled out. When he jumped, though, the boat didn't quiver and the four went on to win by eight lengths. However, they were immediately disqualified for 'having thrown their cox overboard'. When his mother heard, she apparently remarked, "Disqualified indeed, they ought to be tried for attempting to murder the poor dear boy." Coxswainless fours were born and Fred's story has become part of rowing history.

When Fred arrived at Oxford, he admitted that he was swept off his feet and "whatever studious habits I had seemed thrown to the winds." He was appalled at the number of authors he had to read for Mods and Greats. The teaching he thought awful and above his head, but "there were too many distractions". He went to lectures in the morning, there was the river in the afternoon and after dinner the evenings were spent at the piano and writing verses. He thus tried private tutors; these were not much better apart from a Dr Williams of Merton who taught him logic. He said it was no small wonder that he took low honours in both Mods (3rd in classical moderations 1869) and Greats (4th in Classics 1871 leading to BA.). In mitigation, his writing was taking off, verses for both public recitation and to be set to music. However he failed, after attempting three years in a row, to be awarded the Newdigate Prize for Poetry, the prestigious annual university award. It was awarded to a partially rehabilitated William Hardinge in 1876, who, because of illness, did not read it publicly, and later to Oscar Wilde in 1878.

Fred was in at the foundation of the Oxford University Dramatic Society, through which society he met Henry Irving for the first time and who was to become a long-term acquaintance. For the opening of the Oxford Playhouse, with a production of Twelfth Night, Fred wrote a prologue especially for the occasion which was delivered by Arthur Bourchier, later a distinguished actor/manager at the Garrick and Royalty Theatres. The opening lines of his prologue ran as follows:

Lone and dishonoured, lurking in the shade,
Creeping in twilight darkness, half afraid
To meet the eyes of honest men, I stand
With lowered face and deprecating hand
Irresolute whether to remain or flee —
Spirit of Drama, as it used to be.
What's this? A brand-new Theatre? Then 'tis clear
My day is over, I've no business here.
At last instead of Darkness shines the Day,
Arise, thou modern Spirit of the Play.

A stream of creativity was now flowing that was to became a torrent during his life. He certainly wasn't studious and perhaps not an intellectual either, thus he did badly in his exams. Fred became a member of the Apollo Lodge, the University Masonic Lodge as an undergraduate. On the day in 1875 that Oscar Wilde was initiated into the Lodge, Fred was also there being raised to its third degree - so the two must have met.

No mention is made in any of Fred's own writing about being a Mason. The author of the same website that speculated about an affair between Fred and Maybrick also suggested that 'Holy City' was based on the Masonic concept of Jerusalem. The second verse has a Christian reference – the shadow of the cross outside the city wall, but this scene is surpassed by the Holy City bathed in light into which all that wish can enter. In this image there isn't a judgment day before entering and a Masonic tenet equates God to light. More than he in the family might have been involved in Masonry. In a letter to his brother Eddie, Lewis (Luke) indicated that he was trying to join a lodge in San Francisco to be eligible for subsided health care and thus wanted to resurrect his earlier contacts with the Apollo Lodge. Lewis was apparently a common name given by Masons to their sons, so perhaps Dr Fredrick was one too.

Oxford - tutoring and marriage

After coming down in 1871, Fred took a post as second master at Christchurch Cathedral School, at the same time securing some undergraduates as private pupils. However by now his verse writing was progressing, particularly for children's books and songs. A book of poems was published in 1871 called 'Muriel, the Sea King's Daughter'. This, his first volume, he sent to Gladstone under the persuasion of Owen Cole. Gladstone wrote back on March 22 and again on March 25 1871 from 11 Carlton House Terrace. In the first he said that he will peruse the book with kindly interest. Also writing that the life of his old friend (Cole) had been darkened by a dispensation of Providence, but that he was glad that his influence should have been felt in quickening and strengthening the development of other minds. Four days later, Gladstone having so perused, wrote that 'he had the pleasure of assuring you (Fred), though it must be hastily and I fear abruptly, that it impressed me much with feelings both of pleasure and admiration.'

By 1872, Fred's tutoring was established and his literary work was growing, so he gave up school mastering. At the end of 1872, he married. Until now, the only reference in 'Piano and Gown' to any kind of romantic attachment or girlfriend had been to someone called his childhood sweetheart, a musical girl with brown hair and laughing eyes in Portishead. It seemed a long distance affair as they barely spoke to each other. During his undergraduate years he does not mention any female in his social life. The marriage immediately at the end of his undergraduate years aged 24 seems thus unexpected. In his memoirs Fred mentions this marriage, but doesn't provide his wife's name for his readers, nor any details of how they met. His bride on 31 December 1872, was Anna Maria Hardwick, aged 30, 4th daughter of a John Hardwick, surgeon at Worle (near Weston-super- Mare) in Somerset. The Weston Mercury of the 4th of January 1873 gives this detailed and informative account of the wedding:

WEDDING FESTIVITIES AT WORLE

'On Tuesday thirty-first - the last day of the old year - the village of Worle was thrown into a state of pleasing excitement by the marriage of Frederick Edward Weatherly. Esq. of Brasenose College Oxford, to Miss Anna Maria Hardwick, fourth daughter of John Hardwick Esq. of Worle. The village was very prettily decorated with flags and mottoes and soon after 9 o'clock, the wedding guests began to arrive in well-appointed carriages and greys. Nearly all thought of business was laid aside, and people began in serious earnest to keep a general holiday. In addition to the very profuse Christmas decorations in the church, there was a very beautiful motto, in white, over the chancel to face the welding party as they passed up the aisle of the church, "Blessed are they who are called to the marriage supper of the Lamb", and another under the belfry to face them as they retired, "Live together in holy love". The bridal party consisted of John Hardwick, Esq., father of the bride; F.

Weatherly, Esq. and Mrs Weatherly (Portishead), parents of the bridegroom, Miss Hardwick, Mr and Mrs John Hardwick junior, Mr and Mrs Charles Day, Mr and Mrs F. Lucas, Rev O and Mrs Fletcher, Rev F.T.Brown (Brasenose College Oxford) and Miss Pienitz. The bridesmaids were Miss Agnes Hardwick, Miss Weatherly and Miss Elsie Weatherly (sisters of the bridegroom), Miss Lucas, Miss M. Lucas, and Miss Day (nieces of the bride). Best man, F.A. Pritchard (Pembroke College, Oxford), groomsmen Mr Edward C Weatherly, Mr Alfred W Weatherly, Mr Arthur J Weatherly, Mr Herbert H Weatherly, Mr Lewis J Weatherly, brothers of the bridegroom. The bride's dress was of white satin, tulle polonaise and tulle dress with orange flowers in hair and dress. The bridesmaids' dresses were of white muslin over pink muslin, trimmed with lace, pink ribbon sashes and bows, tulle veil, and wreaths of pink azaleas.

There was a very large congregation in the church amongst whom we recognised many of the leading gentry of village and neighbourhood. The service was performed by the Rev 0. Fletcher, assisted by Rev. F.T. Brown, (Brasenose College Oxford), with full choral service by the choir. After the wedding breakfast, which was of the most recherché description - served by Mr. Wickenden of Weston-super-Mare - the happy pair started on their wedding tour by the 2.45 train.

At three o'clock in the afternoon, an excellent dinner of roast beef, boiled mutton, and plum pudding was given by Mr Hardwick to a large number of old people also to the church ringers and others. The dinner, which was of the best description, was served up by Mrs Cook, of theNew Inn, in her usual sumptuous style. The chair was taken, at Mr Hardwick's request, by Mr E.M.Watson, assisted by Messrs Scotford, Lee and E May. During the progress of the dinner, Mr Hardwick and nearly the whole of the wedding party visited the guests, and together with a large number of the inhabitants of the village, remained until the end of the proceedings. At the close of the repast 'The Health of the Queen' was drunk and one verse of the National Anthem was sung by all the company. The Chairman then said that he had a toast to propose in which all the assembled company had a deep and special interest that day, and that was 'The health of the bride and bridegroom'. He (the Chairman) had known the bride nearly all her life but had never known or heard of her saying an unkind thing; truly, the law of kindness had always been on her tongue. She had been brought up in a well ordered and well regulated home, and she had gone in and out among the parishioners, always honouring her position and dispensing those blessings which lay in her power, gladdening and enlivening those with whom she came in contact, like a gleam of sunshine. She had that day been called, by the providence of God, to enter a new relationship of life, but there was not the slightest doubt that the dutiful daughter, and the kind friend, would be equally the amiable and affectionate wife. The only consolation which the village of Worle would feel in her loss was, that she had gone to enliven another circle of friends, and it would be the prayer of all that she might still continue to sow good seed, which would yield fruits of blessed ripening, and which would in its turn, scatter fresh seeds of fresh fruits. With regard to the bridegroom, the Chairman, said he had not the happiness of an extensive acquaintance with him, but that he knew him to be a member of a very worthy family, moreover, he had an established reputation of his own, having gained some of the highest collegiate honours at the University of Oxford that it was possible for a young a man to obtain. In conclusion, he (the Chairman) begged to propose the 'health, long life, and happiness of the bride and bridegroom'. The toast was most enthusiastically received; after which John Hardwick Esq. rose, and, in a feeling and eloquent speech, returned thanks for the kind manner in which the health of the bride and bridegroom had been received. He said that his feelings and emotions must be of a very mingled character that day; feelings of joy because of the happiness of his child and sorrowful emotions because of her loss. He wished continually to live in reference to his last day of which that day, the last in the year reminded him. Mr Scotford then proposed the health of Mr Hardwick, to which that gentleman again briefly responded. Mr Lee then proposed the 'health of the bridesmaids', which was rapturously received. F. Weatherly Esq, father of the bridegroom, returned thanks on behalf of the young ladies. In a speech which was fraught with Christian feeling and kindly sentiment he drew a parallel between Mr Hardwick and himself as being both members of the medical profession and said he had no doubt but that many of Mr Hardwick's friends, who were met to congratulate him that day, had had reminiscences of some of the most painful events of their lives (alluding to illness) with which that gentleman had been mixed up. Little did people generally think of the sleepless nights which medical men had, when overwhelmed with anxiety respecting the convalescence or otherwise of their patients. He (Mr Weatherly) was very favourably impressed with the people of Worle and intimated that he should be pleased to renew his acquaintance with them. Mr E May then proposed the health of Mr John Hardwick junior, and his lady, which was gratefully acknowledged by that gentleman. Mr John Hardwick senior then proposed the health of the Rev. 0. Fletcher, to which that gentleman replied, with his usual earnestness and humour. Mr Hardwick having spoken very kindly of the services of his friends who had carved the joints, the day's festivities were brought to a close amidst great satisfaction and congratulation.'

It is clear from this description that the Weatherlys and the Hardwicks did not know each other at all well. For instance, Mr Watson's description of Fred's undergraduate achievements was hardly accurate. Fred maybe came across his wife because their fathers were both doctors practising in neighbouring areas. The description of Anna Maria's character is very similar to that of Fred's mother - dutiful, charitable etc. She was 6 years older and from photographs considerably taller than Fred, handsome rather than beautiful; she doesn't sound the most exciting choice for a young man just out of Oxford who was getting known in the literary world. She sounds as though she was in the mould of a wife for his father's generation, with the clear division between masculine and feminine virtues and roles in the family. Perhaps there was an element of seeking mother, remembering that his mother remained an adored figure all his life.

Fred and his bride returned to Oxford and he continued his living as a private tutor while his verse writing continued. In 1876, in partnership with Michael Maybrick, he had his first 'hit'. This was 'Nancy Lee', a ballad about a sailor's wife - one of several sea songs that this partnership published. Seventy thousand copies of the song sheet were sold in the first few weeks and two hundred thousand over the next two years. With this earning, Fred was able to build his own house - Seven Springs in the Parks. This house was designed so that he could accommodate his family and have rooms for boarding pupils. This enterprise was possible as Minnie (Anna Maria's name in the family) was, Fred writes, 'a devoted wife who, in addition to her love and affection, was a perfect genius in domestic economy and management'.

I have an unpublished short story, typed by Fred called 'Under the Limes, a true storyof a Commemoration Ball'. In this Fred and wife were to chaperone five girls to the Trinity College ball. His wife in the story is laid up with a cold, not very flatteringly described, so Fred has to go on his own with the girls. At the ball, he dances with an unknown woman who metamorphoses into his 'First Love' as he dances with her. Memories flood back of their meetings by the old church in the village, a kiss, but also of her father's anger at their involvement. Suddenly, he feels a stabbing pain in his chest. Fred believes that this phantom has stabbed him in the heart and notices a red mark spreading out on his dress shirt. Afraid of appearing like that in front of his wards, he rushes home to change the shirt, hiding it from his wife, who is in bed; her cold symptoms are again graphically described. He returns to the ball but the phantom lady had gone and he escorts his wards home. Next morning, he discovers that red stain is from crushed geranium flowers from the corsage on this woman's dress, presumably because they danced closely together.

Not exactly a story of genius, but it does tell us something of Fred's fantasy life. His wife is put out of the way and made unattractive, while Fred makes contact with a past flame. The red stain, presumed to be blood, reflects a broken heart or may be an expression of his guilt. The relief that the stain was only from geraniums must also reflect his relief that he had only acted in fantasy. However this story seems an important premonition of what happened later to his marriage.

In old age Fred could only recall some of the 'hundreds' of pupils he taught. One was Coningsby Disraeli, nephew of Benjamin Disraeli and later a Conservative politician. But the most interesting period in his coaching days was when Prince Swasti Sobhon, brother of the King of Siam moved in as pupil. Two noblemen Nai Snai and Nai Rong Bam Rung Botomai accompanied him. Also in the house at the time were two Greeks - Ambrose Argenti and Spyridion Mavrojani. Fred said that introducing these five young men to local girls at dances he held for them in his house was 'a quite longwinded affair'. Prince Swasti was one of the 170 or so sons of King Mongkut, Rama IV, and thus brother of the reforming King Chulalongkorn, Rama V. The Siamese trio became very attached to Fred and, at their request, he would accompany them on official trips round England that had been arranged by their Embassy - such as to Worcester porcelain makers, Cammell Laird in Belfast, John Brown, Cutlers in Sheffield and Fry's Chocolate in Bristol. Fred noted that the Prince was one of his brightest students, mastering English in the first year and passing Smalls easily. When the time came for the Siamese to go home, Prince Swasti asked Fred to accompany them to become tutor to his nephew the Crown Prince Maha, offering a large salary. However by now, Fred had decided to study for the Bar and declined. He said later, 'There might have been another book called Fred and the King of Siam'.

Prince Swasti returned home to found his own dynasty of Royals in Thailand. He remained an anglophile. His daughter married his nephew the Crown Prince, later Rama VII, to become Queen Rambao Barri. Prince Swasti would thus be great uncle to the current King. He must have met others in the Weatherly family and kept in touch, because Fred's younger brothers Herbert and Luke, when very short of money in America, wrote to him to ask for financial help.

Fred and Minnie had three children, Alec born in 1873, Muriel in 1878 and Christine in 1879. Minnie was already 31 when Alec was born, quite late by Victorian standards but the usual family size was reducing to 3 by the 1870s. Fred writes little about his children in Piano and Gown. There is a story of Alec who, on receiving a gift from his godfather, Hugh Gough later the 3rd Viscount Gough, handed back a sixpence from his pocket telling his godfather to buy what he wanted with it. Alec was attached to one of his aunts, Agnes Hardwick which occasioned one of Fred's more, by today's standards, sickly poems called 'Auntie'. Set to music by Arthur Behrend, it had its first performance at the Crystal Palace with Madame Patey (a famous contralto of the day) singing it. Fred said that it was received with a standing ovation, but the next day it was panned in a daily paper. 'A song of a little boy in love with his aunt; a disgrace to the author, to the composer, to the singer and the publisher!'

Opening lines-
You're my little true lover
You're my little boy blue
But, I'm your old auntie, darling,
And I cannot marry you."

Much of Fred's fame and income at this stage in his career came from his composition of verse for children. These were published, usually illustrated by well known artists of the day. He actually gave Beatrix Potter her first commission as an illustrator ('A Happy Pair', 1890). His songs could be grouped into those with a naval flavour and those he called rustic. Of the latter, 'We come up from Somerset' is the most enduring. He also wrote and was commissioned to write verses to commemorate special national days and events. Around now, he wrote the Old Brigade, which has become the signature tune of the Chelsea pensioners. However he did keep his academic side going, publishing two books on logic – the Rudiments in 1878 and Questions in logic in 1883.

The illustrated books of children's verses and songs are still in circulation and collected. There are usually two or three available for purchase on ebay – price now £10 -£30. 'Punch and Judy' and 'The Three Maids of Lee' appear most often for sale. His biggies, the enduring songs that are still widely sung – Danny Boy, Roses of Picardy and the Holy City were however written when he was much older.

London

In 1887, Fred was called to the Bar. He had had enough of coaching in Oxford ('the drudgery') and moved to London, having another home built in Raynes Park, Wimbledon. This he called Hardwick House after his wife's family. He was now 39 and wrote that, if he was going to make anything of himself at the Bar, it was time to start. His Chambers were in 1, Hare Court in the Temple, headed by Henry Dickens QC, son of Charles Dickens. Fred is full of praise for the tutelage and experience he was given by Dickens. His song writing, for which he now had considerable fame, was never mentioned at work. His two worlds met occasionally as when, with two other young colleagues, he wrote a small handbook on musical and dramatic copyright. The author, however, of the standard work on copyright law lifted a section of this handbook for a new version of his own book on the subject. The three young authors sued. The action was settled but Fred wrote, 'it was probably the only case of an author of a book on copyright being sued for breach of copyright!' A second time was a case that he defended as a junior concerning the copyright of 'Ta-ra-ra- boom-de-ay', which he recalls had to be sung in court in front of the judge.

Beside the sea in a dark fir wood
a little ruined Chapel stood,
Where peasants met for prayer & praise,
long ago in distant days.
O sweet the tale the organ told
O sweet the voice of young & old,
but deepest prayer would ever be
for those in peril on the sea.

No organ plays, no choir sings, now!
no sunshine falls on upturned brow,
no priest to bless the hallowed seat,
and Yet — the little shrine is blest.
For there the birds the whole day long
send up to Heav'n their thankful song,
and there to God the ancient sea
sings ever of Eternity!

Fred. E Weatherly

Unpublished verse.

He writes of this period that 'he was in the London of his hopes and dreams, busy at my Piano and getting busy with my Gown'. He commented that both occupations (song writing and law) had little in common except knowledge of life but that he had managed two trades in Oxford so 'why not in the new life?' As his verses arose spontaneously in his head, he could jot them down in spare moments in court or while travelling on the train to appear out of London.

He was to be seen writing verses on the starched cuffs of his shirt. Any anxieties about his song writing interfering with his law pupillage were not great enough to prevent him getting thoroughly linked into the musical and theatrical world of London. Despite his junior status in the law, he belonged to the Arts Club in Hanover Square and dined at Pagani's restaurant in Great Portland Street; at both he met musicians, poets and painters. He felt it necessary though to comment in his memoirs that such life didn't appeal to him, that he wasn't a clubbable person and that he had always been a home bird.

Fred did become a Bar pupil late. He could undoubtedly have kept himself and family by his writing but some part of him had determined that he should take up a serious profession. He claimed to have found his interest while at school in Hereford, but law is not mentioned throughout his Oxford days.

Having started the training, he now reassures the reader of his memoirs that he was taking the law seriously; pointing out that song writing was so spontaneous that it took virtually no thought. He would have been considerably better off, through his royalties and sales of sheet music than his fellow pupils in chambers - did he fear that they or his superiors regarded him as a dilettante? Was he worrying that his father was thinking that he was wasting his time in London? The tension in his mind between his two worlds is becoming apparent. As he gets older his self-identity as a lawyer will dominate.

He was very busy in town, so evenings in Wimbledon with his family must have been infrequent. The Boosey and then the

Chappell ballad concerts had begun in 1867 at St James Hall in Piccadilly. They were immensely popular. If a new song by him were being aired at one of these concerts, Fred would be present behind the scenes, as he was when Mrs Diehl described meeting him. Their first performances were advertised in the press. Fred spent thus much time with aspiring composers, some like Maybrick, Squire and Diehl becoming personal friends. He also got to know the leading singers of the day; Antoinette Sterling, the American contralto, and the tenor Charles Santley were famous exponents of his songs. If song sheets had the statement on the front 'as sung by Madame Antoinette Sterling', sales increased enormously. Her son Sterling McKinley, in his book of the life of his mother, describes the excitement of the time:

'THE ST. JAMES'S HALL BALLAD CONCERTS'
They were flourishing times for music and musicians, the years between 1880 and 1890. I am taking this decade because it was the one during which Antoinette Sterling was at her zenith. Every one connected with music seemed to be making money more or less easily. Publishers, concert-givers, choral societies, agents, artists, composers, lyric-writers, and those thousands who were less prominently connected with the profession - printers, engravers, travellers, and the like - all were enjoying unexampled prosperity. Yes, the world was indeed a pleasant resting-place for musicians in the eighties.

Those were the days of 'The Better Land', 'The Star of Bethlehem' (FW),' The Holy City' (FW), and 'The Lost Chord, of the Three Fishers', and an equal number of' Beggars', of 'Darby and Joan' (FW), of 'Anthea and Nancy Lee' (FW), of 'The Owl' and 'The Midshipmite' (FW), of 'Life's Promise', and of that 'Love-Song' which was both 'Old and Sweet'.

Those were the days when the Popular concerts were in full swing at the St James's Hall. The Pops popped out merrily on Saturday afternoons while the public popped in with equal light heartedness. Nor did the Monday evening ones meet with less satisfaction.

Mr McKinley cites five of Fred's songs among those that he recalled his mother singing. The ballad concerts, latter renamed Popular concerts, continued in some form until the 1920s when they were abandoned because of the competition from the BBC.

Through Mrs Georgina Weldon, a notorious figure in London at this time, he met Charles Gounod who stayed with her in London probably as her lover. Mrs Weldon was a very eccentric lady who turned her house in Tavistock Square into an orphanage, collecting street children in a wagon and taking them home. Unfortunately the conditions there were of considerable squalor and her husband with others tried to get her certified as insane. She successfully avoided this but then set about suing those involved. Mrs Weldon was a compulsive litigant having usually ten suits or so on the go at once. Fred had known her since Oxford days, so she kept trying to get him to appear for her. He purposely refused, claiming that he was too inexperienced but, when it was possible, he would go into court to listen to her cases. She conducted these herself, wearing her own version of a barrister's gown and performed according to Fred with a consummate skill. He further describes her as a fascinating woman with beauty of voice and wonderful intelligence. This would have been a minority opinion; most thought her a real nuisance, even a danger, as she rattled around central London looking for children to collect in her wagon, labelled Mrs Weldon's orphanage. In the account of her life, 'Plaintiff and Person', her nephew Philip Treherne quotes an unnamed barrister (? Fred), who knew her well and described her in the midst of a sea of litigation as follows:

"She saw the world moving round and round like a vast piece of machinery and she saw that in the course of its motion were worked numberless acts of infinite oppression and wrong. It was useless to tell her that the machinery as a whole worked admirably. Her attitude was that of the old knight errant, who did not trouble herself about abstract principles of law and justice, but rode out to discover individual cases of oppression and to decide them on her own authority and to redress them according to her own judgement."

This was a kindly view of a chronic litigant as Mrs Weldon viewed herself as the oppressed one most of the time. Any way Fred, through his friendship with her, had some courteous letters from Gounod who set some of his verses to music.

Alongside, came Fred's contacts with more serious music. He got to know Sir Augustus Harris of the Drury Lane theatre, father of pantomime and known as Druriolanus, and D'Oyley Carte and his wife. Fred was commissioned to write for Covent Garden, where Harris was then in charge, English versions of French and Italian operas. These were to be available for those in the audience who couldn't follow the original language, but the English words also had to fit the music perfectly so that they could be used when the operas were performed in English. His versions of Cavalleria Rusticana (Mascagni) and Il Pagliacci (Leoncavallo) became commercial successes immediately and are still in use today. He writes of the necessary skills of a translator - knowledge of the host language, knowledge of the structure of the music to which the new words must fit and most important the matching of the emotional tone of words in the new language with old. He states however that the translator is unappreciated and often not properly rewarded. As an example, the Times review after the first night of Pagliacci in English mentions Fred's role only in the first sentence – 'Pulcinello by which word it has pleased Mr Weatherly translator of the libretti to render the title of the piece.' On the other hand, he received a warm letter of thanks from Leoncavallo himself after the first English performance of Cavalleria Rusticana. Other ventures in opera were less satisfactory. His version of the libretto of Andre Messager's Mirette, was soon replaced by another more romantic one. The Times review of Fred's version –'M. Messager has not given us of his best as exemplified in La Basoche or the pretty ballet Scaramouche. No doubt the effort of writing his music to Mr Weatherly's English version of the French verses cramped his style and every excuse is to be made.' Later, 'There is little that is strong enough in the music to compensate for the weakness of the book.' His collaboration with Frederick Cowen on an Italianate opera Signa led to a near flop. Even Fred said that the opera was dull. The Times review stated, 'The first production of Mr Cowen's Signa attracted an enthusiastic if not very large audience.' The opera had been compressed from four acts to two which meant that the libretto has passed 'through complicated processes, for which Mr H Rudall and Mr F Weatherly are responsible and they have not resulted in a very successful book. The composer's qualities as well as the limitations of his powers have been kept well in view.' Fred was upset and angry about such remarks, saying that he wanted to improve and criticism should help him do that.

He also pursued another enthusiasm from Oxford days, the stage. It was the time of the Lyceum Years with Sir Henry Irving in charge of the company there and Ellen Terry as the principal actress. He was acquainted with Irving from OUDS and said of him, "I saw him all through his great progress. Although his mannerisms and pronunciation were weird, he was a great actor, a fine manager and a good friend." Fred had been a fan of Terry since he saw her on stage in Bath when he was a teenager. "I fell in love with her the moment I saw her, and if I may dare to confess it, I have loved her ever since." A high point was watching her with Irving in 'The Dead Heart' from a box at the Lyceum in the company of his friends, the Diehls. He wrote some verses on the subject of the play, which he sent to the two protagonists who each replied with a personal note and a signed photograph. Among other actors of his acquaintance were Mrs Sarah Siddons, again known from Oxford days and the actor- managers, the Bancrofts.

When Fred wrote of this period in London, he says nothing about life in Raynes Park. It doesn't seem likely, from the way he describes them, that Minnie Weatherly was with her husband on the jaunts to the theatre or the opera. His children would be going through their teens, so presumably she was with them and managing the house – the skill for which Fred so praises her. Alice Mangold Diehl doesn't give Minnie a name when describing a visit with her husband to Fred Weatherly and his wife. She writes of 'their beautiful artistic house built for them at Raynes Park near

Wimbledon - a gem of architecture of a bygone romantic period with a central hall and wide staircase, upon whose gallery opened the suite of bedchambers'. Later in her book she provided another domestic detail. The Diehls gave up living in Regents Park Terrace and moved to Brighton. They took with them 'a beloved spaniel called Carlo and the exquisite fox terrier puppy, given me a few months earlier by Mr Weatherly. She was the daughter of his well-known West Country fox terrier Doctor, whom I named because of her lissom grace, Fairy'.

It shouldn't have been a surprise to me that Fred once had a dog, common for the gentry of the period, but it was, as he doesn't mention it. Devoted owners often do in memoirs. A West Country terrier would be a Parson Russell terrier, aka Jack Russell. Calling a dog Doctor is unusual, but not as inappropriate as Fairy for a member of a feisty breed. In Fred's case, perhaps there was impishness. He must have heard a respectful 'Yes, Doctor, No Doctor' all the time as a child in Hillside, all the household would be expected to defer to the old doctor. Now he can call the shots 'Come here Doctor, Sit Doctor'. Was this a way of rebelling against the old man?

During the first few years in London as a junior, Fred appeared at the Surrey Sessions. The next step was to join a circuit of which there were eight. He followed advice and joined the South Eastern circuit, which began by his having to lodge in Maidstone for the Assizes. He didn't like this posting, once it dawned on him that he didn't know a soul in any of the other south-eastern towns either where Assizes would be held. Fortunately, solicitors from the West Country were now sending briefs to his chambers, expecting him to appear down there, as they knew him to originate from their part of the world. He was granted permission to transfer to the Western Circuit, for which he wrote, 'the gods be praised'. Soon, he had much more work in the west than in London.

As Fred was beginning to identify himself with the law, his son Alec moved in the other direction. Alec had obtained a place at Brasenose College in the steps of his father to read law but, in 1893, he threw it in to go on the stage. The tussle between the law and the arts thus continued in the family. Fred was displeased but he remained sufficiently sympathetic to artistic ambitions to write, 'When my boy was mad enough to leave Oxford and go on the boards, it was to Irving's fatherly care I entrusted him. I felt that the smallest part under the great actor-manger was the best luck that could happen to him.'

The West Country

At the end of 1893, Fred decided to move west, buying a house in Clifton in Bristol. It was near the home of members of his mother's family. Apart from the pleasure arising from work with colleagues he already knew, he drew more from re-familiarising himself with the countryside and the history of the locality. This was from a Burns Night speech, that he was asked to give shortly after his return to Bristol:

"It was a happy hour that brought me back to settle in my country of the West – to walk once more over the green hills of Somerset, to dream again of Arthur and of Avalon, to see again in fancy the earliest Christian Church planted by Joseph of Arimathea, to stand by the shores of the Bristol Channel and in dreams to watch the great sea-venturer, John Cabot, as he sailed past the stormy hills of Wales; in dreams to hear again John Wesley's silver tongue, the stirring speeches of Burke and the songs of the ill starred poet, Chatterton."

He continued song writing; important collaborators now were Sir Paolo Tosti and the young Eric Coates. He wrote two songs about Somerset which have endured –'We Come up from Somerset' and, with Eric Coates as composer, one of his most beautiful songs, 'Green Hills of Somerset'. 'Parted' was the most renowned result of the collaboration with Tosti. In a newspaper article about Fred after his death, it was stated that they both travelled to Balmoral Castle to perform this for Queen Victoria in a recital for her diamond jubilee. Fred doesn't mention this event in his memoirs, surprising given how many encounters with well-known people do appear.

In 1901, Fred moved from Clifton to Bath, arguing for Bath because of the convenience of its railway connections as several lines ran into the station, which simplified the travel for his legal work. He continued to occupy chambers in Bristol though; the short journey between Bath and Bristol being a useful interlude to jot down songs as they came to him. He noted that by then the aristocracy and county families that had made Bath one of 'the gayest cities of fashionable society' had gone, to be replaced by more sober but very cultured residents. Fred set up house in Grosvenor Lodge, Combe Down just outside Bath. Despite its name, Fred describes it as a little house, but the spot was 'bracing and inspiring'. Now aged 53, Fred seemed to be set on a civilised life in Bath, a prosperous career at the Bar but with his very profitable song writing as a sideline. The law was now his dominant identity, but his song writing reputation was established and he could continue to publish them away from London. Composers would come to him although Fred always enjoyed train travel, according to my mother.

It all turned upside down. Sometime after 1901, Fred lost what his obituarists called 'the greater part of his fortune, through no fault of his own'. Fred himself refers to the years until 1910 as 'times that I hope fall to the lot of few men, times of sorrow and anxiety, of mistaken steps, of financial loss'. In a letter to Eddie in the US, dated 1919, he refers to a past contact with the Official Receiver and mentions bankruptcy. Luke in a letter to Eddie writes how Lionel Weatherly had been declared bankrupt and thus evaded his debts, 'dirty welcher', and goes on to say that Lionel had never discharged his debts to Fred. Fred may have been caught up in some scheme with Lionel which went bust and which came under the aegis of the Official Receiver, costing Fred most of his money but with only Lionel being declared bankrupt. Precisely when this financial disaster occurred is not clear. The 1901 census states that Fred and family were boarding (lodging) in a house in Clifton, rather than owning their own house in Whiteladies Road. Were they lodging now because they were about to move to Bath or because their house had had to be sold? How he lost his capital is unknown. There is no suggestion of his ever being a gambler and this is not implied by the obituarists' comment. He couldn't have been declared bankrupt for he continued with his Bar practice as he himself reports and is confirmed by entries in the local press during this period. He also continued song writing – ones enduring today from those years were 'Holy City' and 'Thora'- so income must have held up but he may have been obliged to repay his creditors.

Bankruptcy records from that period no longer exist. I find it hard to believe that a psychiatrist could be declared bankrupt and go on in practice, but that is what his brother Luke wrote. Lionel was an ambitious man and did buy properties to make into licensed houses for the care of the mentally ill. Maybe he persuaded Fred to invest heavily in the business side of his plans, which didn't succeed. The Weatherly brothers could be critical of each other but with sympathy; Herbert, Luke and Fred actively disliked Lionel.

Between 1901 and 1905, Fred separated from his wife. Minnie, who had never been a strong personality, had now become mentally ill. The separation from her was sometime after 1901. By 1905 Minnie is recorded as living in Wooton Villas in Portishead with her daughter Christine. Fred had another partner, one Maude Francfort, who was to live with him for nearly twenty years under the name of Mrs Weatherly, confirmed by the entry in the 1911 census. She was in Bath in 1903 and probably had moved into Grosvenor Lodge. When Fred wrote about stresses, he must have been thinking of this upheaval as well. He would now have additional outlay to keep Minnie's household on top of whatever else he was forced to pay. His children became estranged.Alec away in London, now married, was always closer to his mother and her sisters than to his father. Muriel, recently married to a wealthy Bristol man, was building a social life and would not welcome this scandal, while Christine his younger daughter showed her loyalty by moving in with her mother. Fred should have been ostracised socially and professionally in Bath. Having a mistress was hardly uncommon, but the form was to remain publicly loyal to your wife and not break up the family. However it is possible that Fred got away with it by producing a Mrs Weatherly shortly after his arrival in Bath. Minnie would have been unknown there, as they had been living in Bristol for the past eight years. Unless her behaviour had changed from the London days, she would have anyway been invisible in Fred's professional and social life in Bristol. If there wasn't much overlap between society in Bath and Bristol then, maybe people in Bath didn't doubt that Maude was the real Mrs Weatherly. Minnie by now was too withdrawn to make a fuss and the children absented themselves rather than cause scandal. Doctors and lawyers involved in Minnie's care would be bound professionally to keep quiet and presumably Fred didn't bring any domestic staff from Bristol.

What had happened to Minnie? My mother described her as having become strange and having to be put away. My mother who was born in 1906 said that when growing up in Fred's house in Bath she never heard Minnie spoken of. She was taken to visit Minnie once in a nursing home shortly before Minnie's death in 1920 telling me that she looked like a very old woman, unlike Fred who always looked young for his age. Peggy, Fred's niece, never met her aunt but thought that Minnie had premature senility, inherited from the Hardwick family. In fact, Minnie lived on for nearly twenty years after the

Minnie Weatherly.

separation. This is far too long for someone with an early onset dementia – she would have been nearly 60 when the separation happened and, with dementia onset at that age, would have had a life expectancy of around five years. She died of heart disease, without mention of senility on the death certificate. There is no suggestion that she was institutionalised, rather the evidence is that she lived a normal if limited life in Portishead, visited by her children who remained loyal to her. The daughter of her principal housemaid told me that her mother described Minnie as a very kind woman but 'very very sad'. Perhaps for my mother as young girl, 'put away' must have been what she thought had happened.

The likelihood is that Minnie developed depression. A photograph of her taken in her sixties shows a sombre looking woman in dark clothes. Depressions have an inherent component in their origin, but any such propensity usually needs adverse life events (sudden shocks, a loss) or long term stresses or both to produce a clinical condition. Minnie had experienced both - the financial setback that had overtaken Fred and the break-up of the marriage. Loss of both home and husband are seen as major risks for depression today but in Minnie's days they were the main things that gave a woman a social identity; their loss would be shattering. One could guess that the marriage had been failing for some time. Minnie seemed an odd choice for Fred at the time of his marriage and, though seen by Fred as loving and dutiful, she filled the role for him of a wonderful housekeeper. By the 1900s, she would have served that purpose now that the children were grown up and leaving home. Fred must have become used in London to more amusing female company. It was the time of the New Woman who was refusing to live by patriarchal rules and was asserting emotional and economic independence; the campaign for woman's suffrage would be in the background. Maude in contrast to Minnie was an attractive, experienced, travelled and independently wealthy woman whom Fred must have found an exciting companion for his later years.

Minnie's personality was not a robust one, feeble by family account, so she would not have fought her corner, coping instead with Fred's loss of interest in her by silent suffering and turning in on herself, blaming herself for her inadequacies as a wife. It would not have occurred to someone described as gentle, dutiful and Christian that her husband would actually desert her. While it was not uncommon for well to do men to have mistresses and the wife to accept these liaisons, provided they did not embarrass family or social life, Minnie may not have been brazen enough to do that. She would have responded by withdrawing, becoming silent, weeping, staying in her room and not eating as depression took over. Her behaviour would seem reproachful even punitive to a man intent on a new life with a free spirited woman. Making an arrangement for her to live quietly elsewhere on the grounds of health would be easier to countenance than doing this because he'd rather be with someone else. The children's loyalty to Minnie suggested that they saw her as the injured party in this situation. When they visited, the other woman (Maude) could not be mentioned. Fred himself did not visit her, only appearing to carry out speaking engagements in Portishead after her death. Yet, in all documents after the separation (deeds and wills) Minnie still refers to Fred, as my dear husband - the status of wife must have been crucial to her. Fred and Maude referred to each other in their wills as 'my very dear friend'.

Before there was any effective medication, the treatment of depression was in fact seclusion with nursing supervision with an expectation of remission in three years or so. Nowadays, Minnie would have been prescribed anti-depressant medication to reduce the symptoms of depression. One hopes that the children or sister of today's Minnie would have insisted that she saw her general practitioner. If it was thought that the depression was centred around a marriage breakdown, then psychological support would be added to help her deal with her loss, anger, the probable divorce and then to focus on what she might do from now on. If not getting a job, then being involved in some voluntary work would be a start to social rehabilitation. Hiding away at home would be discouraged. It would be easier today for Minnie's equivalent to start a social life on her own as there are fewer stigmas attached to her situation. There *would be no referral to a psychiatrist, unless the patient was expressing suicidal intent or had self harmed.*

Treatment, were she offered any, for Minnie would have been in the hands of a general doctor or perhaps a neurologist, not an alienist who saw the 'mad' patients. Diet, tonics and sleep aids would be prescribed with nursing supervision to see that the patient was kept both active and safe. Psychoanalysis was being widely discussed among members of the medical profession but its approach would not influence general practice in Portishead. The difference from today would be that the focus of treatment was then on restoring Minnie to a healthy physical state. Minnie's lack of robustness, nervous debility, was the target rather than helping her to neutralise or overcome the events that had caused her collapse. It is unlikely that anyone would discuss with her how she felt about Fred living with another woman called Mrs Weatherly only a few miles away. Even if it were thought relevant to her condition, it would have been embarrassing for doctors who knew the family socially, as they would in Portishead, to bring the subject up. This undiscussed humiliation could have been enough to maintain Minnie's sense of failure, preventing recovery of her self-esteem and meaning that she remained until her death 'a sad woman'. Divorce was becoming more common and the grounds for women to initiate it easier but, even if her religious principles allowed it, a divorce would have meant accepting her loss of status. She hung on, with sad dignity, to the knowledge that she was still the real Mrs Weatherly.

Eugenia Beatrice Maude Letouzel, born in 1858, came from a prosperous Jersey family who had been prominent landowners in Normandy. Two brothers John and Jacob fled France because of religious persecution and settled in Jersey marrying into local families; Maude was a great granddaughter of John. There must have been a continuing connection with relatives in Normandy because, during her lifetime, Maude inherited land there. By all accounts, she was beautiful and charming. Fred's brothers in America were always nice about her in their letters, while making disparaging remarks at some stage about everyone else in the family in England.

She married Colonel Alfred Frankfort, a military engineer whose career was in India. While stationed there, she met Arthur and Lizzie Weatherly who were living outside Darjeeling. Whether separated or widowed, Maude was back in the UK in 1901 living alone in Latchford, Cheshire but Arthur Weatherly's three daughters were staying with her at the time of that year's census. Fred was very fond of his widowed sister-in-law, Lizzie, and took an interest in the upbringing of her children. This may have been the way that Maude met him.

Fred and Maude seemed to have been accepted as a couple by his brothers including Alfred the parson who came to stay with them in Bath, supporting the idea that Maude was Mrs Weatherly so far as Bath society was concerned. My mother growing up in the house referred to the couple as grandpapa and grandmamma. However, while Fred's activities at the bar continued with many successful appearances as defence counsel in criminal cases, he didn't take silk until the extraordinarily late age of 75. The Lord Chancellor offered him this promotion immediately after he married for a second time, when Maude and Minnie had both died. He didn't become member of the Bristol Savages Club either until that same year and almost immediately was elected to life membership. Those cannot be coincidence; he was not being recognised by the powers that be until his home situation had regularised. Presumably this breach of convention was the reason too why he never received a national honour.

Maude was wealthy. If Fred had been in financial difficulty, then this must have been very welcome. They lived at first in Grosvenor Lodge in Combe Down and later at 10 Edward Street near the centre of Bath. Maude definitely owned the latter house that she made over to Fred before her death. During the twenty years they were together, Maude also made over much of her capital to Fred. According to Herbert, she did this to ensure that her husband had no claim on her money. Inheritance planning may have been a prominent topic for this couple because, about ten years into the relationship, Maude developed the first symptoms of the spinal cord degenerative disease that was increasingly to disable her and then render her bed bound.

I have traced no photographs of Maude; so can only speculate about her looks. Her great-niece Miriam was a childhood and lifelong friend of my mother. She and her mother, Maude's niece, were both indeed beautiful women. My mother told me that most of her memories of Maude when she was a child were of an invalid. She was firmly of the view that Fred did not marry Maude (and there is no certificate), in fact explaining to me that she was a friend who helped Fred in looking after her as a child. That she was expected to call Maude Grandmamma is of course inconsistent with this but my mother was always keen to have me respect Fred's memory. I inherited a rotating library side table that came from their house. In it, my mother used to keep a series of novels by F Marion Crawford, most of the volumes being autographed at the front by Fred or Maude. The earliest is signed by Maude 'Bath 1903', showing that she was established by then. My mother always kept these novels in the rotating table, which is how she must have known them. Crawford was a prolific writer, an American living in Italy who wrote mainly historical novels set there.

Fred's story is nearing 1913 when Danny Boy was published. To understand the congruence of events that led up to the song's creation, its time for the stories of his son Alec and his brother Eddie.

7. ALEC WEATHERLY

Alec John Frederick Hugh was Fred's only son and his first-born. He was born in1873 on Milton's birthday December 9th, thus called John. A friend sent Fred a piece of oak from Milton's house to commemorate this event, which Fred had made into an inkstand for the boy. Alec turned out better looking than the usual Weatherly-taller, with his mother's handsome features. He was sent to board at Whitelaw House, Rugby School where records reveal nothing apart from his presence for five years. Fred said of him then that his greatest interest was carpentry. From Rugby, he followed in his father's footsteps to Brasenose College arriving in 1892. He left at the end of one year to 'tread the boards' as his father called it. Since a teenager, he had wanted to act and was part of an amateur dramatic company while Fred and family were living in Wimbledon.

According to my mother, he fell in with an acting crowd while at Oxford and she thought it included the Barrymores. This seems unlikely as, although Lionel, John and Ethel were approximate contemporaries of Alec's, they hadn't started their careers in 1892 and there is no suggestion that they were in Britain when young.

Furnished with an introduction from his father to Sir Henry Irving, he set out to make his career on the stage. In fact, it wasn't a bad time to be doing this. Acting had become more respectable. Squire Bancroft and his wife had formed the first theatre company as would be recognized today. Because of them, the lot of actors improved – better salaries, proper dressing rooms and much more practical scenery that made performance easier. An actors' association had been formed in 1891, the first union to safeguard pay and conditions. The Bancrofts had retired from the Haymarket theatre in 1889 but, by the time Alec arrived to try his luck, there were several other London based actor-managers forming their own companies. The most illustrious was that of Sir Henry Irving at the Lyceum theatre. Henry Beerbohm Tree who took over at the

Haymarket after the Bancrofts, was so successful that he had a theatre built - Her Majesty's - for his company. Charles Hawtrey and Cyril Maude were other names. It was also a time when provincial theatre was becoming an important source of income, meaning that it was worth London based companies to go on tour. Each such company employed a stock of actors in training. Most of these young recruits did time on tour before they might be picked for a role on the London stage. Though perhaps perceived as a grind, it does seem that a career structure was developing with the possibility of advancement for a young actor seen to be talented. Long runs were becoming usual as they met the demand for more people to be able see the "stars" of the time. For a young actor in a small part, long runs gave job security but at the same time they meant that he or she could be stuck in a role rather than being able try out a range of similar parts, necessary if touring was meant to be training and a means of showing talent.

Another change was in the nature of the plays being produced. Henry Irving exemplified the old school of acting – dramatic and mannered in the great classical works. However, demand had grown for contemporary comedies, gentle and more true to life. Emotion in these plays was nuanced, passion hidden, as would be expected at home. The audience understood that they themselves were part of the social group that was being gently mocked in front of them on stage, but the vehicle for this sending up had to conform to the norms of polite society. As a result, actors from middle and upper class backgrounds were in demand to play parts of men and women of society, so it was no longer shameful to be of good birth and 'tread the boards'.

Alec Weatherly.

EVERY EVENING AT 8

ROBESPIERRE

A Drama in Five Acts by

VICTORIEN SARDOU

Rendered into English by LAURENCE IRVING

Maximilien Robespierre	HENRY IRVING
Clarisse de Maluçon	Miss ELLEN TERRY
Olivier *(Son of Robespierre)*	Mr. KYRLE BELLEW
Augustin Robespierre *(younger Brother of Robespierre)*	Mr. F. D. DAVISS
Benjamin Vaughan *(of the House of Commons)*	Mr. H. COOPER CLIFFE
Lebas *(Member of the Convention)*	Mr. FULLER MELLISH
Buonarotti *(a young Corsican)* *(devoted to Robespierre)*	Mr. LEONARD CALVERT
Couton } *(of the Committee of Public Safety)*	Mr. LOCKE
St. Just }	Mr. TAMWORTH
Old Duplay *(a Carpenter—Robespierre's landlord)*	Mr. BOWN
Simon Duplay *(Secretary to Robespierre)*	Mr. S. JOHNSON
Maurice Duplay *(Son of Old Duplay)*	Mr. F. HAYES
Didier } *(Police Agents of Robespierre's)*	Mr. C. H. KENNEY
Gerard }	Mr. W. GRAHAM
Billaud-Varennes *(of the Committee of Public Safety)*	Mr. LOUIS CALVERT
Jagot }	Mr. HATCH
Amar }	Mr. SHARP
Voulland } *(of the Committee of General Security)* *(hostile to Robespierre)*	Mr. BARTON
Ruhl }	Mr. F. M. PAGET
Vadier }	Mr. JAMES CRAIG
Thuriot }	Mr. W GARSTIN
Tallien }	Mr. LAURENCE IRVING
Fouché } *(Members of the Convention)*	Mr. C. DODSWORTH
Lecointre }	Mr. FERGUSSON
Legendre }	Mr. MORRIS
Héron *(a Police Officer of the Committee of Public Safety)*	Mr. F. TYARS
Count Harday de Hauteville	Mr. JUNIUS BOOTH
De Bussey *(a Prison Spy)*	Mr. L. J. S. WOOD
The Recorder of the Revolutionary Tribunal	Mr. GILBERT YORKE
Haly *(Head Jailor at Port-Libre)*	Mr. R. P. TABB
Another Jailor	Mr. W. MARION
Collas *(a Jailor at the Conciergerie)*	Mr. J ARCHER
Barassin	Mr. T REYNOLDS
Urbain *(a Servant)*	Mr. ERIC BLIND
A Workman	Mr. JENNINGS

Imprisoned at Port-Libre :

Maréchal de Mouchy	Mr. ELLIS	Charles Legnay } *The elder Legnay*	Mr. LIONEL BELMORE
De Broglie	Mr. PERCY NASH		Mr. FRITH
De Kersaint	Mr. EARDLEY HOWARD	Gournay	Mr. YOUNG
De Pans	Mr. FRANK LACY	Lavergue	Mr. SNOW
D'Armaillé	Mr. ALEC WEATHERLY	Mancière	Mr. HERBERT INNES
Prévot D'Arlincourt	Mr. SINCLAIR	Sourdeval	Mr. H. G. LANE
Cottant	Mr. CHARLES VANE	Maleyssie	Mr. ERNEST MARTIN
Dossain	Mr. PARSONS	The young De Maillé *(aged 15)*	Miss MAY HOLLAND

Marie-Thérèse *(Niece of Clarisse de Maluçon)*	Miss WINIFRED FRASER
Madame Duplay *(Wife of Old Duplay)*	Miss CROSSE
Madame Lebas }	Miss SUZANNE SHELDON
Cornélie } *(her Daughters)*	Miss GEORGIE ESMOND
Victoire }	Miss IDA YEOLAND
Madame de Narbonne	Miss MAUD MILTON
Madame de Lavergue	Miss EDITH CRAIG
Mademoiselle de Bethisy	Miss CECILIA RADCLYFFE
The Maréchale de Mouchy	Miss MAUD ANSTEY
Madame Maleyssie	Miss NELLIE HUNTLEY
Charlotte Maleyssie	Miss WINIFRED KEAN
Claire Maleyssie *(Imprisoned at Port-Libre)*	Miss MARTIA LEONARD
Madame d'Avaux	Miss E. F. DAVIS
Madame de Choiseul	Miss GERTRUDE CLARIDGE
Mademoiselle Lacroix	Miss EMILY ARCHER
Madame Héré	Miss ADA MELLON
Madame de Narbonne's little Girl *(Aged 5)*	Miss TARVIN
Shade of Marie Antoinette	Miss ROSITA TENNYSON

Members of the Convention, of the Committees ; Ushers of the Convention ; Gendarmes of the Convention ; National Guards ; Police Agents ; Jailors ; Townspeople, &c. &c.

Programme for Robespierre 1899.

The first recorded stage appearance by Alec was in 1891, the year before he went to Oxford. He was classed as 'juvenile' in performances of Jim the Penman at the Lyric, Hammersmith. This was a detective drama about a famous eighteenth century forger. There is nothing to discover of his activity in the theatre over the next few years. Fred described his son's career as a long struggle, so one guesses that parts were hard to come by. In 1896, he was in 'Bitter Lemons' at the Lyric. Then came Lord and Lady Algy, a very popular play of the time, which exemplified the new lighter real-life style of writing. Opening in April 1898, it lasted for over 50 performances. Alec played Mr Jeal, a reporter for the Searchlight paper. By RC Carton, it was reviewed as "a play of pleasant cynicism, of worldlings who know and smile". The story is of a spendthrift, gambling son of a duke being saved by the craftiness of his wife. A year later, the Telegraph reviewer wrote, 'The public had taken kindly to Carton's comedy; the play was a good humoured satire on the idiosyncrasies and failures of people in the high mould.' And, 'The audience didn't see themselves as the people being targeted, but they are.' The play opened in New York at the Empire in 1899. The audience again loved it and indeed it was made into a film in 1919. The NY times reviewer said that of the dialogue, 'It would be difficult, if Mr Carton's light comedy were printed, for a 21st century antiquary to comprehend the language of its fleeting sentiment and humour as it is for any of us to laugh at the robust fun of Ben Johnson's comedies.'

In 1899, Alec went to a very different play – 'Robespierre', translated from the French original of Victorien Sardou by Lawrence Irving, which opened on April 15 1899 at the Royal Lyceum with Henry Irving as Robespierre. Although it had a huge cast, it was a vehicle for the one actor who played the dictator and was barely off stage. Ellen Terry played Clare de Montlucon, mother of Robespierre's illegitimate son whom she struggles to save from the guillotine. There were 69 speaking parts and 250 supernumeraries. One of the former was D'Armalille, an aristocratic prisoner played by Alec. Because it was a magisterial performance by Irving who was returning to the stage after an illness, the play was warmly received at first, indeed watched by the Prince and Princess of Wales on the second night. However, it was generally rated as long and gloomy, a character study of one man. All other characters were ephemeral, including Ellen Terry's, though her role was meant to provide the love interest. Ellen Terry wrote in her memoirs, "'Robespierre' was a grand success last night (opening night). It's a bad play but a showy one. Much variety in scene and no development in character. A one-man piece. Henry and over 250 supers. He acts the third act superbly.' By June, Terry wrote that the play was 'good business but not as crammed as at first'.

In July when the play closed in London, Henry Irving told Terry that he had lost £4000 on it.However there was a New York tour in the offing. Terry wrote, 'All the supers are asking my advice about going to America. I will have nothing to do with it. I don't believe that any of 'em will go except me and I am a fool to do it, but after all these years ....' 'Robespierre' opened at the Knickerbocker Theatre in New York in October 1899. The next day, the New York Times reported the warm welcome awarded to both Irving and Terry. There had been queues around the block during the day. The reviewer described the play as 'an opportunity for a great actor to portray an intelligible idea of a famous personage'. Later, 'The play is far from a masterwork and its performance with an actor less majestic and interesting than this great Englishman in the dominating role would be accounted tiresome.' Mention was made of the prisoners who were 'clearly individualised'. The play required them to practise ascending a makeshift guillotine in their prison cell so that they would be graceful when the time came for their execution. The audience found this gory. Alec must have ignored any advice from Ellen Terry for he was in the same part in New York.

Alec is recorded in the Green Room Book of 1907 (the Who's Who of actors) as being a business and stage manager, rather than an actor. He had changed direction in his career and this must have been what Fred meant by reaching calmer waters after his struggling start. He was stage manager of a production of 'Lord and Lady Algy' for Charles Hawtrey's company at the Avenue Theatre in Northumberland Avenue, now the Playhouse. He is listed as business manger for tours by the Harrison-Maude Company and with Beerbohm Tree's repertory company. There is only evidence of his being on stage again in 1908, at the Lyceum as one of Capulet's kinsmen in Romeo and Juliet and then playing the Salvation Army Captain in 'The Prince and the Beggar Maid'. A special matinee performance on July14 of the latter's first act was given as part of a mixed programme in aid of Kings College Hospital, which was being relocated to its new (and current) building in Camberwell. Ellen Terry was in the cast; the young Sybil Thorndyke sold programmes and Queen Alexandra was present.

In 1898, when 24, Alec married 21-year-old Gertrude Dorothy Thomas in the St Giles Registry Office. The address given for both of them was also in Bloomsbury, 6 Bedford Place; they were listed as actors on the marriage certificate. Gertrude was the daughter of one of the witnesses Dora Koch. Born in Ballarat in Australia, her schoolteacher father was dead. There were no signatures by any of Alec's family. At the time of the 1901 census, the couple were living in a boarding house at 21 Upper Woburn Place where Dora was housekeeper. In the house, as well, were two Indian law students, two dental students from New Zealand and two young Welsh singers. There were no children from this marriage. Gertrude appeared as a fairy in a pantomime at the Lyric Hammersmith in 1900.

In January 1903, Gertrude sued Alec for divorce, which became absolute a year later. Divorce was now easier for women to initiate, the courts allowing mental as well as physical cruelty as grounds. The records report her complaints that she was physically attacked on four occasions by him in 1902, pushed to the ground, then kicked in the back and, second, that he was having a liaison with an unnamed woman in Hitchin with whom he was living as man and wife. Alec didn't contest the divorce, which seemed to be granted expeditiously.

Alec then found another 20-year-old actress, Louisa Ethel Balcombe, whom he married in May 1905; now aged 31. This ceremony took place in Brentford Registry Office. There were again no family witnesses but one was Reginald Bacchus – a theatre reviewer, a satirist with some notoriety for publishing pornographic and macabre stories. He was said to operate in a 'sub world' of louche parties. Alec and Ethel were listed as living together in Queen Anne's Gardens in Chiswick. Judging by her appearance later in life, Ethel must then have been an attractive young woman with thick, dark, almost black hair but slight and pale in complexion. However at the time of her wedding she was four months pregnant.

The Balcombe family were long-term residents of Ticehurst in Sussex. Ethel's grandfather George Franklin Balcombe was the local printer and post master. One of his sons took over the business; the second son Charles became a solicitor qualifying in 1886. He married in 1881 and was living in Hastings when Louisa Ethel the first of his four daughters was born in 1883. George Balcombe died in 1898 and his son Charles in 1899 aged 44. There must have been little money left as, by 1901, his widow still living in Hastings was working as a needlewoman with a daughter May, only 14, listed as a nursery maid. Ethel had left home and was in digs in Tunbridge Wells training in costume making. Other lodgers with her were also training in dress or hat making. The costume making must have led Ethel to London and to the stage. Writing much later, Herbert Weatherly commented that she was a much better actor than Alec but she doesn't appear in any lists of actors of the time.

Betty, their first daughter was born in Portishead. Alec gave his address in the Green Room Book as Wooton Villas, which was his mother's address, and it was there that Betty was born in September 1905. A second daughter Marjory Ethel was born in December 1906 in Burnham Beeches.

Alec, since the separation of his parents, was estranged from Fred. Muriel, his older sister, had married well to a Bristol business family linked to Wills tobacco. She was living in a large house in Clifton and producing Fred a series of grandchildren. Muriel was a capable woman much given to good works but bossy and a snob. Her younger sister Christine, a much gentler soul who inherited some of Fred's talent for music and verse, moved with her mother to Portishead. Alec's modest career, two marriages and a child conceived out of wedlock must have been a disappointment to his father and made him a black sheep in his sisters' minds. He showed which side he was on vis-a-vis his parents by taking his wife to his mother's house to be confined and delivered.

In 1910, Alec, Ethel and daughters were living in a rented flat in Hackford Road, Brixton. In February of that year, his grandfather Dr Frederick died at the age of 90 in Portishead. The small town closed down for the funeral. Male members of his family led the mourners. Fred was there with four of his brothers – Eddie and Luke by now being in America. Alec attended; also present was Blayney Owen Cole, the son of 'the patient' in Hillside. His sons' wives and his female grandchildren sent wreaths but missing from the list of donors was Minnie. That autumn, Alec went on tour as manager with Percy Hutchison's (an Edwardian actor, later manager) touring company who were performing 'Smith', a new play by Somerset Maugham that had recently opened in London. In Torquay, he was taken ill with pleurisy but according to his obituary in Stage, he stuck to his nightly work and travelled on to Southampton. There he rapidly developed pneumonia followed by heart failure, which proved fatal within ten days on 31st October. His uncle Herbert Weatherly, rather than his father Fred, travelled from Hillside to notify the death and accompany the body to Portishead. The obituary goes on, 'He is to be buried in Portishead near his grandfather and it is a pathetic circumstance that his body passes through Bath where his company is now playing and his father resides.' He is buried at the opposite side of the churchyard in Portishead to the grand tomb containing Dr Frederick, his wife, mother-in-law and daughters. The local paper reports Alec's funeral without details of mourners. He was to be joined in the same grave by his mother and favourite aunt. He left £110 in his will for Ethel.

Pleurisy occurs when the outer cover of the lung becomes inflamed, usually as a result of a viral infection. It is very painful to take a deep breath. For that reason and that the cavity between lung and chest wall fills up with fluid, the lungs are not properly inflated and become susceptible to secondary bacterial infection - pneumonia. In the days before antibiotics, the pneumonia was usually fatal, the organs of the body being starved of oxygen. 1910 was not a year of a major flu epidemic, but such a death would have been common when there was one.

It is difficult to get a grip on Alec's character or what happened during most of his life. There are no first hand accounts. He died when my mother was three, so she had no personal memory of him. Muriel never spoke of him to her family. In the Green Room Book, he lists his hobbies as billiards and cycling, both new enthusiasms of the Edwardians. His education, appearance in photograph and these hobbies would suggest that he would have presented socially and spoken as an upper middle class young man of the time. There must have been a rebel in him to break from Oxford to take off for the stage. Fred certainly professed great admiration for the theatre and actors, so Alec would have heard a lot about that at home when growing up. He acted in Ealing as a schoolboy showing early commitment. He conformed enough to start at Oxford but the call of the theatre, on the look out for young men such as him to appear in the new lighter comedies, was too much it seems.One can imagine that Fred would have pointed out the uncertainties of seeking work as an actor in London and, when arguments failed to change Alec's intention, 'Here's an introduction to Henry Irving, you're lucky to have it and now you are on your own. Don't come running when things get difficult.' It was ironic for Fred who himself had tussled with similar conflicting interests to see his son reject the law for the stage.

It would have been a nice outcome if Alec had turned out to be a star, but the evidence is that he never progressed beyond minor speaking parts, despite being furnished with a gold plated introduction by his father. Presumably he had little ability as an actor, but fared better when he went into management and could take advantage of opportunities in the growing number of touring companies. His obituary implies that he was conscientious in that work. He must have scraped by on his earnings, as Fred wouldn't have helped him financially even if he had wanted to - it was the time when Fred himself was stretched.

Marriage and later divorce from his landlady's daughter must have shocked the family, (assuming they knew) confirming his outcast status. Alec didn't contest her action, which means the account of violence goes unchallenged and unexplained, perhaps rather reckless on his part. But by not challenging, he would ensure that the details would have remained out of the public eye, whereas a challenge might have meant press publicity, given who his father was and the details of the case. It could therefore be that his family never knew the grounds for Gertrude's complaint.

The summary of the divorce action by her against him was remarkably still available in the national archives at Kew - only a tiny minority of such files remain, a stroke of luck. I noticed that the solicitors acting for Gertrude were the same firm that I use today - another coincidence. Unfortunately no personal files remain with the firm from so long ago. Assuming Gertrude was not perjuring herself in court, the grounds for divorce are worrying. I had expected to read about adultery but not domestic violence, which does not fit with the picture of Alec that I had been building up. Nothing is said in the court papers of alcohol being a factor, the common trigger for such domestic attacks. Was Alec a wife beater, an inadequate man taking his frustrations out at home on her? It could have been that Gertrude, a feisty, independent Australian woman goaded him - you're useless, no money, no talent etc. One can imagine Alec being very sensitive to that.

Whether or not he wanted to remarry so soon, his second marriage was necessary if his older daughter was to be accepted without stigma. It must have been a great help that he could take his new wife to Portishead so that they could be near his mother when she delivered. Ethel was of a more ordinary background than he.

Her father moved up into the professional class by training as a solicitor but his early death left his wife and daughters without money. Ethel moved from Kent to London to be an actor but three years later at 21 was pregnant and married - a death knell for a career. Without family support or the possibility of paying for childcare, her life would be confined to the house, doubly frustrating if, as suggested, her acting talent was greater than her husband's. The contrast to the life of her sister-in-law Muriel would be marked – she had a large family but with staff would have found her life little inconvenienced by childrearing. There would be no question in those days that it was Ethel's duty rather than Alec's to stay at home, a view reinforced by social judgement that this early pregnancy would have been her fault - a result of her loose morals or fecklessness. Ethel's father died young when she was 16 leaving her family without money and the same happened to her with Alec's death at 36. She was now a 26 year-old widow with two small children and pretty well penniless.

The situation has not changed today for young women without means, despite government promises to subsidise childcare. A way out for middle class women today is to delay child-bearing until a career is established but life in the home after a first pregnancy at a young age without the chance to live as an independent person remains a risk for later depression and alcohol dependence. I was given no information by my mother about Ethel's own family. For instance I had no idea that she had three sisters, my great aunts. I went to Ticehurst where the parish church has a large and dilapidated churchyard but all the occupants of the graves are listed in the church, indicating that over twenty Balcombes are buried there, including Charles and his wife, Ethel's parents.

Alec's death had saddled Fred with a new responsibility - a near penniless Ethel and two granddaughters living in a rented flat in Brixton in London. Ethel's first move was to a rented house in Weston super Mare looking after her children with the help of one of her sisters. Fred then made a decision that would resonate down the next generations; he decided to take over the upbringing of his granddaughters, now aged six and five. They moved to Bath without Ethel where they would grow up in his house with him as a surrogate father. The reason for taking them away from Ethel can only be speculation. The family did not approve of her; indeed her sister-in-law, Muriel, refused ever to receive her. This may have been snobbery; she was of a lower class than the Weatherlys and an actress. Fred said to one of his sisters-in-law that Ethel was 'common'. Ethel had also conceived a child out of wedlock. However, Fred may have had more emotional reasons. He was mourning his son and feeling guilt, brooding perhaps about his role in their separation and about Alec dying without his family with him in Southampton. It may be that Ethel's physical presence, grieving herself, was just too painful to tolerate near him. Did he think that she entrapped Alec by her pregnancy? Did he blame her for Alec having to work all hours even when he was ill? Herbert Weatherly's view was different, that the main motive for Fred and Maude taking the girls in was to give their irregular household respectability, but he, at the same time, conceded that they were determined to give the girls everything they needed.

It may have all come down to money, for Fred made it plain to Ethel that he wouldn't support her and that she must work. Supporting Ethel in Weston with her family would be another drain on his finances on top of paying for his own household and Minnie's in Portishead. Ethel returned to London and worked for the next three years as a resident floor manager at the Piccadilly hotel, ensuring that the rooms under her supervision were properly prepared for guests. Then she was sent to America by Fred to live with one of his brothers.

Fred was 62 and Maude 52 when they took these two small girls into their house. A nanny was employed. Yet it must have been very disruptive for a couple who were living happily and comfortably together. Their action would have been altruistic but for the fact that the girls had a mother. There is no evidence that Ethel had neglected her children and thus wasn't a fit mother, though she could never have provided for them without financial help, which was not to be forthcoming from her in-laws given the disapproval she met within the family. Her own relatives in Hastings were impoverished since the death of her father, so would not have had the wherewithal to help her out of dependence on the Weatherlys.

Ethel would have no ammunition to fight against this decision to remove her children from her. Her emotional state must have been very low and then it is very difficult to stand up for one's rights. There is no evidence that she contested Fred's decision. By acceding, she was now set on a track of powerlessness and dependence, which in time she seemed to accept as her lot. She becomes a victim, to whom bad things happen.

In 1910, there was little understanding of the emotional needs of a developing child. These girls had lost their father and now their mother was to live away from them to be replaced by a nanny and an old man and woman as their parents. Betty at 5 would be old enough to mourn her father and to ask questions as what had happened to her mother. Marjory perhaps depended on the more dominant Betty to explain. The separation would last nearly fourteen years. Fred and family would not understand the child perspective. Rather the loss of an unsuitable woman as their mother would, in their view, be more than compensated by a comfortable middle class life in a well-regulated household. Damage to a child's development from such loss can be minimised if time is spent with the child to explain the reality of what has happened and that it's not the child's fault. Fred is unlikely to have thought it appropriate to explain to a child what had happened to Ethel. There is no mention in the family letters of her visiting Bath to see her children while she was still in London. The impression given to me was that Maude became the mother.

8. EDWARD AND MARGARET (JESS) WEATHERLY

The obituary of Edward Weatherly dated December 7 1934 from the Durango Herald and Ouray Plaindealer describes the facts of his life summarised:

He came from an aristocratic family, grew to manhood at his place of birth and then entered Oxford University, graduating with an MD degree. He then followed the profession of an educator before practising medicine at the Bristol Royal infirmary and St Bartholomew's hospital. He settled in the United States in 1888, abandoned the practice of medicine and became a sports editor on an Omaha newspaper before moving to San Francisco. In 1889 he married Margaret Anastasia Enright who survived him. He moved to Ouray in 1907 when he became interested in (silver) mining, becoming an authority - his knowledge of the San Juan mines was such that no other man could match him. He owned the Combright properties and was agent for several other properties. He wrote over a hundred articles on mining and the monetary question, described as scholarly authentic works, which commanded attention of newspapers, magazines and high government officials. His influence was felt in the fight for re-monetisation of silver. Finally, 'Mr Weatherly came from a wealthy and accomplished family but it was not necessary for him to bask in their light, a thing he never did because his own accomplishments, brilliance of mind, culture and education were sufficient unto themselves.'

Then there was another obituary which is worth quoting in full:

'It is with sadness that we chronicle this week the death of E. C Weatherly. With his passing something has gone out of Ouray - and our life - which cannot be replaced: but as Solon said that a man has not lived until he has died, so it is that we do not know the fullness of the influence of another until the personal contact with that one has been removed. Personal contact with E. C. Weatherly will be no more, but his influence upon many individuals and the community, will never pass. Impressions left on others by his remarkable mind will know no death, kindnesses to his loved ones and his friends will only increase with his passing, many of his thoughts and data and the results of his careful research have been embalmed in everlasting print. Had those who knew him best and loved him had control of the hand of fate he would still be among us, administering to his mate, writing scholarly articles carrying on the fight for silver, keeping in touch with the guiding influences of at least three governments and keeping himself posted on every mining operation, large and small, in the San Juan and the world — but that is not the way of life. Through a Devine Economy E. C. Weatherly's active, cultured and useful life on this sphere is ended and, in sorrow, the fact must be accepted.'

In 2003 I visited Ouray. The Historical Society kindly agreed to accommodate me in the town in exchange for a lecture on Fred Weatherly to them. Just before I left, I heard from Petey's grandson who had travelled through Colorado some years ago. He went to Ouray in search of information about Eddie's life, so that he could tell his grandfather about an uncle whom he had never met. His report was not optimistic; he saw the Combright property, but otherwise found out little. Eddie's grave in the local cemetery was unmarked and did not contain Margaret.

The small plane from Denver to Montrose passed over the spectacular Rockies still thick with snow. It was early May and I had expected a warm alpine spring with grass and flowers everywhere. The car ride from Montrose up the Uncomprahgre River valley to Ouray however showed me a brown/grey countryside still with patches of ice everywhere. No spring and, shortly after I arrived in Ouray, the temperature plunged and a snow storm followed. Ouray lies in a valley at 7792 feet, enclosed by mountains - the Brown Mountain to the right, the amphitheatre to the left and Mt Abrams straight ahead. These peaks are over 10000 feet and of course snow covered. The scenery was awe-inspiring for someone not used to mountains.

This road in to Ouray continues straight on through the town up round Mt Abrams to former mining settlements, such as Ironton, now largely derelict and then to the larger town of Durango. The section from Ouray to Durango is referred to as the million-dollar highway, presumably reflecting its construction cost and its importance to the town when it was built. The Combright property lay to the right of this road.

Ouray has a main street with side streets in grid pattern. Notable is the uniformity of architecture in the centre of town, Victorian in style. Along Main Street is the large, turreted Beaumont hotel in the process of restoration and Wrights Opera House, not in current use. St Michael's Church built in the 1880s is still with an active congregation; it was where Eddie's funeral took place. I learnt something of the history of the town from Ann Hoffman's husband who became my guide. Ouray was developed in the 1870s as a back-up town to support those working mines higher up in the mountains. It provided r and r for the usually single silver miners, with bars, beds and brothels. But, it was also where mine owners set up home; hotels, restaurants and shops flourished. At the beginning of the last century, when the silver mines lost their profitability, Ouray lost its purpose and did not develop further. Its buildings remained untouched, which gives the town charm now and in fact enables it to be a heritage site. Its stable population though has fallen from about 2000 in Eddie's day to 700 today. A role as a tourist centre has emerged both for winter sports, being called the Switzerland of America, and summer hiking. The old houses are in many cases becoming second homes.

During my stay, I was taken to see Eddie's grave in the Cedar Hill Cemetery. Indeed it was unmarked, either because no stone was paid for at the time or it could have been that one had washed away in the not infrequent floods. As I was to be trampling through Eddie and Margaret's lives, the least I could do was to arrange for a small stone to be laid on this grave. Then I was taken up towards Silverton to see the Combright, Eddie's mine. It lies at 9000 feet and on what seems a vertical side of the mountain. Nowadays it can only be viewed from the highway across a gorge carrying the Uncomprahgre River from the Bear Falls down to Ouray but, in Eddie's day, there would have been access direct from Ouray up the other side of the gorge, made easier with tracks up the hillside for carts to be dragged by burros or by hand. Now it is a four-hour steep climb up rough ground to get there. Apparently the site never yielded any useful silver ore or other metals.

I was shown a pretty one-storey house, which might have been the one, the couple rented on arrival, but no one could trace the wooden house where they lived later. A member of the historical Society provided me with copies of accounts of litigation proceedings that pitched Eddie against a Henry Jackson – it seemed a family with whom he had had many disputes. There was a reference in a diary of the period to Eddie having an expert historical knowledge of the mines, but no idea of practicalities of the business at which he was a failure. I also was given a newspaper cutting reporting Margaret's death in 1938 in an institution for the insane and destitute in Pueblo. It didn't look as if either of their lives had ended well.

Unfortunately no one still living in Ouray had been traced who had any knowledge of them, but all the information I had gained so far was at variance with the glowing obituaries of Eddie and confirmed what the previous family visitor had thought. One question no one could answer - as I read that there was always a shortage of medical help in the town at this period - why on earth didn't Eddie practice, if things were not going well with mining? There is a memorial to him of sorts in Ouray. A small hut still sits on the Combright to which has been attached a sign saying 'Antiques'. It is a tease for tourists who see the sign and ask how to get there and are then told it's a four-hour climb. Poor Eddie, a local joke as a legacy.

The effect of altitude was marked on me. As mobile phones had no signal there, I had to walk from my hotel to the general stores on the main street to buy an ATT card. This was a walk of about 200 yards uphill. I thought the combination of the cold and breathlessness would finish me off. How did Eddie and Margaret manage?

Boulder is a pretty and relaxed university town; the campus of the University of Colorado there is built in Italianate style. In the basement of the library sit the archives. The archivist helpfully had arranged for a student helper to go through all the 31 boxes before my visit and identify the ones potentially useful to me containing personal papers, photographs and letters. The rest contained all Eddie's collection about the mining claim in the San Juans. Those researching the history of silver mining in Colorado periodically consulted these other boxes. With further student help, I was able, in the three days that I had, to sort through the relevant 5 boxes and photocopy material.

In the 1930s, the University of Colorado was keen to collect as much information as possible on the development of the state in which silver mining in the San Juan's had played an important part. 1936 must have been the year that Margaret was taken from Ouray to the hospital in Pueblo. Eddie's collection was evidently well known, but whoever did the collecting up of his files for the University seemed to have carried out a form of house clearance, for every bit of paper in the household was boxed up. Fortunately for me, those loose papers included letters to Eddie from his brothers, his draft replies, Margaret's copious and often illegible writings, recipes, health tips, gardening plans and shopping lists. There were photographs of Eddie and Margaret and of their life in Ouray. The letters were mainly from brothers Herbert and Luke to Eddie, written in the 1920s and 1930s but few were precisely dated. There were some from England, including ones by Fred. To my surprise, a Mrs Mitterling who was listed as completing the cataloguing of the contents in 1975 was still alive and in Boulder. I telephoned her - she was astonished to hear of anyone's interest in the Weatherlys after all this time. The cataloguing was a task that she was put to after joining the library staff – she had no personal knowledge of the Weatherlys, as I had hoped. She must have read the material as she classified, for she remembered thirty years later that the Weatherlys came to a very sad end. I hope my call was a small acknowledgment of all those hours of work.

In the letters now in front of me, I read of my grandmother being sent to America by Fred, her hard life, then her return with her daughters - my mother and Betty - for a four year stay in Richmond Va. There was a graphic account of the onset of Betty's mental illness leading to their unwilling return to Britain in 1930, confirming what Peggy told me. The letters told of the Eddie, Luke and Herbert's hardship during the Depression years, their attempts to support each other emotionally and financially and their bitterness about Fred back in Britain. Herbert seemed to be the strongest of them and played an important role in helping my grandmother and her daughters. Margaret's copious writings usually to herself included poetry, some music, but mainly were expressions of her devotion to Eddie. Later she wrote bitterly about their hard times in Ouray. As she got older, her writing became mostly indecipherable scribble, describing visions and other frightening experiences. The most anguished accounts occurred mainly after Eddie's death when she felt that there was nothing left for her. She wrote on old envelopes, seed packets, baking paper – it seems anything that came to hand.

But amongst all this, I did find her account very different to Fred's, of the origins of Danny Boy, confirming that she was indeed the unnamed sister-in-law and, for that discovery, my trip achieved its purpose. A whole new vista for research had opened up for my return home - what happened to Betty?

Edward Christopher was the third son and fifth child of the family, born in 1855. His education followed the course of his older brothers - first school in Portishead, Hereford and then Brasenose College in 1874. It was a promising start, as he obtained a Somerset Thornhill Scholarship, established by the Duchess of Somerset in 1686. In old age, he recalls happy social occasions at Brasenose, for example:

"It's summer term at Oxford. I am in my old rooms at Brasenose - the rooms that were occupied by Heber where he wrote the Newdigate Prize poem, 'Palestine'. And I'm giving a Wine, a college supper party, and Alice the dear sister is here and other fellows' sisters too.

 We've just come back from the river and we are singing and the girls singing with us – the Eton Boating Song. Now they are calling for a song from Alice. She is standing at my side at
the little piano and brother Fred is playing for her, while she sings Way down upon the Swanee River. Then we are calling on Dolly Jones for John Peel, though he has never followed hounds in his life. At the end of the last verse, a knock is heard. It's the vice Principal's scout. 'What's up? The Vice Principal's compliments, gentlemen and he hopes you'll soon be done 'cause he wants to go to sleep.'"

Fred of course was by now married and tutoring in Oxford; it's likely that Alice was staying with him. Perhaps because of such jollity, Eddie did very badly at Oxford. In October 1876, the College records show him as being suspended from the emoluments and position of scholar for three months because he failed the first public examination, Mods. Three months later he was deprived of his scholarship for failing again and in 1877 his name was removed from the College books.

This Oxford record is at variance with Eddie's glowing obituary - no mention of the study of medicine (it wasn't a possible option at Oxford then). I found no trace of him as student or graduate at Bart's or Bristol. His name has never been on the medical register. The medical training described in the obituary in fact was that of his father. Thus his story of being an ex-doctor was an affectation that he must have used to beef up his status in the US.

His doting wife, perhaps realising that there is some explaining to do, later writes that "Eddie has been at medical school all his life". He probably read widely on the subject, absorbed much and would have sounded informed. This is the first example of what seems to be a feature of his life style – amassing and retaining considerable information, thus appearing an authority. It's now clear why he didn't earn a living through doctoring in Ouray. Margaret also wrote that 'Eddie falls short of being able to face the brutal business of the world and should always have been provided for at least to the extent of having food and shelter all his life. It's been no secret that he has suffered these attacks since he was a child.' Attacks could mean epilepsy or panic attacks. What she described sounds like anxiety. If Eddie were an epileptic, she would have said so in her personal writings. Being subject to disabling anxiety attacks at times of stress could explain his exam failures at Oxford. While epilepsy, if not socially acceptable, was recognised and treated, anxiety attacks would not have been diagnosed.

San Francisco

After Oxford, Eddie worked for the Sassoon family acting as a private secretary. This family was now part of the establishment. Beginning with businesses in India and China, their trading and shipping empire had become global by the 1860s. Several of the family settled in England and became important players in Victorian and Edwardian society. David Sassoon (1792-1864) the founder of the modern dynasty had eight sons. The eldest, Albert, led the family in Britain, receiving a baronetcy. Two brothers, David and Reuben David became intimates of the Prince of Wales (later Edward VII), the latter acting as his private banker. Eddie was employed as secretary to two of the brothers, Reuben and Arthur, and at times to Sir Albert himself. Eddie's wife proudly writes that he had to correspond with Prince Leopold of the Belgians and the Shah of Persia in this role. He prepared Reuben's son David for Eton, apparently the first Jewish boy to go there. This must be the work as educator, described in his obituary, in which role he travelled extensively accompanying his employers. The Weatherly family photograph shows Eddie, the most handsome of the brothers, in a frock coat. He would have been working for the Sassoons at the time.

In 1888 Eddie emigrated to the United States. His obituary reports him as working as a sports journalist, first in Omaha and then in San Francisco. His younger brothers Luke (Lewis b. 1863) was already settled in San Francisco, having emigrated after he finished his studies as a non collegiate student at Oxford. They shared an apartment near Golden Gate on Lygon St. In April 1890, Eddie married a young widow Margaret Anastasia Carrillo, nee Enright.

Her father Dennis Enright was from Tarbert on the Shannon in Co Kerry. In 1860 he emigrated to America as part of the mass escape from poverty and British rule. Already married to Margaret Brassel with two sons, he settled with his family first at Port Henry near New York before moving to Jo Daviess County in North West Illinois. Four other children were born including Margaret in 1864. In 1868, the family moved on to San Francisco but, because there was a major earthquake immediately after they arrived, they fled from there to settle in Napa County, near Sacramento. Margaret's mother died in 1869 soon after their arrival there, leaving Dennis to bring up 6 children. Dennis was a railroad worker. Margaret recalls her father with tenderness:

'It is the memory of how my own dear father looked when he heard of one of us being sick, hungry or homeless – how quick the mist of sorrow crept up from his honest Irish heart and covered the most precious grey blue eyes on earth.' Margaret identified throughout her life with her Irish roots, seeing them as the source of her strong Catholic faith, her love of singing and of her thick lustrous red brown hair. She attached a lock to a piece of paper and writing about that later in life said:

'My hair is a dark brown with a decidedly glow of red in it and is naturally a most unusual and beautiful shade of brown. I belong to a family of wonderful and abundant hair -mine own at the present being long enough to sit on easily being very thick; my sister's at this date being to her ankles, full and fine and thick on her head.'

She recalls running out across the fields in the Napa Valley at dusk to meet her father on hearing in the distance his singing or playing on his 'low, mournful whistle' the traditional Irish songs and tunes – Come-all-Yes. A great heartbeat rose up in my throat on the words 'Spring in Old Killarney'. She learnt his repertoire of Irish folk music and songs as she was possessed of a musical memory and good singing voice.

The family later moved into Sacramento itself where life was less idyllic. Later in life, during the time of prohibition in Colorado after 1916, she rails against alcohol, hinting that she had experienced problems at first hand.

'It is because of the knowledge of what drink has done to my family that I condemn the Catholic Church for not lending every effort they possess to wipe out saloons forever and to help abolish the accursed bootleg and help give us a clean world for, in my own life, I have seen and lived through the truth of how the drinking habits (and all the depredation that attends it) of those we love can almost destroy your own life – although we never touch it. Keeping company with those who drink has ruined more lives of young men than anything else.'

This would suggest family drink problems as she and her siblings were growing up. Margaret wrote that her sister Hannah was lucky to survive but did so as an invalid because of her experiences and writing to her states that she and her husband 'would have done far better here in this little mining town (Ouray) than in that low-tread, foul beast-hearted place (Sacramento) that you hate so much and for a very justifiable cause.'

Margaret's first marriage was to Albert Francisco Carrillo, son of Don Julius Carrillo.

These accounts of Eddie and Margaret's early life come from her disorganised reminiscences that I found in the Boulder boxes. Much was written in old age when Eddie and she had failed in their enterprise in Ouray. She is now bitter and blames others. But Margaret still comes across as a spirited woman with a vivid turn of phrase. All San Francisco records were destroyed in the 1906 earthquake, so the dates of her first marriage and subsequent widowhood cannot be checked. Carrillo, judging by the Internet, is a common name in California. Despite her strong Irish roots, both of her marriages were out of that culture. The second to someone of British origins probably pained her family.

In April 1890, Eddie and Margaret were married in a civil ceremony; he was 35 and she 26. There was a second ceremony at Holy Cross church in 1896. It seems possible that she was divorced from Carrillo before she was widowed, thus a church marriage was only possible when her first husband had died.

Eddie and Jess Weatherly, portrait photograph ca 1905.

A photograph of Margaret around this period taken at the San Francisco Irish Fair shows a fashionable woman, hair piled up and wearing an elaborate frilly blouse. She seems determined, even a little stern in expression, nose rather pointed, chin prominent and lips set. Eddie by now had lost his hair on top with the rest brushed towards a full cut at the back. His expression seems rather haughty, the look real or feigned of an aristocrat.

From the time of the marriage, Margaret was called Jess by Eddie and is called that in correspondence with Eddie's family and refers to herself as such. The marriage was one of passion and devotion, emotions that were to last through all their tribulations until their deaths. Eddie had a sense of his superiority, was well read and inclined to amass information about many subjects of interest to him so that he would be seem as authoritative and be asked to write articles and give lectures. He was ambitious, still wanting to prove himself to his father and brothers. Unfortunately his academic attributes were not combined with any practical ability at business or money making, which is what he hoped to do in Ouray. Furthermore, a stubbornness or rigidity in his character meant that he wouldn't modify his plans according to the reality of the situation. Jess provided him with uncritical admiration and support, interpreting every adversity as not being due to the unreality of his plans or his pigheadedness but due to being thwarted by others or not being given adequate financial backing by his family. Nothing was her darling Eddie's fault. For Jess, the marriage led to an almost magical entry into what she saw as a grand, wealthy English family. She writes in respectful tones about the Weatherly lineage and revels in the contacts of Eddie's parents. When labelling her photographs, she always refers to herself whether its subject or the person taking the photo as Mrs E. C. Weatherly. Her attitude to Eddie was of unadulterated admiration; he had for her nobility that was divinely inspired.

I came across nothing written about their life together in San Francisco; presumably Eddie continued work as a journalist until their fateful move to Ouray. His obituary said that he became interested in mining and moved to Ouray 27 years before his death (1907). In fact Margaret was writing letters from Ouray in 1905, so the move must have been soon after the turn of the century.

Ouray ca 1905. *Courtesy of the Ouray Historical Society*

Shortly after the move to Ouray, they prepared wills. Eddie, in his formal script, drafts out for her the lines that she should use to begin her will:

'I, Margaret Weatherly make this my last will. I give devise bequeath my estate and property, real and personal to my husband Edward C Weatherly and appoint him executor of this my will without bounds.'

Her response attached to his page takes up five, beginning:

'It is the solemn wish of my soul that everything that I have ever owned in this world –every scrap of lace (including that which you Eddie bought for me in Dublin), every scrap of everything I possess shall be burned to ashes at my death and that no living soul in this world shall lift the cloth from my dead face to look at it (excepting my husband) and that everything be locked away until this wish is carried out in full. Not even a post card, not even a scrap of ribbon or string nor pin that ever belonged to me must ever leave your dear precious hands (Eddie's) in any state but ashes.' Despite this proposed bonfire, she then makes several bequests before launching into her feelings for Eddie and her wishes for him after her death.

'May God's greatest blessing ever follow you and may God's light ever shine upon your blessed soul, may the right friends ever be around you and help you. You were God's message to me, my guardian angel, my answer to my prayers to the blessed Virgin Mary from the depths, the light and joy of my world and my life, my comfort, my only blessing, my salvation and saviour. If we ever meet again through out the long years of eternity, I shall know your beautiful face and kneel down before you in gratitude for the blessings you have been to me.'

There was no equivalent paean from him to her in the archive, but letters and notes always began 'My darling' and ended 'Ever your own loving Eddie'.

This adoration might be expected of a religious writing about their feelings for Christ, but it seems over the top when written by a woman approaching her forties about her husband. There is perhaps a clue to the origin of her attitude to Eddie when she says that he was the answer to her prayers to the Virgin from the depths- if one adds of despair. Did Eddie rescue her from an abusive marriage helping her divorce? Was she in poverty? There is something sexual in tone here too; I wonder whether Eddie's arrogance yet insecurity demanded physical adoration in the bedroom of the sort that she described here? Whether her devotion feeding his sense of superiority helped Eddie or whether this couple would have done better if this intelligent woman had been more objective about him is an open question.

Ouray

After American independence, free coinage of gold and silver was adopted, implying that gold or silver could be taken to the mint for conversion into coins that reflected the weight presented. Gold was always more valuable than silver and the price ratio between them per unit weight was fixed at 16:1. After the discovery of gold in California, the value of gold started to fall in relation to silver. To compensate, free coinage of silver was dropped save for the silver dollar that remained totemic in American minds. After the civil war, when both sides printed worthless paper money, there was pressure to drop the silver dollar in favour of a hard gold-based currency. In 1873 silver was demonetised, an act called by some the crime of 1873. Its effect was to create hardship for poorer people who could not aspire to hold gold. To satisfy demand for silver once again to become legal tender, two acts were passed - in 1878 (Bland Allison Act) and in1890 (Sherman Silver purchase Act) that ensured that the Treasury would buy each year a fixed quantity of silver at a guaranteed price. Silver value was thus guaranteed but without a return to monetary silver. The silver mines and the towns in the western states, particularly Colorado, supporting them bloomed. It was worth now investing in the technically challenging task of pushing railways through the mountains to link the developing towns there, to bring the ore out cheaply but also to enable the inhabitants to be connected with rest of the country commercially and socially. But, huge quantities of silver were now produced leading to a glut. People wanted to get rid of it and to buy gold as security, leading to shortage of gold. Other countries were also buying gold, so it was necessary to reverse things in the US. The Sherman Act was repealed in 1893 and the value of silver was immediately halved, leading to closure of mines, joblessness, strikes and economic depression in the western states. To counteract this and redevelop the importance of silver, a subgroup of Democrats, called the silver Democrats, ensured that William Jennings Bryan ran as presidential candidate in 1896 with a return to a bimetallic monetary standard as part of his programme. It was a west versus east coast and bitter election. Bryan lost to William McKinley and with him went an early return to the silver standard.

The mining areas went through a recession until the early 1900s, when more gold was discovered in western Colorado and the newspapers were full of optimistic news for future discoveries. World War 1 increased demand for metals of all kinds including rare ones such as molybdenum and tungsten keeping the mining industry buoyant. The ensuing Depression finished the mining industry off. This, combined with droughts affecting farming, its other source of prosperity, reduced Colorado to starvation levels in the 1920s. But snow sports and tourism in the 1930s brought new life to the mountain regions. There is very little current mining activity but it is said locally that only a small sample of the available minerals were ever got from the ground.

The economic background to Eddie and Jess's life there between 1900 and 1936 was thus a very turbulent one. Ouray like other towns in the mountain region of Colorado went through the vicissitudes of the western states; its prosperity or otherwise was largely determined by events outside local control. Ouray was named after a chief of the Ute tribe of Indians who led his people to cohabit peacefully with the new explorers and settlers in their lands. It was established in 1876 as a staging and back-up town for the more rough ad hoc settlements that arose near the mines themselves – Ironton, Silverton and Red Mountain Town. In a valley alongside a river with local hot springs, it was well positioned. Over the next twenty years, the population grew to approximately 2500. Water is brought down from a local creek that has hot spring water feeding into it so it doesn't freeze in winter. The town has always been subject to flooding when the weather is warmer than usual, the snow melts and there are simultaneous thunderstorms. Two flash floods greatly damaged the town in 1909 and 1929, while Eddie and Jess were there.

The building of a branch line to Ouray from the Denver-Rio Grande railroad enhanced the town's prosperity. Important brick buildings –Town Hall, Beaumont Hotel, Hospice and Opera House were all put up, along with substantial Victorian villas for more prosperous families, giving the town a sense of permanence. By

1900, it was possible to make a circuit by rail from Ouray through the mountains to Durango, called the 'most magnificent mountain trip in the world'. Tourism thus started, producing demand for hotels, shops and restaurants. In this respect, Ouray differed from its neighbours higher up as it could withstand the down turn in silver mining, which occurred after the repeal of the Sherman Act in1893. Most mines closed then with attendant unrest and hardship, but several near Ouray stayed open because of their promise of producing gold. The town was also helped by a local man Tom Walsh who became one of America's richest men from his ownership of Camp Bird mine nearby. He was the town's benefactor until his death in 1910, endowing churches, the hospital and library.

By the early 1900s when Eddie and Jess arrived, the town was an established community, some mining activity in the mountains nearby still underway with excitement that more was to come. Through tourism and the railway, it would not have seemed that remote, nor would they be deprived of current necessities or even luxuries. However a description from the time indicates that there would have been several differences from the quiet heritage town of today. Trees were scarcer as they were chopped for timber for building scaffolding in the mines and for fuel. The air was thus polluted from wood fires everywhere and often the water was too, as mines and mills discharged into local streams. The town would also have been noisy – steam trains, building works, sawmills, horses and mules and the occasional brawl, even gunfire in the street.

Eddie and Jess coming from San Francisco would be exposed to a much harsher climate and had to manage daily life at an altitude of 7800ft. There are on average 140 days of snowfall each year in Ouray, settling at one foot depth or more during the winter months. The temperature then is around freezing point during the day and falls to minus 15F at night. In the summer residents could expect two months of daytime temperatures in the 70s, dropping to 50F at night. The sun is dangerous at this altitude because of unrestricted exposure to UV light. The wettest months are in the autumn.

For most people the effect of altitude starts to become noticeable at 8000 feet, where Ouray lies. Breathlessness, light headedness, clumsiness and perhaps nausea are common symptoms; fatter and less fit individuals are more susceptible. The pressure of oxygen at this altitude is about 80% of sea level, so the body needs to adapt to compensate for the resulting reduced amount of oxygen in the blood to protect the organs in the body. Its initial responses are to increase breathing rate and heart activity, as shown by a raised pulse rate and blood pressure. After a time at this altitude, the body makes some structural adaptations – it increases the absorbing surface of the lungs so that more oxygen can enter the body, it produces more haemoglobin, (the oxygen carrier in the blood) and increases the numbers of small blood vessels that deliver blood to key organs. Memory and concentration are impaired at first but these usually recover. However, the whole body does remain somewhat less efficient physically even at 8000ft than it would be at sea level. Ouray is much lower than the mines themselves, which could be often 2 or 3000 feet higher. The loss of efficiency in physical work, fatigue and probably impairment in mental function must have been more problematic even dangerous for labourers in the mines. Women would find life hard; the uv light causes freckles and aged, wrinkled skin on the exposed face. In the winter the dry cold chapped and caused cracking of the lips and ears. Various lards had to be applied to protect the skin. In the winter all fashion was discarded in favour of fur hats, floor length skirts and coats and fur boots. The altitude also affected cooking – water boils at a lower temperature.

 Eddie and Jess rented a single story villa near Main Street. Jess helped out with teaching in the Catholic school. There is no evidence of anything in Eddie's background to equip him for a career in silver mining. His interests were British history and the Constitution and seemingly matters medical - not geology or engineering. Nor does Eddie tell his brothers how much money they brought with them to Ouray; they only speculate about this. Meanwhile Eddie must have set about informing himself about mining. Fortunately, as there was still mining activity in the area, he would have found expertise around.

Silver, because of its lower sale value had to be mined in bulk. Placer mining is the simpler procedure, involving washing surface rock with water under pressure and sieving through the resulting sludge with a filter. This can be done by a single individual and is best for gold, where the reward for the discovery of a small nugget is high. For silver, the prospector looks first for a possible end of a lode or vein in surface rock. This lode has to be followed deep into the rock itself. But first, the possible prospector had to register a claim to the land ,if not already owned. Attorneys sited themselves on a regular basis in temporary sheds in the town for this purpose. A team had then to be assembled – an expert in drilling, an expert in explosives, many basic labourers to take away rubble and any ore. Carpenters were crucial to construct a stable tunnel in the hole left after the explosives. By the1900s, electricity had become available to provide power for the drills, light in the tunnel and power for pumps to keep the tunnel free of water. The first samples of ore drilled were taken to an assay office to measure its likely yield of silver. A poor result should indicate to the prospector that the boring should move elsewhere, but many believed in their instinct rather than evidence and pushed on. It was after all a form of gambling, staking some money in the hope of a huge reward. There had been a few remarkable fortunes made locally, such as Tom Walsh's, to fuel a gambler's instinct - after all anyone could be next with a lucky strike. For the tiny few that made fortunes, many lost everything.

Over the next years, Jess and Eddie acquired properties – the Combright mining property to the south of Ouray and a shared interest in two others, the Old Lout and the Wedge both to the north east of the town. They also bought a wood house to the east of the town with Mt Hayden rising above.

Eddie and Jess in front of Ouray house.

Eddie and friends in front of Combright property.

Combright property today.

Jess describes it as follows:

'Our little home is in Ouray which I was lucky enough to secure by paying £15 down and the rest in monthly rent till the whole £60 is paid. It is a desirable property, 55 feet front by 159 feet deep, 3 good sized rooms, a stable with place for two horses, coal shed, wood shed chicken shed and one small one room cabin, city water in the front yard and just one block from the new radium baths.' (Hot outdoor baths today).

They also bought a log cabin near the Combright. The mines and the cabin were bought with a loan from the banks, which also provided money for the exploration of the Combright. They had thus regular payments on their house in the town as well as on their bank loans to keep up. As a security for these, Eddie had a plot of land in Florida, acquired before Ouray and Jess owned some land near Sacramento, maybe inherited. These last two assets were never developed. Instead Eddie set about using his English connections to raise money to invest in his and other local mines; Eddie was probably able to name drop sufficiently to persuade others that he could act for them in London. Britain was then wealthy and a source of finance for such exploratory ventures worldwide. He had printed a letter heading made calling himself mine manager.

It was now necessary to go back to Britain fairly regularly. In 1907 and in 1908 Eddie and Jess came to England spending several months on each visit. The 1907 trip was Jess's first trip to England since one shortly after her marriage in 1890, thus her first encounter with her in-laws for some time. The trip was by rail from Denver to New York and then a steamer to Liverpool. En route, they stopped in Illinois with her brother Dennis and family. For his business, Eddie established an office in the City and presumably did the rounds to drum up investment. He recalls in old age his hopes at the time of these visits:

'We are safe in London, busy all day in the City around London Wall among the mining engineers. I see my hands carrying the bags of ore samples; I had taken home to show. I have told my story and they are interested and will find the money for more development so that we can begin production and then sell. I hope and tremble.'

There was sight seeing of Westminster Abbey – 'We are standing in the crowd, I feel Jessie's hand trembling as she presses mine. And the organ plays and the hymn we have loved of all others is falling on our ears. 'Abide with me.'' They visited music halls for what he calls an hour of merriment and went across to Dublin, but no details are given of that trip.

Most important for Jess was the visit to the Weatherly family. Eddie's father would by now be 88, but surprisingly she doesn't leave a description of meeting him or her impression of Hillside. Visit she must have, because she kept a chutney recipe, dated then and written in someone else's hand, from the Hillside kitchen. The occasion must have been daunting for her, coming from such a different life in the mountains of Colorado. Her intelligence, honesty and enthusiasm should have won her in-laws over.

They visited Fred and Maude in Grosvenor Lodge in Bath and the four went to Downside Abbey to visit Hugh Ford, Eddie's first cousin on his mother's side who in 1906 had just retired because of ill health from being the first Abbot there. The Fords lived at Wraxall Court near Portishead while the Weatherly family were growing up at Hillside. James Ford, Mayor of Bristol, for thirty years leader of the Conservative party in the city was Eddie's uncle, brother of his mother. He had married an Irishwoman Jane Hammill and, to the consternation and disapproval of friends, family and business colleagues in Bristol, converted to Catholicism. Jane Hammill Ford created a chapel with a relic on display at Wraxall Court. After this visit Margaret wrote approvingly of these Irish and Catholic links.

Eddie and Jess returned from England to their most successful period in Ouray, which lasted until 1920. Eddie must have gained financial support from his trip, for he began excavating at the Combright, hiring labourers to help. He also attracted potential investors to visit the region, such as Mr M Rylott from Boston in Lincolnshire, with whom he was photographed on horse back outside an assay office. Eddie in the caption is referred to as the manager of the Chrysophia Mines Company, Ouray, named after the owner. His own mining activity apart from being financed by bank loans was also backed by promises from investors in England. Eddie by now had educated himself on mineralogy and mining and began his extensive collection of papers - survey reports of local mines with copies of blue prints and diagrams, the Colorado Scientific Society bulletins, reports from the US Government Department of Commerce and Bureau of Mines and US geological surveys. He received the reports of the American Mining Congress and attended their meetings. He subscribed to the Engineering and Mining Journal and other technical monthly publications. With no scientific background, it must have been heavy going at first, but his acquisition of technical knowledge in this field continued until the end of his life, so that he was recognised as an expert as reported in his obituary.

Eddie had joined the Elk Lodge in Ouray. The Elks Order founded in the 1870s was a charitable organisation that had lodges (actual buildings) in most US towns by the 1900s, to which members paid dues and in turn could rely on for help in times of financial hardship and illness. There was strong emphasis on fellowship with dinners and meetings at which there would be invited speakers. The Ouray lodge is a fine Victorian building off Main Street. Getting silver recognised again as a currency was still a goal for some local Coloradoans. Eddie joined a pressure group that made representations in Washington and even went there to lobby Congress. One of Eddie's ideas was to recruit countrywide membership of the Elk Lodges and Lions clubs in support of this pressure group. In a letter to members, he first rehearses the history of demonetization and then describes the consequences in the aftermath of the World War that left nations with huge debts that could never be paid with the limited supplies of gold. Then:

'Legislation by demonetising silver at times of peace has destroyed much actual wealth by robbing silver using nations of their outside buying power, to the extent today of four–fifths of it, and has disturbed and retarded commerce in the same proportion. Legislation though has the power today to recreate that wealth by a general international agreement or agreement between four or five of them to put back silver in its original status as a monetary basis in a fixed ratio to gold, thus liquidating in one act the worlds indebtedness and at the same time opening the streams of commerce to a free and increasing flow.'

He calls on the memberships for wide support, thereby keeping the movement out of partisan politics.

Eddie and Jess acquired a black and tan long-haired dachshund named Buster who is photographed regularly by them in the town with Jess and coping with a foot of snow in their back garden. The couple were out and about a lot inspecting their properties. In Eddie's case, as he managed several apart from his own, this meant long trips by horse back to distant mines. Each left notes at home to explain to the other where they were. Some examples remain - him to her, 'Darling, gone to Giannino's (a person) looking for you – right back. Why didn't you leave word? Ever your own loving

Eddie.' Her to him – 'Dear loving heart, I've gone up to the church to say a few prayers. Forgive me and forgive me for not being at home tonight. God bless you. Your own Jess.'

Jess spent time writing poetry and verses for songs. Much in the archives is indecipherable but examples are these separate verses:

" When the book of life is closing
Sails are set for beck'ning shores"
 " Good bye old timer from our scene,
From friends that are and long have been
From friends that are and ere will be."
"Oh spirit of poetry - divine
Come, to possess my soul
That I may write just one word
Which completes the whole"

And a longer poem-
"When winter comes and you're not here
 In our garden next to mine
 I know there'll be another ache
 In this Irish heart of mine
When peonies have gone to sleep
And the irises are lying down
And lilacs up against your shed
Have let fall their emerald crown
And wild sweet peas that deck the pole
Of purple shades and grey
Have wearied of their crimson sport
Like children tired of play
When I peer through the old iron fence
I shall miss you walking there
With the sun on Hayden's peak
And upon your silvering hair."

In April 1911, Eddie and Jess set off for a long tour to Europe, only returning to Ouray in July 1913. While it would be a business trip, there were family visits including one to Bath to stay with Fred and Maude. To be away for so long, Eddie must have had confidence in his job security and finances back in Ouray.

9. (1910-1915) THE BIRTH OF DANNY BOY

Fred and Maude were still living in Grosvenor Lodge. Fred writes:

'In 1910, two special blows had fallen on me. My father and only son died within three months of each other, the former at the age of ninety, deserving well his name of 'the Grand Old Man of Somerset', engaged upon his public work till three weeks of his death; and my only boy, an actor, who had only just after long struggles got into smooth water.'

Although Fred and Alec had not seen eye to eye since the separation from Minnie, they would have met at the old man's funeral. Fred wrote no more in his memoirs about the loss of his son, but Jess writing twenty years later, just after Fred's death, commented:

'He was a father and I know what he thought of his son (his letter is before me now, in which he said 'I never knew the depth of sorrow until now') and I know too that he loved his daughters with the same love – but in dear Alec's case.'

Elsewhere in 'Piano and Gown', Fred states that he had written verses, later to be the words for Danny Boy, in March 1910 and then rewritten them in 1911. He makes no connection in the book between these verses and the grief he was experiencing over those two years. If they were intended directly to represent his feelings about Alec's death, he is likely to have said so, as he did with 'Friend o' Mine' for Michael Maybrick. However the final version of the words, which were modified again to fit the 'Londonderry Air', do concern loss, grief and reunion after death. None of the earlier versions of these words have yet been found, so their evolution through three modifications cannot be examined.

In 1912, Eddie and Jess came to stay in Bath as part of their long visit to the UK. Fred's account in 'Piano and Gown' was that, in1912, a sister-in-law in America sent him the 'Londonderry Air'. It was a melody that he had not come across before. The 1910/1911 song fitted 'by lucky chance, that beautiful melody' with a few alterations. Jess writing in old age when bitter, widowed, poor and alone tells a different story:

'How he could he leave the false statement that he had Danny Boy sent to him, it is a bitter pill to me. We, Eddie and self, were stopping with Maud and Fred when, while in the drawing room having tea and discussing old airs, Eddie turned to me and said, "Sing that old Irish air to Fred that your father used to sing," I objected saying, "No, I won't because many people don't care for Come-all-Yes," but Fred began to play quietly on piano, turned to me and did his share of persuading me to sing just the melody-saying, "I love the old Irish airs."

Fred's piano, above, and drawing room below.

He little suspecting that I had put words to it years ago and had my heart set on someday publishing the words but, after hearing the melody just once, he turned to Eddie and said, "It is one of the most beautiful melodies I have ever heard." He then urged me to sing it again and again, while he played an accompaniment to it. Then he said, "I shall write some words to that." While I was pleased that he recognised the beauty and pathos, I always felt pain that I lost something. My Kerry Irish father would go to a quiet corner. He (Fred) must have guessed because after the sudden smile he gave me, a shadow followed it. He read my thoughts and my blasted hope was gone of ever making it- the songs of my father's blood bred in his bones and handed down from generation to generation through the very blood of his family, my hope was gone of ever sending it (as I often dreamed of doing) down the Napa Valley stream on the wings of my father's voice.'

Jess's words for the melody, a draft and hard to decipher, were:
Oh Kerry boy, my Kerry boy
Who sleeps in Irish f....
You are not dead
But live in the heart of every Gael
I can hear the words 'I love you'
With an eye obscured by tears
Come again your golden voice, dear
Singing of a love we knew.

Her father was from Co Kerry, so these words must have been meant for him. Fred says nothing of this encounter in Bath, but goes on in his memoirs to discuss the song's publication in 1913. However Eddie and Jess did not come away empty-handed. Maude loaned £500 (£10,000 today) for exploration in the Combright at the time of the 1912 visit. This was interest free and only to be repaid in the event of a successful strike. A few years later, Fred sent money himself for the mine and began an allowance to Eddie of £10 per month, when they were in grave financial difficulties in Ouray.

There are thus two accounts of how Fred got hold of the melody Londonderry Air. Both accounts were written many years later. Given the details of encounters he recalls elsewhere in his memoirs, it seems unlikely that he could have forgotten Eddie and Jess's visit - especially as it concerned one of his most famous songs.

Eddie and Jess returned to the US in 1913. It was to be their last visit to Britain. For Fred, the next few years were painful ones. Apart from the deaths of his father and son, he lost three of his closest musical collaborators - Michael Maybrick, James Molloy and Walter Roeckel. There were continuing financial anxieties. However, he said that he didn't carry his heart on his sleeve:

'Those who met me in the law courts, in Chambers, in the train and in the street, those who read and heard the songs which I was still writing, only saw me gay and active, and knew nothing of what I was suffering, or if they did, gave me the kindest sympathy of all, the deeper fellowship that says nothing but feels the more.'

In fact some of his most lasting songs came from this period. Danny Boy was published in 1913 and was recorded by Ernestine Schumann Hank in 1918, enabling it to be heard throughout the English-speaking world. 'Friend O Mine', the tribute to Michael Maybrick, set to music by Wilfred Sanderson after Maybrick's death, became instantly popular. Up from Somerset, with the rousing chorus 'Oh we'm come up from Somerset where the cider apples grow' was published in the same year. He lists ten other successes in 1914 and 1915, working with among others Eric Coates and Ivor Novello. When the war came, it was for Fred a distraction from his worries for it brought to his law practice the novelty and excitement of Courts Martial. He said it (the war) did not crush but seemed to stimulate his power of song writing.

In 1916, Fred published, with Hayden Wood's music, 'Roses of Picardy', which he regarded as his most commercially successful song:

Roses are shining in Picardy
In the hush of the silver dew
Roses are flowering in Picardy

But there's never a rose like you
And the roses will die with the summer time
And our roads may be far apart
But there's one rose that dies not in Picardy
'Tis the rose that I keep in my heart

And the years fly on forever
Til the shadows veil their sighs
But he loves to hold her little hand
And look in her sea blue eyes.
And he sees the rose by the poplars
Where they met in the bygone years
For the first little song of the roses
Is the last little song she hears
She is watching by the poplars
Colinette with the sea blue eyes
She is watching and longing and waiting
Where the long white roadway lies
And a song stirs in the silence
As the wind in the boughs above
She listens and starts and trembles
'Tis the first little song of love

This song is said to be one of the best marriages of words and music ever produced. Although set in Picardy the site of the fighting in World War 1, Fred didn't write it as a war song as such ,rather as an oldish man (68) imagining a young man's feelings at finding love while away from home. It gave a glimmer of hope in difficult times. This song remained very popular until the 1960s since when it has faded in comparison with Danny Boy. Published in French in 1918, it became a favourite there too, developing a French mythology of its own. Weatherly was thought to be a young officer who fell in love with a young widow (Colinette in the song) who had a garden full of roses that he admired. He supposedly penned these words before he went into battle. The widow has been identified (Germaine Bertaux) and the desk at which he wrote the words is preserved in the bar in the village of Warloy-Baillon. One story continues that he married Germaine, took her to London and then Paris to live. Germaine died, so Fred returned to Warloy-Baillon to marry a friend of hers, then lived happily on the Cote d'Azur. Another story is that he was nursed in the hospital at Corbie, where his pretty nurse put roses by his bed.

This story of the English soldier can be still be found in promotional material to encourage tourism in Picardy. In 2005, to celebrate the centenary of the Entente Cordiale, a rose named Rose of Picardy was baptised by the Duchess of Gloucester in the gardens of the Abbe de Valloires, inland from Le Touqet. Giles Gousset, a local historian, contacted me and a descendant of Haydn Wood in order to prepare a book on the song, telling the lives of author and composer. That is now on sale with various Roses of Picardy mementos in the shop in the Abbey grounds. Fred visited France several times. Many French girls' names come into his songs. Apart from Colinette, there are Fleurette, Minette, Annette and 16 more. He wrote songs with French words –Mon Ami and La Petite Francaise.

9. ETHEL AND HERBERT

In 1915, Herbert Weatherly returned to America to make his life there. The fifth son Herbert Henry was born in 1861. He followed his brothers to Hereford school and Oxford but his name doesn't appear amongst the alumni of either place. He started studying medicine but he took off to travel extensively, trying different work around the world. He describes himself as a rolling stone:

'Life has taught me in the16th Royal Hussars in the British Army, the North West Mounted Police of Canada, a diamond digger in the Kimberly mines, a trader in the Transkei of South Africa, an orange grower in Florida, a newspaper reporter in US.'

He was back England in1910 and was there to help Fred by traveling to Southampton to collect Alec's body and travel with it to Portishead for burial. He was in Vermont in 1913.

A small man, perpetually untidy in appearance, he was talkative, often irascible and opinionated but at heart was kind and helpful. He was hands on, un-snobbish, saw everyone as a friend and thus took readily to life in the US; he was the only one of the three brothers there who didn't dream of a return to Britain when things got hard. He acquired a wife Madge and they had a daughter Freda. Madge sent a wreath with the other Weatherly brother's wives to old Dr Frederick's funeral in 1910, but didn't travel to the US with him. She is not mentioned in any of his correspondence during the 1920s to Eddie. Herbert describes his return to the US at the age of 54:

'It was the Great War, my services were no longer required in the Army. I landed in New York in 1915 – penniless. I didn't seem to quite fit in. Becoming disheartened, I resolved to return to England and enlist under an assumed name. A genial skipper of a tramp steamer offered to carry me back 'dead hand'. The corner of Wall St and Broadway found me late one night in a blizzard making the turn for the East River. Just then the chimes of Old Trinity rang out seeming to say "turn back again, you have not done your best". With no ambitions to become the Lord Mayor of New York, I obeyed what these beautiful chimes seemed to say. Going up Broadway, I turned into a pawn shop; I left my last and only possession there and found a room in a good hotel. Next day, wandering down 4th Avenue, I noticed the sign of that famous publishing house – Longman Green and Co. Venturing in I found the gateway of my come back.'

Herbert was employed as salesman of their science books. Working largely on commission, he traveled the length and breadth of the US, so that he could write later in life –'I have now visited every university, college and all the important public libraries in the forty eight states.' He did this travel mainly by automobile alone, usually being away two or three months on the road each trip. He stayed in hotels, which gave him time in the evenings for letter writing. His work trips allowed him to visit his brothers Eddie in Ouray and Luke in San Francisco from time to time. He writes about this job:

'Entailed a lot of learning about colleges and faculties. It's a hard life and very interesting - I originated it and no other man has ever attempted it. I know 1000 librarians and over 5000 professors; I

Silver Fox Farm at Ballston Spa, New York.

Silver foxes at the farm.

Freda at fox farm Ballston Spa.

never intrude or make those upon whom I call think I have come to tell them any thing. Can't believe my own eyes when I look at a map and see where I have travelled.'

According to his notes he made over $30,000 per year in the first years for the company. Longmans had set up a New York branch in 1875, moving to 434 4th Avenue in the 1890s. The firm soon started to publish independently of their London parent company. The managing director was a Charles Mills; he and then his sons were in charge of the company until it was sold in 1961. Herbert described many letter exchanges with Mills senior and junior, usually arguing for greater remuneration for himself. As he got older, he became worried about being replaced by younger men, but his vast network of contacts supported him over younger salesmen recruited by the company. Nevertheless this work took its toll. He developed hernias from carrying bags of books, had regular bronchitis in the winter and

endless trouble with his teeth. He depended on his car, which would breakdown causing him great expense. His daughter, Freda, accompanied him to do some of the driving when it became too much. He was thus able to carry on until he was 70.

As a scheme to make money, Herbert bought a small farmhouse and land in north New York State in order to breed silver foxes. The Robin Hood Farm near Ballston Spa was his base and Freda's home for the next twenty years. The land round the farm, the equipment and the breeding foxes were bought with local loans. Luke, a soft touch for both his brothers, loaned some of his savings to Herbert but depended on being paid back to fund his old age. Breeding animals were expensive to buy - $150 dollars for common silver, several thousand dollars for the best silver foxes.

Silver fox farming was catching on at this time. Silver foxes in reality have black fur with silver edges and are genetic variants of the usual red foxes; one or two turn up in a litter of red fox pups from time to time. If one of these is selected for breeding with another of the same colour, then a strain of silver foxes is started. The first breeding farms were in Prince Edward Island in Canada, but they spread south into the US as demand for silver fox pelts grew.

Initially they were made into coats and hats for use in the Canadian cold, but silver fox fur became a fashion accessory - evening stoles, tippets, linings, collars and cuffs of expensive coats. Queen Mary and the Duchess of York both regularly appeared with silver fox accessories. In 1914, the average price at auction in London of a fox pelt was $110 (around $2000 today). There was money to be made. So Herbert, without previous experience, in true Weatherly style, aimed to be someone who did that.

In view of the interest in new fox businesses, the US department of Agriculture put out in 1915 an information sheet for potential investors. The following points are made. The most valuable furs are those in which the entire pledge is dark at the base and overlaid with greyish white. Selective breeding will encourage production of foxes with the better coloured coats but inbreeding can produce very nervous animals, which are disadvantageous for breeding. Money can be made both from selling the pelts and live foxes for breeding. The industry fares best when the prices of the two are similar so that rearing and killing animals are equally profitable. The animals need the colder latitudes to produce the best furs making the states on the southern border of Canada the most suitable. The animals should be kept in pairs in yards, surrounded by high wire netting that is sunk into the ground to prevent the foxes from tunnelling out and curves inwards at the top to prevent them climbing out. After mating, the couple are kept apart until whelping. Each compound should be about 2500 square feet, contain a wooden hut or den and be in shaded and drained land, away from noise or interference. The foxes are not friendly animals but they do fare better if the human contact is familiar to them, rather than constantly changing. The vixen becomes very protective of her pups and will destroy them if she feels threatened. After whelping, the vixen will stay hidden in the den for several weeks and cannot be disturbed for risk that she will endanger her pups. This confinement of course is very frustrating for the breeder who will be eager to know the size of the litter, their sex and fur colour – all of which will determine later income.

Herbert wrote of his relief when Freda could inspect a new litter as the vixen came out with her pups. Gestation is fifty days and the litter between two and seven pups. The coats thicken with age and in the winter months, thus December is the usual month for slaughter. In the last weeks, honey and oats to give sheen to the fur are added to supplement the diet of meat. Pictures of tens of dead foxes hanging in rows were part of the positive publicity of the fox farms at the time - as after pheasant shoots.

As well as the foxes, Robin Hood Farm contained cows, horses and dogs that Freda wanted to breed for profit. Her particular interest was the dogs, Alsatian–Airedale crosses that she wanted to sell as police dogs. Luke Weatherly who went to recuperate on the farm disliked the experience of being there intensely. After San Francisco, the weather was very cold. He describes his day. Herbert was on his travels and Freda and he were in charge of the foxes:

'I go out at 9 o'clock to clean up the 24 kennels – 40ft by 10ft and don't get through until 12.30, sometimes 1.30, and then there are the 96 pans I have picked up to be washed and scalded. Then, 25 lbs of beef hearts, liver and cow melts are to be cut up and ground, that takes another 2 hours and has to be ready by 5 o'clock and you can imagine how many other things there are to do. In fact I have had to give up the idea of letter writing; I have so many dear friends in 'Frisco I should like to keep up a correspondence with.'

Herbert, in his many letters to his brothers, showed wild optimism at the outset about the likely proliferation of his foxes and then pessimism in the late 1920s, when there was a glut of pelts that weren't selling in the then depressed economic times. He depended on Freda to be at Robin Hood Farm but notes how lonely, depressed and friendless she was – the farm was 9 miles from Ballston Spa and in the winter was very exposed to wind, the track leading up to the farm often being blocked by snow. When later, to give her a break from the farm and to help him manage his bookselling Freda travelled with him, it was necessary to get help in – a couple called the Lampkins were employed for that – but they had to be paid out of any profits from the sale of foxes and other animals.

Because I have read many of his letters that give his opinions, hopes and fears, I feel I know Herbert better than the other brothers and have come to like him. Herbert's life is the hardest to trace through records today. He left virtually no trace - he is not listed in England on any census. He appears in the American 1920 and 1930 census living in the Ballston area with Freda, a co-resident in the second one. There is no record in the US or the UK of his marriage or the birth of Freda; perhaps these occurred while he was in South Africa or Canada. Or, he didn't marry and Freda was born under her mother's name. Freda must have spent her childhood with her mother because Herbert was thrilled to have her around when she was in her twenties to help out on the farm. He keeps repeating what a nice girl she is, as though it's something he has just discovered. He didn't keep his brothers informed about her; they had no idea of Freda's existence, suggesting that Herbert had had a long period out of touch. Luke wrote to Eddie to ask who she was.

A friend spent a couple of days in the Ballstom area looking round on my behalf. She could find no trace of the Robin Hood Farm, though she discovered that there were US Government fox breeding stations in the area. No-one knew of Freda, though she could have lived on until the 1980s.

Both Herbert and Eddie embarked in middle age in business ventures about which they knew nothing. Both started up with loans; both believed until the end that wealth would come so that they could repay them. Herbert at least had another source of income from Longmans which he kept going.

Sometime after Herbert had set up Robin Hood Farm, probably 1918, Fred asked him to take Ethel there to act as his housekeeper - it may have been before Freda turned up. Herbert confirmed in a letter to Eddie that Fred was desperate to get Ethel off his hands. Herbert later regretted agreeing, as he felt he had been pushed into colluding with Fred's plan to separate her from her daughters. Indeed he became an ally and support of Ethel, the only person who was such in the family. Ethel's name does not appear in the passenger lists available now, so the year of her first arrival in the US cannot be precise. Fred provided her with £1 weekly, paid quarterly, to live on. Herbert reports that she was detained in Ellis Island - presumably lack of funds - and he had to go and sponsor her in order for her to enter the US.

Ethel would have found the farm a shock to the system. It was isolated, not well heated and surrounded with animals - a contrast to the Piccadilly hotel. Then there was Freda. Although described by her father as a charming and good girl, her appearance was forbidding – tall and masculine looking. She was a top rank skater and could ride any kind of horse. Despite her rather masculine appearance, she was heterosexual, for Herbert writes of her wanting to marry a local farm worker, Tom Sweeney, which he wouldn't allow as he reckoned there would be wealthier people around. He was right, an older man he refers to as Monte wanted to marry her. But, to Herbert's annoyance, Monte died suddenly leaving $350000! When travelling with Herbert, Freda visited Eddie and Jess in Ouray, and then Luke in San Francisco, both described her as a charming girl, Luke commenting though that she wasn't so pleasant when she had been drinking. She was certainly devoted to her dogs, which seemed to have top priority.

Luke describes the interior of Robin Hood Farm when he was there to Eddie:

'I can't find the newspaper that you want but I am sending you the only date that I can find. Freda throws everything away on account of 'making rooms untidy', yet she will have dishes, cups and all kinds of things laying on the floor for the dogs to eat out of. They are all (4 of them) allowed to stay in the kitchen while we are having our meals and of course are a darned nuisance, besides costing $25 per month for food with three cats. I can't even get a glass of milk and I was told I could get all the milk I wanted - yes canned milk.'

At first Ethel settled, sending a cheerful post card to Luke from Ballston Spa where she was then living rather than the farm. However trouble arose when Freda's friends the Fitchams arrived from New York to visit. According to Herbert, Ethel Fitcham had a hold over Freda and dominated the household when she was staying, so that Herbert didn't feel comfortable in his own home when she was there – which was frequently. Herbert describes her as a 'whale of a woman with a worm of a husband who must be enveloped in folds of fat in bed'. Mrs Fitcham came across Ethel and the said worm in some kind of embrace in the sitting room of the farm. Mr Fitcham immediately blamed Ethel whom he claimed came after him. Mrs Fitcham passed this onto Freda who insisted that Ethel was thrown out.

From now on, Herbert had to do what he had promised to Fred - to keep an eye on Ethel -away from Freda's knowledge, instructing his brothers not to refer to her in any letters addressed to the farm. Freda usually looked at these and would go into a rage if Ethel were mentioned. Herbert of course depended on his daughter's hard work to keep the farm going and wasn't going to cross her. Ethel moved down to New York and went back to hotel work as a floor clerk at the Biltmore earning $65 a month. The Biltmore was a luxury hotel of the day, part of the complex at Grand Central Station. It had a big clock in the lobby from which the idea of meeting 'under the clock' was said to have originated. Luke wrote to Eddie that she was settled and the hotel was doing well. Her finances must have been stretched though, partly because Fred's allowance was often delayed or missed. One Christmas, Herbert writes that she was completely alone in New York with no money left to cover the holiday season. She took casual work washing up to make ends meet as Herbert described:

'Working alongside a dirty Greek, putting up with insults – the shame and humiliation of it all. The whole episode is sickening, imagine such a condition for Alec's widow.'

Herbert sent her $2. All the time, Ethel was fretting about her daughters expecting letters from them.

By the early 1920s Ethel had left New York and was trying to develop an income giving dancing lessons while working in hotels. She spent time in Washington, Baltimore and Los Angeles (Hollywood). Herbert was now writing to Fred telling him that her exile should end, to which Fred responded by hinting that the girls could come out to join their mother and finish their education there - Vassar College was mentioned. But then Fred said that Ethel's hotel work meant odd hours so that she couldn't look after them properly. Herbert deemed this outrageous, as it was Fred who insisted that she worked and had encouraged the hotel jobs in London. Also he claimed that Fred was taunting Ethel with the social life that he could give the girls in Bath and with the snobs of Bristol (Muriel's family presumably), while she was in the laundry room of a hotel. He had denied Ethel sight of her grandfather's will and was not paying proper interest on the sum she had been left. Fred had power of attorney while Ethel was away, so received Ethel's legacy. According to Herbert, she should have been receiving £218 p.a rather than the £13 quarterly that she was getting.

In 1922, Ethel drove with Herbert across America to San Francisco; by now they seemed to be close and Herbert was giving her money from time to time to survive. Ethel was to stay in San Francisco, much to Luke's horror. He believed that Herbert was over-involved with Ethel and should let her fight her own battles with Fred. He also saw Herbert spending money on her and saw the chances of his getting his loan back from Herbert were diminishing. Luke's life was in a rut in San Francisco, living in a bed-sit on Mission Street and going each day to sell cigars. He did have an escape place in Hearst to the north of the city where a widow friend Mrs Hall used to invite him. He helped her look after the land and relaxed there; usually losing stress symptoms that had been preoccupying him. It was to Hearst that he fled before Herbert and Ethel arrived. However they tracked him down and stayed with Mrs Hall too. Luke describes to Eddie preparing a roast lamb dinner.

Everyone noted that Ethel looked unwell, thin and with a bad chest - they wondered about TB. The doctors in San Francisco advised her not to stay on there because of the notoriously damp weather, so Herbert sent her to Tucson, Arizona, paying for a new hat and coat for her journey and providing the first two weeks rent. He promised an introduction to a dance teacher at the University. Ethel agreed to stay there until the girls came out or until she returned to England, adding that she was looking forward to giving dancing lessons, the work that she liked best. Nevertheless she wrote twice to Herbert asking for more money, which decided Herbert that she had to go back to England.

In 1925, with Herbert's financial support, Ethel went back to Bath to claim her daughters. Fred telegraphed to tell her to let him know of her arrival, but then added that she must find a cheap room in Bath and find her own fare there.

10. FRED 1915-1929

From 1912 onwards, Fred's household was enlivened and complicated by the presence of his two granddaughters. Betty the elder was described as a wild child, active and the leader of the pair, while Marjory, quieter and more dutiful, followed in her wake. Their education was first at a private local school in the company of a great niece of Maude's. Their first cousins, Muriel's five children of a similar age, were not far away and Fred arranged for the two girls to spend as much time a possible at their aunt's.

Around 1913, Maude developed the first symptoms of the neurological disorder that soon would render her disabled and then bed bound. This was diagnosed as having descending spinal cord degeneration. She began also suffering what Fred wrote of to Jess in 1919 as cardiac attacks. These were intermittent but Fred said that he was afraid to be too confident about the outcome; that Maude could not stand visitors and as an alternative had a very dull time – for he had to be away all day. To provide some nursing help and to be a companion, Miriam Bryan moved into the house. Miriam Bryan was born Miriam Lewis in Llanfechan, Montgomeryshire where her father was stationmaster. She had training as a singer and married John Bryan, a tenor of some repute in Wales. She was now widowed and aged 40 when she took up this post in Fred's household. She soon became close both to Maude and to Fred. Herbert and Luke in America saw her, from the start, as wheedling herself into everyone's affection including that of the girls and being behind Fred's intention to keep Ethel away. In 1919, the household moved closer in to the centre of Bath to10 Edward Street, which was bought by Maude.

Fred continued publishing songs, listing in 'Piano and Gown' five or six for each year from 1915 to 1920 but comments, when writing in 1925, that fewer songs were now being produced, as concerts at which they would be sung were fewer and home singing had declined. Broadcasting and the gramophone were taking over. If it weren't for the great increase in gramophone records, he said composers, authors and singers would be having a hard time. One of Fred's long term gripes was the relative lack of recognition and remuneration for the authors of the words of a song compared to the composer. With the advent of the gramophone record and thus payment of mechanical royalties as well as the performing ones, he must have been pleased to be in at the formation of the British Society of Composers, Authors and Publishers to protect all their interests. The organising committee was elected in 1912 with Sir Edward Elgar in the chair and Fred, along with Edward German and Lionel Monckton, as committee members with representatives of the publishing houses.

In 1919 a dinner was given in Fred's honour to commemorate his jubilee as a songwriter. Arranged by Arthur Boosey, of Boosey and Co the music publishers, the guests were a mixture of lawyers-silks and juniors of the Western Circuit - with composers and publishers. The dinner was at Odeninno's in Piccadilly and the Chairman was J Foote KC, an old barrister friend, who replaced the Attorney General who on the night had been detained in the House. Reporting the event, a music journalist wrote, to Fred's pleasure:

'Tastes have changed enormously in the last fifty years and it is a striking testimony to versatility that the man who wrote the words of 'Nancy Lee', 'Darby and Joan' and the 'Star of Bethlehem', which in the last century circled the world should today be the author of the vigorously blooming 'Roses of Picardy'. It shows that Mr Weatherly has succeeded in writing to the hearts of people and that he has the power to touch the ever responsive springs of humanity.'

After the war, when in Fred's words 'people began to think they were at peace', his legal practice returned to usual after the Courts Martial. He said that he missed his contact with colonials and was sorry that sea lay between him and them. Indeed because of a successful defence, he was asked to give a song lecture in 1919 to about 800 New Zealand soldiers stationed on Salisbury Plain. After this event, Fred was thrilled that eight Maori soldiers performed a war dance for him. He continued proudly his practice in the Western Circuit now always for the defence, appearing up to his 80th birthday. He gained the respect and friendship of some of the leading lawyers of the day, whom he had known as juniors but who had sailed past him in their careers. These included Justice Sankey, later Lord Chancellor in the Ramsay MacDonald government, Lord Coleridge a High Court judge and Justice McCardie. The last, well known for his independent, outspoken often reactionary views wrote the foreword to Fred's memoirs:

'I first met him nearly thirty years ago. He has not changed with the fleeting years. His heart and mind have almost ignored the arrogant grasp of time. Success has gone hand in hand with modesty. Upon the roll of the Western Circuit, the author will occupy a place of distinction. His faculty of song has been combined with a constant loyalty to the traditions of rectitude, courtesy and fair play that give to the English Bar its strength.'

During the 1920s Fred enjoyed living in Bath; he describes with pleasure the literary societies, poetry club and the Theatre Royal. There were performances of the amateur opera and dramatic society, of which his brother Lionel was a keen member, and he supported Citizen House, a charitable institution where children were taught stagecraft. 'But alas', he wrote, 'Bridge and broadcasting seem to have bewitched the citizens of Bath.' Among his friends was Frederic Harrison, who had been a don at Wadham College when Fred was an undergraduate and with whom Fred had maintained contact at the Bar. Harrison became a jurist and, through that role, helped to establish the statutory position of the Trades Union movement. Madam Sarah Grand, the New Woman novelist, and the Williamsons, authors of travel books were also friends.

A particular pleasure was to be asked to give a speech at a lunch given by the Mayor in honour of the visit of Ellen Terry and Squire Bancroft to unveil a memorial tablet to Mrs Siddons. In it, he recalls his first memories aged 8 in 1856 of Ellen Terry in Bath when she appeared as Puck in Midsummer Night's Dream and then, in the same play, as Titania at a performance to celebrate the reopening of the Theatre Royal after a fire in 1873. He commends the live theatre for 'its educational possibilities for children' and he asserts that certain plays, which he lists, 'might have educational value for people such as public servants, for social reformers (who are turning our world upside down) and economists (who repay old debts by creating new ones).'He refers to the beauty of live performances when 'one can witness the genius of the players, their imagination, personality and knowledge of life', but continues, 'the mechanic's millennium is approaching when the moving pictures oust the living voice and the theatre is reduced to a central station for broadcasting. I shall not live to see it, thank God. Long live the stage, long live the players! And when one by one the great players pass, when into the night go one and all, for those that remain let us pray – God keep their memories alive. Drink then to the stage and the illustrious players – Ellen Terry and Squire Bancroft.'

Bancroft responded to the toast 'in his old courtly manner and the dear Ellen herself made one of her sweet little speeches that brought the tears, if not to our eyes, then to our hearts.' She wrote on an old photograph Fred that had brought with him –'I listened to your beautiful speech with high appreciation, dear Mr Weatherly, Yours very sincerely, Ellen Terry.'

The outward appearance of Fred's life in the period from 1919 was thus of comfort and success. Yet at home and in private, he was still preoccupied with money matters. This was shown by his regular contacts with publishing houses, chasing up royalties and complaining that he was owed money. He had in his first years of song writing, as was the custom, sold his verses to a publisher for a fee usually of ten guineas and thus deprived himself of any royalty for these early but still popular songs. Now, he had the performing and mechanical royalties but their collection became a matter of importance for, as he complained to Hebert, the expenses of his household and of bringing up his granddaughters were considerable. They were often ill. He was still supporting Minnie's household in Portishead. There were further demands on his purse from his brothers and sister, none of whom were financially successful, who were regularly looking to him for help. He was sending Eddie the monthly £10, but Elsie, his surviving sister, with the alcoholic husband (the bum, in Herbert's words) needed money regularly. He made loans to Cecil (never repaid) and to Alfred (repaid). He helped finance the education of Alfred's children and paid the last two terms' bills for Cecil's son Jim at Sedbergh School. Cecil's business had folded and he was out of work but Fred wanted the boy to finish his schooling. Lionel was, in contrast to the rest, now well established but never, to Fred's fury, offered to repay the loans of many years earlier that had so impoverished Fred. Nobody in the family even bothered to ask Lionel for financial help as, in Herbert's words, he was always keeping himself fully occupied looking after himself. The continuing financial problems of his brothers as they were getting older, and their view of Fred as a source of cash, stressed and annoyed Fred to the extent that he would dread getting letters from them. Somehow he never said no. His nephews whose education he sponsored were always grateful.

All his important songs had been written by 1920; his output after that date was mainly verses for national or family occasions. He himself saw how the song world was changing with the arrival of the gramophone record and of broadcasting that enabled people to hear professionally produced music at home whenever they chose. Fred had been quoted in a newspaper article some years earlier as saying that neither would last but he was sufficiently flexible to grasp the opportunities of both when they did. He was becoming a local celebrity in Bath and respected in the musical world, judging by regular speaking invitations and the dinner to honour his jubilee.

It was sometime around 1920 that Maude made over all her capital to Fred with the proviso that he honoured her personal bequests to her friends and family in his will. The Edward Street house remained in her name. According to Herbert, this transfer of capital was to prevent her husband or his family having a claim on it after her death. At home, Maude was becoming more and more disabled. Fred wrote to Luke in 1920 saying that she was helpless but mentally alert and that it was necessary to employ an extra nurse.

Luke comments with some awe that Fred's bill for nurses and servants was now £23 per week.

In 1920, Minnie died aged 78 with her daughter Muriel at her bedside. She had moved to a nursing home in Bristol before her death. The certificate records a common cause of death for older people – heart failure with superimposed pneumonia at the end. She was buried in Portishead in the same grave as her son Alec. In her will drawn up in 1911, she appointed Fred as trustee and left her small estate to be divided equally between her daughters Muriel and Christine with the third part in trust for her two granddaughters until they reach the age of 21. Fred could choose and keep any of her personal effects that he wished. Now he was free to marry Maude but they didn't, maybe because of her frailty.

At home, he was watching Maude's slowly deteriorating functional ability. Being with someone suffering from a neurodegenerative disease is painful particularly, as in Maude's case, when the sufferer remains mentally alert and thus aware of the progressive debility. Being in the courts all day must have been, as he implies, something of a sanity saver for him. This is probably where Miriam came in. With a companion at home rather than just the servants, Maude had some intellectual distraction and Fred could feel more comfortable about leaving her all day

There was in addition a problem with Betty's schooling. The two girls had moved onto the local High School, but Fred found it necessary to send Betty to a special school, commenting that she couldn't cope at the High School, 'because it could only teach clever children not delicate ones.' The chosen school was residential – Buxted Court in Snaresbrook, Essex. Marjory was diagnosed with anaemia; the treatment prescribed for her was a daily intake of raw liver, which she ate in sandwiches.

Betty's schooling difficulties with the reported wild behaviour suggest she might qualify today for a diagnosis of Attention Deficit Disorder - ADD. That she was intellectually impaired was not formally recognised until later in her life when she became mentally ill with manic depressive psychosis in her twenties. Given her later breakdown, this behaviour could have also been a teenage manifestation of hypomania, though that condition is rare. Marjory, more anxious and dutiful, was in photographs at the time extremely thin and remained so until her marriage. She probably had developed an eating disorder, not uncommon in young women with a conscientious and compliant personality trying to cope with family disruption and being in the background as the 'good' girl while Betty received much more attention by being' bad'. A limited food intake might explain her anaemia. Difficulty in eating and thus enjoying food lasted through her life.

Miriam Bryan was now playing an important supportive role to the entire household, beyond that of housekeeper and companion to Maude. Herbert's suspicions were much aroused, believing that she was setting about seducing Fred. He strongly infers in a letter to Eddie that the two were having an affair before Maude died. He expostulates about Fred and his three women (Minnie, Maude and now Miriam). He says that 'Miriam arrived as Fred's housekeeper and Maude's nurse, fully knowing about Maude's illness and Fred's age. She pulls the carnal gag.' Then he remarks in the same letter, 'Fred has sowed so much bad seed everywhere that bad crops can't help but out. Don't mention to Freda, I don't want her to know all our ghastly skeletons.' Herbert unfortunately doesn't return to this theme again in any other letter available.

In January 1923, Maude died at home in Edward Street. Miriam was present at her death. The immediate cause was a cerebral haemorrhage but the diagnoses on the certificate also included spinal cord degeneration of seven years standing. In the Bath newspaper, the announcement was of the death of Maude Weatherly after an illness of nine years. She was buried in Brookwood Cemetery in Surrey as Maude Frankfort, next to a group of graves from the 1870s of members of her Letouzel family. Her will was first written in 1919 with codicils in 1920 and 1921. The last codicil was signed by a cross being witnessed as the mark of Maude Frankfort. Fred and Miriam, the latter described as my friend and companion, are executors. Miriam is left £1000 for her own use and Fred has the residue of the estate repeating the wish that he honours her bequests in his will. In the case of Fred predeceasing her, Miriam is charged with selling up and dividing the estate into four parts between her friends the sisters Selena and Annie James, her nieces the sisters Blanche Fletcher and Ethel Ford and Fred's granddaughters the sisters Betty and Marjory with the fourth part to Miriam. The first codicil clarifies that Maude's residence (Edward Street) goes to Fred and the second that, if one of the pair of sister's dies, then the survivor inherits her share. Her estate was valued at only £11690, presumably because much was handed over to Fred and excluded from probate valuation.

Degeneration of the spinal cord as described on her death certificate, has several causes. Pernicious anaemia and multiple sclerosis would have been known in those days and might have been put as the actual diagnosis on the death certificate. Less common conditions, more likely if the condition progresses in descending pattern, are syringomyelia and the spinal form of motor neurone disease. Both these involve death of nerve cells in the spinal cord. Descending implies that the part of the cord in the neck was affected first, symptoms occurring in the arms with weakness and clumsiness as likely openers. Fred describing Maude as helpless but mentally alert would be characteristic of both these two conditions where the brain is unaffected. Both remain even today untreatable and slowly fatal. On top of this, she had arteriosclerosis giving the heart problems that Fred worried about and her final stroke.

Miriam was according to my mother a quiet, gentle person, very Welsh in her speaking voice. She suffered from bad asthma. She appears without make-up in photographs wearing rather drab dresses and thus doesn't appear like someone who would pull the carnal gag (in Herbert's curious phrase). Fred on the other hand was always a bit of a goat, so he might have made some advance on her. I had a story from Eric Coates's son Austen about Fred as an old man. He would purposely call at the Coates house, knowing when Eric was out. Fred would pay court to his much younger and attractive wife, Phyllis. One day, Eric came home to find Fred *chasing her round the kitchen table. So from then on, Eric Coates asked to be telephoned when Fred was calling, so that he could drop everything and rush home.*

In August 1923, as he described 'to my unspeakable happiness', Fred married Miriam at St Mary's Bathwick. Fred was now 75 and Miriam 46. It was a simple ceremony. From the Bath Times:

'Mr Weatherly in full morning dress motored to the church with his two daughters, who wore frocks of pale grey with hats to match. The bride who wore a simple dark blue frock with broad brimmed black hat arrived with her friend Miss Mitchell. There were no bridesmaids and the utter absence of music was singularly curious, in view of the bridegroom's reputation as maker of songs. Simplicity of ceremonial had been the object and this was undoubtedly obtained even to the point of the absence of ceremony.'

The wedding party consisted of the five above with Walter James; Muriel's husband - no other Weatherly family members including his granddaughters were recorded as being present. His brother Alfred didn't officiate at this wedding as he did at other Weatherly events. However the church was filled with well-wishers and others were gathered outside the church.

'Mr Weatherly looked in the best of spirits as he left the church with his bride and very readily paused at the church door to enable the waiting cameramen to ensure a good picture. The bridal party returned to 10 Edward Street after the ceremony prior to embarking on their journey through London to the Continent (Holland and Belgium) for their honeymoon.'

Herbert maintained his disapproval of the marriage, referring to Miriam as the housekeeper and complaining that it took place indecently soon after Maude's death so that Bath society should not recognise her. Herbert never visited or met Miriam so his statements about her are conjecture, but perhaps based on his knowledge about Fred's sexual behaviour. He was also partisan for Ethel and saw Ethel's position with Fred being further weakened by his second marriage.

Freda and Miriam , on holiday Margate 1925.

Unobtrusiveness, sympathy and quietness, if combined with competence, must have been very appealing traits for a tired old man to find in someone at home. She certainly was rewarded in Maude's will – executor and beneficiary to the tune of £20000 in today's money. It is hard to say that she got it by scheming - Maude must have liked her. Herbert's other objection was that the wedding was soon after Maude's death. It was indeed only seven months afterwards and Miriam remained in Edward Street in the interim. This suggests that a domestic arrangement was in place and the wedding just formalised it. Quite what his snobbish older daughter really thought of Miriam – Welsh and a companion - can never be known, but she accepted her for social occasions. Fred was evidently really happy and he now had someone to be there in his old age – relieving the daughters of this responsibility. Fred commented in a letter on how pleased he was that his daughters got on so well with Miriam.

Fred's life was transformed by his marriage. Miriam and he went travelling to Paris, cruising on the Rhine and in 1924 enjoyed a lengthy stay on the Italian lakes. This was at the house of his old friends, the composer Franco Leoni and his wife, which was part of an old palace at Bergamo overlooking the Lombardy plains. 'He and I finished an opera, while our two wives and Lucie - their little artist daughter - amused themselves in the garden and left us alone to our work, criticised and applauded when Franco played and sang to us the result of our labours. I will only say this of this work: the story, which is his, is one of love, superstition, quarrels and fun in a little seaside town of the Abruzzi and the music is melody from beginning to end. When will it be produced? I cannot tell. Only those who have produced an opera know the difficulties. I may however record the fact that on the day that my wife and I passed through Milan on our way home, Boito's opera Nerone was produced at La Scala for the first time, fifty years after it was composed. Franco and I said to our anxious wives, "There is at least a chance that our great-grandchildren will hear our work."' Afraid not!

Back home, a dinner in early 1924 with the Bristol Savages indicated at last his social acceptance. This club, founded in 1904, was a place for artists, writers and entertainers and some lay people to meet each other for convivial events on a regular basis. The members meet in the specially constructed Wigwam building, which is reached through Red lodge, a famous Bath building of Elizabethan origin. It was extraordinary that a man of his national distinction had not been a member from the beginning, a black ball because of his private life until his second marriage maybe. He was soon made a life member and given the right to wear a blue feather in his lapel, that being the colour for writers, red being that for artists. He describes the club as binding its members in pleasant bonds. In the same year the Lord Chancellor called him within the Bar and gave him silk. He was now a Kings Counsel.

The current Secretary of the Bristol Savages told me that there is a portrait of Fred hanging in the Wigwam today. It was a mystery to him why Fred had become a member so late and then was so rapidly made a life member. That was most unusual. I think that I provided him with the explanation, that it followed his regularising his

Ethel Weatherly beck from USA, 1925.

domestic life by marriage in 1923. But a club for artists and writers shouldn't have been that prudish – one would have thought.

In 1925 Ethel arrived from America to reclaim her daughters. There are contradictory comments in the letters about this. Luke wrote to Eddie that Fred was getting old and was tired of the responsibility of two girls, now 18 and 19. Also Fred had wanted to be free to be with Miriam and thus he, Luke, was sure that Fred would be relieved that Herbert had enabled Ethel to return for them. Herbert, who was already fixed in a malign view of Miriam's motives, said that she was still encouraging Fred to keep Ethel away, so that she Miriam could gain respectability by caring for the girls. The girls were growing into attractive women. Lizzie Weatherly comments that Betty was exceptionally beautiful and that Marjory was pretty in her dark way. Fred writes to Eddie that 'they are both pretty girls especially Betty who plays and sings well.'Betty, in the year before her mothers return, was in Italy staying with friends of Fred, while Marjory had moved into her Aunt Muriel's house with a paid post as governess to the youngest of her cousins. She was to prepare herself to go to Bristol University.

When Ethel returned, Herbert wrote to Eddie that 'Muriel's door remained firmly closed to her', so Marjory left her aunt's house in order to be with her mother and sister. The three lived in a flat in Maidenhead. Ethel must have reclaimed her grandfather's inheritance from Fred and thus had a little financial independence. While Ethel had had her difficulties in America, she did survive there; she saw a lot of the country and received kindness and acceptance from Herbert. Settling there must have seemed a better bet for her and her daughters than overcoming the hostility of the Weatherly family. The three of them left early in1926 on the S.S. President Roosevelt for New York.

Invitations to Fred to give song lectures arrived – these were first in familiar settings in Portishead and in Essex near where he was used to staying with his brother Alfred. The lectures were a mixture of reminiscences, comments on the art of song-writing and how fashion had changed over the years in the demand for songs. Several would be performed to illustrate his lecture. Then the lectures became organised and promoted by Keith Prowse and took place in London in large venues, such as the Aldersgate Street Hall and the Steinway Hall. The promotional blurb for them said that 'the recital is unique as it presents the music of various composers to the verses of one man and every song has already become a household word.' A typical review was in the Musical Herald which included this description – 'His clear enunciation made whispers audible and his unaffected and dramatic reciting of these lyrics charmed everyone.' It must have been the success of his lectures that led to his broadcasting on the BBC, usually from the Cardiff or Birmingham studios. He gave half hour talks every other month from 1926. Ironically, someone, who only a few years earlier was bemoaning the malign effect of broadcasting upon the performing arts, was being made a familiar voice in the nation's homes. One of his talks was entitled 'A Log Cabin in Colorado' and was heard by both Eddie and Herbert in the States.

No recordings of Fred's broadcasts remain. I remember my mother being annoyed when the BBC broadcast a radio programme about him in the 1980s, 'The man of a thousand songs', and chose an actor with a West Country accent to be him. She made it quite plain to anyone who had heard the programme that her grandfather had a proper Oxford accent. The film interview of him made by Pathe News in 1928 to celebrate his 80th birthday was made in his garden in Bath. Miriam, his grandson Guy (Muriel's eldest child) and Guy's son Michael, Fred's first great-grandchild are in the background. Unfortunately this film is silent with captions, so I can't confirm the accent. In 1927, Fred published his last book of poems for children, 'Songs for Michael', dedicated to his first great-grandson.

There was another dinner in1926 in London to honour his diamond jubilee as a songwriter. It was the year that 'Piano and Gown' was published, having been completed the year before. In the preface he writes that he hoped he had set down nothing impertinent and presumptuous, nothing unkind or conceited. 'The feeling that is uppermost within me is one of gratitude for the happiness that my long life of hard work has given me and for the crown of love, which is better than any of life's honours. Amor coronat opus.' Miriam writes to Jessie of Fred's birthday that year, 'We had such a happy day yesterday, dear Fred's 78th birthday. We gave a big (for us) luncheon party at the Pump Hotel. He just loved being amongst his friends of his own kind. Then we had a quiet tea at home and at 8 o'clock we went off to another party of friends and they gave him a tremendous welcome and were so proud that he came to them on his birthday. I am sure he felt it had been a happy day. Our drawing room and indeed the whole house is a mass of flowers sent to him and he had lots of presents, letters and telegrams. I am glad to say the he is in perfect health and looks years younger than his age.'

It's evident from his writing and from photographs of the pair, how happy Miriam made him. The description of his birthday shows that he and Miriam were now part of a warm and admiring group of friends in Bath. National recognition of various sorts had occurred after this marriage but not an honour from the King. Was this because of the bankruptcy or that he had openly lived with a mistress or because of some other dark event that Herbert hinted at? In Fred's mind, however his love for Miriam was all that mattered.

Sometime in the mid 1920s, Fred had what he believed to be a personal contact with Christ, an experience that preoccupied, excited and comforted him. His account of this event, personally typed, was as follows:

"TEN MINUTES WITH CHRIST"

'All my household had gone to bed. I sat in my study, trying to write, for I had to write. But nothing came to me. The fire burnt warm and comfortable at my back -- The sofa, at right angles to my table, looked inviting. The old oak chair on my left stood dark and straight, looking just as it did when the little Mother used to sit in it darning our stockings.

I took up my pen again, but to no purpose. I turned out the lights and sat in the light of the fire. I went to the window and drew the curtains and pulled up the blinds. It was a clear starlit night that should have shone over my garden and the city sleeping below. But city and garden were not there. In their place a range of low undulating hills and, huddled together in the starlight, were flocks of sleeping sheep. I saw the dim figures of the shepherds who watched them. It was no dream. I dropped the blinds and drew the curtains for a sudden urge to write had come to me. I went back to my table. Just for a moment I sat on the sofa and looked into the fire, and as I looked, I felt a soft hand laid on mine and, as I gazed at the hand and at my own, I saw that I was dressed as a child again and that it was Mother who was sitting on the sofa beside me.

I had not seen her enter or cross the room. But she was there. I felt her hand. She was there just as when she was young, and she was telling me what she had told me more than seventy years ago. "There were shepherds abiding in the fields, keeping watch over their flocks by night."

And I whispered: "Mother, I have just seen them. They are there, out there," and I pointed to the window and got up to draw the curtains. But when I turned to lead her to the window, I found myself alone. I drew my chair again to the table, but before I could turn up the lights to begin my task, without thinking I looked over my left shoulder to where Mother's chair was standing. And there in the firelight I saw One sitting in the chair. Oh yes, I knew Him. I remembered what she had told of the child who was born at Bethlehem and of the Man who died on the cross at Jerusalem. And I seized my pen . But still no words came. I could have wept for vexation. Then suddenly the room was all aglow and He said, "Write!" And all that He told me I have written down and what He said was this:

"I have come back once again to the Earth where I lived hundreds of years ago. I have been back to Earth before -- many times -- But only a few people in all My visits, only a few have ever recognized Me. The last time I came to London I was at what men call an aerodrome. Wonderful machines like birds were rising from the Earth and flying in all directions. One was starting, I heard men say, for Palestine. And I thought Nazareth and Jerusalem again. Two young men were in the machine and as it rose I stepped on board. They did not see Me, where I sat between them. Up we rose into the air, till first the trees, then the hills and then the clouds were beneath us, and Earth, with its rivers and seas, was faint below. Soon, it seemed, the stars were shining above us. The engines roared as we shot onward, and presently the wind blew wildly and we rocked and swayed as though we should capsize.

"Is it safe?" I said. And then for the first time, I think, they saw Me. For one said: "Who are you? How came you aboard?" And the other laughed, "Safe! Oh yes as safe as Earth!" "You must believe in your machine and in your own skill," I replied. "You believe in its wonderful power to carry you safe -- Do you believe in God?" They stared at me. "You can touch and see your machine. Do you believe in God whom you have never seen?"

"Not I," said the one at the wheel. "I believe in what I can see." And the wind blew more wildly and the wheel seemed almost wrenched from his hand.

"I believe in Him," said the younger. "Mother told me. He is a loving Father, and loved men so well that He gave His only son to them to teach them -- until men crucified him!"

"Impossible," laughed the other.

"But I can believe it," retorted the younger. "My father gave his life to save Mother and me from our burning home."

And the engines roared and the wind beat us about and suddenly something snapped and a flame shot up into the air and we fell, down, down through the night till we crashed upon the Earth. There in the wreck the two boys lay crushed and mangled. But it seemed to Me that the younger looked at Me with his dying eyes and knew who I was as I stood safe and unharmed beside them.

And then the scene changed, and I was on board a mighty ship. All was in confusion. Passengers and crew were rushing up and down the deck. Boats were being launched. People were crowding into them, till there was no room for more. And only the ship's officers and crew were left on the sinking ship. They were all standing in a ring round the Captain and I heard them singing,

'Abide with Me!' And, when I moved into their midst, they knew Me and we knelt together and I prayed, "Father, into Thy hands we commend our souls." And I knew that the Father heard as they sank beneath the waters.

And afterwards I was in a vast Cathedral. The seats were filled with kneeling men and women. The incense rose -- the altar lights shone upon the bright vestments of the Priests. And one raised a golden cup and spoke and one held a golden paten aloft, and a bell rang three times, and priests and people bowed to the ground and made the sign of the Cross -- and worshipped the wafers in the lifted paten.

I saw it all -- where I stood among the priests on the steps of the altar. My blood they said was in the cup, my body was in waters on the paten and they prostrated themselves again.

I knew they were devout and pious souls. They saw my body in the priest's hand -- but Me, the real Christ they did not see. And I passed down the steps of the altar through the crowds of worshipping people. The choir sang and the banners waved. And priests and people saw everything in that Holy Place, but I passed among them unobserved.

But just as I reached the western gate, I saw an old man and woman kneeling by the font. Their eyes were closed. Their lips were moving in prayer. As I passed they opened their eyes and looked upon Me. And I heard them whisper, "See, see! It is Jesus! Lord stay with us, and teach us, and help us to be good."

And I, who was writing all this that is here set down waited for His next words. But there was silence in the room, and Mother's chair, where He had been sitting, was empty.

I can explain nothing. I have written what happened. I have set down all that He said.

And the Christmas Bells rang in the dawn!'

By extraordinary coincidence one of my paternal great-grandfathers also left behind his account of a Visitation. He was the Reverend Alfred Potter of East Leake in Nottinghamshire and on March 20th 1877:

'The Revd Alfred Potter had a beatific vision of heavenly glory which included a sight of the blessed Saviour. It assumed the following character: first, he saw the old world passing away in the shape of a grand primordial forest tree, the top hidden by mist, fine grass covered the ground, a few ferns were interspersed. This disappeared and the blessed Saviour appeared in a frame, three-quarter size. The face was of exquisite gentleness and beauty; indistinct forms occupied the background. This phenomenon remained several minutes. The Saviour's soft gentle features turned towards Mr Potter, whilst he was praying and praising Him. He was assured of the salvation of those dear to him though no word was spoken and, of his own, the effect produced on Mr Potter manifested itself in great drops of perspiration falling rapidly from his whole frame. Passages of scripture came to memory in rapid succession and Mr Potter could not refrain from quoting St Peter's words - I am ready to go to prison and to death for thee. He cannot say how long this vision lasted but it was succeeded by another of great beauty and glory, a new world covered with buttercups of exceeding brightness while here and there was a tree and dim vision of glory like a mist overall. The above reminds me of the poet's fine words, 'One sight of my saviour will make up for all.'It is worthy of remark that Mr Potter had never seen at any time any painting or engraving that at all corresponded with the appearance of our own blessed Lord.'

Each man believed that his experience was a personal contact with Christ. There were important differences in the phenomena, apart from the content. Potter experienced a vision during prayer; only one of his senses was affected. The experience was silent although information was transferred to Potter, who felt overwhelmed; profuse sweating and racing thoughts occurred. He was passive throughout. Fred's experience was more complex, it was both visual and aural. He wasn't overwhelmed by what was happening, able to write what Christ had to tell, a participant as much as recipient.

One's own beliefs determine what one is to make of such accounts. They were real for the two subjects. If one is looking for a *non mystical explanation - to explain them away as some would say - then Fred was dreaming. His experience occurred at night in a warm study and he may have been dozing. In a half asleep state, dream content can be experienced at the same time as awareness of the real world, the two are muddled. The study was reality, the rest a dream. The elements of Fred's experience are understandable in terms of his own life and recent world events – Christ appeared through his beloved mother, the young pilots and their crash are images from World War 1, the liner sinking – the Titanic or Lusitania, the rituals of a high church service in Bath Abbey. Yet Fred was adamant until the end of his life, according to my mother, that it was a real happening and not a dream. In fairness to him, we do know when we have woken from a dream. Potter's experience is more in the tradition of reported religious experiences. A Vision such as his, accompanied by intense anxiety and body arousal can occur in forms of epilepsy where the focus that triggers the fit in the temporal lobe of the brain.*

In 1928, Fred and Miriam moved to Bathwick Lodge, up Bathwick Hill from where they were in Edward Street; the reason being that there was better air up there which was thought necessary to help Miriam's asthma. Contemporary photographs of the Georgian terraced houses in Edward Street show the sandstone facings to be black with grime, indicating sooty pollution even in central Bath. Latter that year, the window that Fred had commissioned to commemorate his family was dedicated in Portishead parish church .It showed St Luke (physician like father) and St. Cecilia (for his musical mother). Underneath these are the names of Fred's parents, Minnie, Alec, all his dead sisters and his maternal grandmother.

In the summer of 1929, Fred required medical help for tiredness and shortness of breath. As Miriam had written, Fred was a very fit man and it is noticeable that, neither in his memoirs nor in what others wrote of him, illness is never mentioned nor any infirmity, loss of hearing or vision with advancing age. On 25 August, he sent a letter to Marjory in America - 'I can only send you a scrap as I am sent to bed for some weeks as I have overtaxed my heart. Fortunately dear Auntie (Miriam) is much better and looks after me by day and a night nurse at night. I am already better.. Now goodbye my best love and blessing for you all. Ever your affectionate. Grandpapa.' A few days later, he wrote a short poem sent from his bed to his granddaughter Ruth who was married on September 3rd.

A friend and former pupil, Fred Wilshire wrote this for the local newspaper - 'On Friday night, Mr. Weatherly read some prayers and the 23rd psalm. He murmured "What beautiful English! How can anyone fail to love the Prayer Book and the Bible?" The next morning (September 7 1929) Mrs. Weatherly entered the bedroom. He was dozing. In a few minutes, he opened his eyes and Mrs. Weatherly smoothed his forehead and kissing him said, "You have had a good night, dear?" "Yes," he whispered, "but ….,"His eyes closed and Mr. Weatherly awoke in the Holy City.'

The funeral was in Bath Abbey, which was packed with an overflow in the street. His brother Alfred took part in the service, Lionel and Cecil the two other brothers in the country attended. There was a wreath signed by all his brothers consisting of flowers from the garden of their old home in Portishead. A wreath came from America – jointly from Jessie, Freda, Ethel, Betty and Marjory. Fred was buried in Bathwick Cemetery, a small burial ground further up Bathwick Hill not far from where he lived and died. Miriam was later buried with him.

Obituaries appeared in all the national papers and in the journals of organizations with which he was associated. His song-writing career dominated their contents. The other theme common to them was a reference to his size and temperament. 'He never pretended to be a poet but remained all his life a modest, good humored, happy-natured little gentleman.' (TheTimes). 'He was always a cheery, happy good humored little man, and very few other men could pass to their grave as he could with genuine knowledge that he had given an incalculable amount of innocent pleasure to thousands of his fellow men.' (The Brazen Nose – gazette of Brasenose College). 'The man was as might have been expected, a little simple, cheerful, generous soul with a little moustache, delighted at his modest success, not overestimating his position relative to real poets, but inclined to rejoice in being something of a poet himself, merrily laughing at his own old unsophisticated humor, and in age, delighted to find wireless audiences pleased to listen to him and his songs. The drawing room song has almost gone and Weatherly's kind has gone with it.' (The London Mercury, the monthly literary magazine).

Fred left £41,638, described as a fortune in the London Evening News. But, Bathwick Lodge was excluded as it was already in Miriam's name and, according to Herbert, Fred had also already made over £30000 to Miriam. Everything, including all copyrights and royalties from Fred's work, was left to Miriam apart from bequests of money to his daughters and a contribution to the trust fund for Betty and Marjory set up after Minnie's death. He honoured Maude's wish for bequests to her own family. A codicil was added shortly before his death to leave £400 to Ethel for her personal benefit. None of his brother was mentioned in the will.

In 1931, in front of a large crowd, the singer Clara Butt unveiled a plaque by the front door of 10 Edward Street, inscribed, 'Fred E Weatherly KC, songwriter, lived here 1919-1928'. That evening she attended a memorial concert in the pump room. Tributes to Fred were read out, including ones from the Lord Chancellor and other legal luminaries and many of his songs were performed. Adrian Boult conducted the orchestra and the BBC broadcast the concert. The purpose of this event was to raise money to endow a bed in Fred's name at the Royal Mineral Water Hospital in Bath, as Fred had given a specific instruction that any memorial to him should benefit the living.

Fred died a happy man, suddenly and without previous infirmity. He was fortunate in that as with much in his life. Whatever her motives, Miriam made him extremely happy in his last years when he relished his grand old man/household name status. During these final prosperous years, he was generous to his family - his sister Elsie and his brothers - by helping pay for their children's education. Eddie continued to receive his allowance. He thus fulfilled his role as head of the family. He made two acts of reconciliation in those years. The memorial window in Portishead Church to his family included the names of Minnie and Alec. The last codicil to his will leaving money to Ethel for her personal use was a recognition of what she had gone through.

There were no instructions in the will for anyone to receive an allowance. Miriam had never met Eddie, Herbert or Luke and was under no obligation to help them. Her advisor and Fred's solicitor in Bath, Ricketts, was of the same mind. Counting in the house and the bequests to Miriam before her death, his estate would be about a million pounds in today's money. His finances had thus recovered from the losses of twenty years earlier.

11. EDDIE AND JESS 1915-1939

Eddie and Jess returned in 1913 from England from what was to be their last visit. They arrived back with the loan from Maude. Eddie continued as a mine manger and continued to be an active participant of the Ouray group pushing for re-monetisation of silver. However he became embroiled in disputes that led to a court hearing with his partner in the old Lout and Wedge mines, Merril Jackson. It concerned money Eddie believed he was owed on the sale of the Old Lout mine. This money was not forthcoming, so Eddie took Jackson to Court. Despite a witness stating that he had overheard Jackson say to Eddie that he was owed money, Eddie lost the case and thus a payment that he had been banking on to secure his future. This failed action, in which both Eddie and Jess believed they had been swindled, preoccupied them from now on and, for Jess, it led to ideas that were to take hold of her that people were ganging up on her beloved Eddie. There was a feud with the Jackson family that continued until their deaths. Because of this setback and general economic conditions, Eddie had to write to Fred for more financial

Mining in the Combright 1920s, photo taken by Jess.

help to keep the Combright going. Fred sent over another £500, clearly stated as a loan to be repaid with interest.

The American and the Colorado economy deteriorated in the 1920s. Eddie lost his work as mine manager and his and Jess's future now depended on the Combright, their mine which as yet had yielded nothing. Eddie couldn't afford labour, so their only option was to do the physical work involved in excavating the mine themselves..

Jess at work.

By 1920, Eddie was 65 and Jess 55; yet every day they undertook hard physical labour at 10000 feet. They used their log cabin near the mine as a base, while they were up there. For Jess living there meant a two-hour journey each way down and back up the mountain to get supplies in Ouray. Each day they waited upon letters indicating that the promises made by English investors during their trips to London would be honoured and actual money would arrive. They kept their spirits up by posting loving notes for each other along the routes in the mountains that they followed. Inevitably, though, the impossibility of it all becomes evident to them and, as they face poverty, they turned to Fred for yet more help. They became unable to pay what they owed on their loans for the wood house in Ouray and were even having difficulties in paying for food. Writing to Fred, while Maude was still alive and thus before 1923, Eddie puts his position:

'Our long silence has been due to the hardest and most desperate times we have ever had in our lives, because after all these years of heart breaking struggles and hard work, we shall lose everything we own in the world unless I can get at least £100 before August 15. It's too long a story to tell you in detail but you must know that I would not write to you to help us in this terrible crisis after all that you and dear Maude have done for us. But it is the only way. The most serious of our difficulties is our house rent and food, we have only been able to secure an extension of credit by saying that we were writing to you in England and thus be able to pay part of our bills in the early part of August. If we fail to do that, we shall be down and out and may as well be dead. Our trouble first commenced when the French Canadian, on whom we spent the money you sent us, came down from the hills with very bad eye trouble –he has become blind in one eye and the other is becoming affected. I am helpless up there without him. The English people are still holding back the balance of their money but unless they want to lose their interest in the property, they must find it before the end of the year. We can protect it for ourselves by living at the cabin. With the loan of £100, I shall be able to hold on

Eddie at work.

through to December and I will make any sacrifice in the way of the price on our other property so that our obligations to you and dear Maude can be met.'

Jess prepared a letter to Fred to describe to him the poor state her husband was in, as he was drafting the above: 'He has begun a letter to dear Maude and you at least six times and each time he puts down his pen from his shaking hands with the exclamation, "Oh it's hopeless, it's hopeless. I can never make them understand. There's too much to explain and even then they may not believe me." Only an hour ago, he cautioned me not to tell you that he has been on the verge of a nervous breakdown for fear that you might think that he might die before help could reach us. I am going to tell you the naked truth about everything if you will bear with me long enough to hear it all. All winter long we have been waiting for our English partners to complete their payment so that we could go on with our work. We are still waiting and looking starvation in the face for the past four weeks. I am without even money enough to get out of here, so that I could get work, which I am only too willing to do to keep my poor Eddie alive. Eddie has gone out the back or front door more than twenty times a day in his slippers and bear headed and his poor gentle face the deathly grey white of despair. The glassy look in his poor dear precious eyes is like a red-hot knife in my heart. You may imagine how we feel when chief Jackson and his family are in rich clover in one of the biggest houses in this town with the town practically at his feet through our efforts and loss. Before my maker, it's all I can do to keep from shooting him. Last Friday poor dear Eddie went to the train in the hope that some man he knew might arrive and the whole Jackson family was there and stood in a row sneering at him and making audible remarks about him.One hundred pounds will barely carry us over our awful crises but he has not the courage to ask you for it. You have been good to all the family and life, but it is not worth this awful struggle, the constant asking for help from those who have always been willing. If I were alone, I would not think of asking but I cannot bear to see him suffering. My prayer is now that some way will open up where I can lead him out of this darkness into conditions which will protect him from anything like he seems convinced is at our very door. I have pleaded with him to cease worrying until he has heard from you. But I started out to tell you all. It gave us such comfort and joy to hear that dearest Maudie is on the whole better when last you wrote. We appreciate all the lovely songs you send us from time to time and the home papers have been such a comfort to dear Eddie.'

It may have been in response to such desperate letters that Fred decided to send financial support to Eddie, the allowance of £10 per month. Herbert came for a visit with Freda during one of his work trips and in his well meaning but bombastic way tried to advise. He wrote to Luke worrying as to how Eddie and Jess would ever manage but how sad he was at leaving them to continue on to Lincoln, Nebraska. 'If only those in England realised what we three brothers have been through.' He wrote from Lincoln to Eddie to say how much he and Freda had enjoyed the sandwiches and jam provided by Jess for their journey. In Lincoln, he spoke to a geologist at the University who told Herbert that capital and management were all that were necessary to get something out of a site in Ouray. He therefore encouraged Eddie to try to dig from 165 to 800 feet to see what they had in their mines. He sent them $100 to cover heat and light for the coming winter, also saying that as soon as he got his own affairs in order he would help more. But that would not be until 1927(two years away!).

When he got home, he tried to interest friends in investing in the mines, but reported that they were too scared to do so. His bright idea was to get Fred more involved in the project, so he wrote to tempt Fred to visit the US and to persuade Miriam to see the Rockies. 'I will make the Welsh bride wet her knickers with excitement. If by then, Eddie has started on the tunnel and has an engineer to hand then, Herbert reassured them, Fred would loosen up.' Meanwhile Eddie and Jess must not 'show the white flag – the little star will drop down from the Combright and tap at their window and tell them to get their tools ready for the morrow.' He repeats this injunction in later letters: 'Keep looking up at your little star over the

Combright each night –remember what's there for you.' Fred's suggested visit came to nothing.

Over the next years, Herbert sent them small amounts of money when he could - $5 or $10 bills, usually saying, 'Have this, no-one over there cares.' Meanwhile Luke was also trying to help with practical gifts - a pair of shoes, over-stockings, a second hand suit - as well as $1-$5 dollar bills from time to time. Eddie returned to journalism, writing articles for the Durango Herald on silver mining and its history, using the considerable reference material that he had collected. He also wrote on general economic matters. He presumably received some payment for these, a tiny income, though it's not mentioned in any letter. The articles were well received and must have contributed to his reputation, noted in his obituary, for scholarliness, for which there is otherwise little evidence. Somehow Eddie and Jess struggled on. One pleasure amongst their hardship was the wireless, by which they heard Fred's broadcasts and the singing coming from England. Presumably Fred's broadcast, a log cabin in Colorado, must have referred to Eddie's life. Hearing the wireless programmes made Eddie long to return the security of the old village, Portishead.

Fred's death and the terms of his will in 1929 were a cruel shock to Eddie and Jess. Herbert was outraged because none of his brothers was left anything and no provision was made to continue Eddie's allowance.Herbert sent for a copy of the will, which he hand copied to circulate to his brothers. When it was thus apparent that Miriam had inherited everything, all Herbert's cynical views of her were confirmed. His initial comments were that the will was unfair and must have been made under Miriam's malign influence exclaiming: 'Bathwick Lodge, $100,000 during Fred's lifetime and $190,000 at his death all to the housekeeper. What will she do with all that money - she's never earned more than £3 a week in her life.' But at the same time, in letters to Eddie in January and February 1930, he wrote that 'they mustn't create in Miriam's mind any idea that we think that the will is unfair, then she might help us and that we must give Miriam time until the estate is settled.'

In fact Miriam, grieving Fred, was overwhelmed by the responsibilities that she now had, for virtually all Fred's family had been looking to him for support, as they got older. In England, his sister Elsie was penniless; Cecil had lost all his money. Apart from Eddie in America, there were also Ethel, Betty and Marjory to think about. Luke was also desperate too but had never had the courage to approach Fred for help. Miriam relied on Arthur Ricketts, the family solicitor in Bath, for help in managing these expectations. Ricketts stuck to a strict interpretation of the terms of Fred's will and gave her conservative advice as to where to place her money. The upshot was that Eddie's allowance stopped and Miriam was advised not to send any money to the US. The latter advice was probably sound, given that the Wall Street crash had recently occurred and America was now in an economic depression, but it completely ignored the plight of Fred's brothers. Once it was clear that nothing was forthcoming, both Herbert and Luke became more vitriolic in their comments about Miriam, referring to her as Lady Bath, the Duchess and 'dressed like the Queen of Sheba wearing all Maude's diamonds'.

For Eddie and Jess, the situation was critical. Eddie drafted a letter to Miriam in January 1930 saying that they were now both ill; Jess with bronchitis and he with serious heart symptoms. Second, he reminded her that Fred was considering patenting their mining property so that it could be passed on to Maude's estate after Eddie's death – un-patented properties can't be passed on to non-American owners. Last year, Eddie wrote, had been busy as miners hired with Fred's money were doing assessment work. Now this work had to stop. He finishes the draft at this point. He was trying to persuade Miriam that without money he couldn't complete this exploratory work, which could potentially repay Maude's investment from all those years ago.

Jess characteristically discharges her feelings in a diatribe on paper. The theme of this was Fred's cruelty in ignoring Eddie in his will, invoking Fred's love for his mother that should have extended to all of her children. His mother would have given her last breath to save her children from 'old age so pitiful that no pen has ever had the power to paint it.' Jess thinks that Fred must have been under some influence, which she was ignorant of, when writing his will. So, 'he has left a black empty void in that corner of our hearts where we keep his memory and where we wanted to write gratitude.' She chastised Fred for expecting too much of Eddie in return for money as Eddie, as she had written before, was struggling from birth to cope with life and should have had some protection. She added that he left a substantial fortune that had been increased by Maude's money and by the royalties from Danny Boy. Of the latter she writes that:

'Royalties from Danny Boy covering 16 years at least has been bringing to Fred a bit; incongruous with his not mentioning a word about it even as far back as 1916 when there was a good occasion to make some reference to it - this was when we had to beg Fred to help us to save our property and he sent us £500, after the war left us suddenly penniless. I contend that he kept silent with the idea that reference to Danny Boy would awaken the thought that we were entitled to something. We were conscious of our right to it all the time. I kept silent because I didn't want him to think we were distrusting him.'

The fact that his and Maude's loan were to be repaid with interest meant to Jess that he wanted to keep silent about Danny Boy – that there was to be no connection between them and any debt to her from the song.

Nothing more ever arrived from England to help them. Eddie was now 75 and Jess 65; the Colorado economy was in deep recession. Jess writes of walking to Denver (a week, over rough ground) to look for work. Herbert does his best, commenting to Luke that the two must be starving and need help. He sent them $45 on one occasion so that they could have their water turned back on. An attempt to breed rabbits failed because they couldn't afford any food for them; they ate their rabbits. Further bad luck followed when falling boulders smashed their log cabin near the Combright. Eddie did his best to rebuild it himself.

Social security for the elderly was not introduced in the USA until 1935 in response to the Depression, when it had been estimated that around 50% of old people during the early1930s did not have enough money to live on. They depended on family or charitable organisations, went into institutions or died. Swathes of the younger population were on the move looking for work; elderly parents being left behind to fend for themselves. Eddie could turn to the Elks, who would have been obligated to help one of their brothers in difficulties. However Jess, writing after his death, to Luke, said that the local lawyer, Mr Siegfried, had been consulting Eddie as an expert on local land ownership disputes. So maybe that, with his journalism, may have produced some money. He must have done something to earn the statement in his obituary that he was a mining expert with an authority that no one could match.

Eddie rebuilding cabin 1930s.

From the early 1930s, Jess started recording what she calls dreams and visions, occurring in the evenings or at night in bed. She received messages from afar; they weren't at all clear but she knew they must be for her and important. She saw figures in front of her; a common apparition was an olive-skinned clergyman usually there after she had woken from dozing. He was holding something which he wanted to give her, that seemed important to her but he wasn't there when she got up to take it. None of these experiences made her afraid; she discussed them with Eddie and then wrote them down with an accompanying note to herself - 'Important, must follow this up.'

Eddie died of heart failure in 1934. After a service in the local Episcopalian church, he was buried in the local Cedar Hill Cemetery. Jess lived on. In a letter to Luke later that year, she says that she was doubled up with worry about paying $85 owing on the house and what was owing to the undertaker. As part of a financial arrangement to keep the house in Ouray, it had been divided up and she complained to Luke that some roughnecks had moved in next to

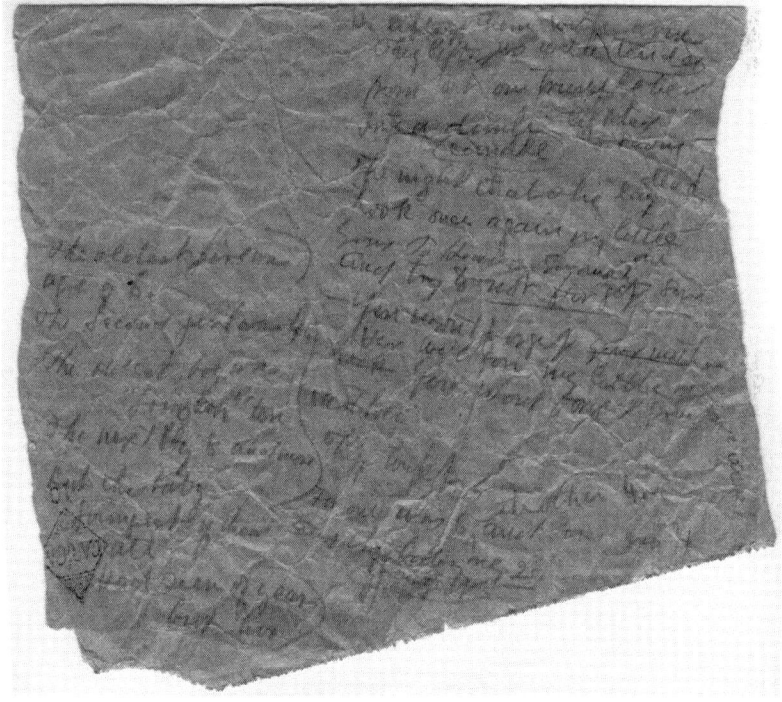

Sample of Jess's writing from Boulder archive.

her. Her failing eyesight and lack of teeth were troubling her, but she took the trouble to commiserate with Luke on his poor health. She ends the letter, 'God help us both'.

Six months later, she wrote again to Luke. She had received her first old age payment of $15 and put it to pay for Eddie's funeral. Most of the rest of this letter is taken up with complaints about Freda whom she says has made a slave and pauper out of Herbert. She accuses, at length, Freda of stealing some personal possessions from her that were her treasures – a photo of Fred and some letters written by Eddie as a child. She can't find them but believes Freda must have taken them during her visit ten years earlier.

Luke died of heart failure in a charity hospital in San Francisco in October 1935. Jess received a note telling her of his death from a former neighbour of Luke's on Mission Street. Jess lost a sympathetic correspondent and that, with the breakdown of relations with Herbert because of Freda, meant an end to contact with Eddie's family. There is a last draft letter to a cousin late in 1935. She is very depressed and longing for death so that she can join Eddie. She has no money and exists off bread and butter, which she can't chew properly because her teeth have gone. Her sight is failing and she can't see to read at night. She believes the people of Ouray are all against her, showing this by laughing at her in the town if she ventures out or talking loudly about her outside her window but disappearing if she goes out to stop them. She is frightened of a three-legged cat that turns up at her house; she sees this as a very malign omen and chases it away. Her great fear is that she will be taken from her home a poor institution.

That is what did happen to her. In 1936, she was admitted to a hospital for the elderly poor and insane in Pueblo and Eddie's papers with her writings were sent to the archives in Boulder. In 1939, the local paper carried a small paragraph that announced the death of Jess Weatherly, long-term resident of Ouray in Pueblo.

Eddie started in midlife on a young man's activity, seeking his fortune from mining for precious metals. In the decade before the First World War, there would still be many optimistic people around in Ouray; he and Jess caught the bug and from then on they were drawn into this gambler's life, as were tens of thousands of others. Someone prone to anxiety attacks since childhood with little ability for finance would seem ill-suited for a rough and tumble life and the cut throat competition that would be operative in a mining community. Eddie must have manufactured the story of his medical training to give himself some status on arrival there. Eddie was scholarly in that he read widely and could store knowledge, so that he could sound an authority. This must have been the case for medicine. He would have to display some knowledge to carry off the role of a former doctor. A similar process enabled him to gain respect in Ouray as an authority on the San Juan mines.

The collapse of the American economy in the 1920s killed off any chance of success in mining; in that sense Eddie was a victim as were millions of others. He threw his capacity for intellectual arguments and acquired knowledge into another doomed campaign for a return of the dollar to the silver standard, which if successful would have revitalized the silver mining industry. When that campaign failed and having had some success as a tutor and a journalist, he could have made these roles a source of income, even if it meant moving out of Ouray. But instead he chose even at the age of sixty-five to continue digging with only his wife as help. The course of his later life was thus progressively downhill - he and Jess put up with harsh conditions. They were probably malnourished, without proper clothes and in fear of being evicted. There was a stupid - not at all heroic- stubbornness in the way he had brought this state on to himself.

This was not a view shared by Herbert and Luke; they looked up to him; they never made any critical comment about the way that he was handling things or suggested he might do something other than mining. Both sent him money, which they could ill afford and actively encouraged Fred to support him, while asking nothing from Fred for themselves. Did this date from childhood? In the hierarchy of eight Weatherly brothers, Eddie some six years older would have been effectively the senior brother whom they would look up to when young children, as Fred and Lionel were away from the home. Or were they convinced too, that the Combright mine would yield eventually? Both had invested money in it and needed a return.

As their situation deteriorated, Jess became desperate about the plight of her husband continuing to see him as a noble man brought low by others and circumstances. While Eddie in desperation pleaded to Fred for help, Jess indignantly thought that Fred owed it to them. Underlying was her belief that Fred stole Danny Boy from her. While she felt that deeply, she was unable to confront Fred or to bring the subject up with Miriam after Fred's death. She knew that these two were a last hope of money and she didn't want to offend them, a reticence that was in contrast to the feuds that she had with some of the locals, whom she believed on much less evidence were doing them down.

Both Eddie and Jess became mentally ill in their seventies. Eddie became disabled by a worsening of his anxiety, described as shaking, pacing about by Jess, but now with a depressed and hopeless outlook. He was suffering an agitated depression. The clinical picture and prognosis would have been complicated by breathlessness and pain from heart disease and weakness from malnourishment.

Jess recorded both visual and auditory hallucinations. In contrast to the hallucinations experienced in a severe mental illness, hers were initially interesting, seemingly trying to convey something personal to her. 'Important, make note of that'. They occurred when she was dozing off or when she awoke during the night and it was dark in the room. They were perhaps similar to Fred's experience, produced by the half-awake brain in darkened surroundings.

After Eddie had died, her hallucinations were no longer intriguing but became frightening. She had become paranoid, hearing voices of people talking about her, believing that she was being shunned or laughed at in the street and interpreting a normal event, the cat visiting, as having a malign meaning. She was psychotic. The underlying diagnosis must have been depression - judging by what she wrote about longing for death. Grief for Eddie, loneliness, malnutrition and restricted activities because of failing vision must all have contributed to its onset and severity. All her life, she had a tendency to see others as the source of blame when things went wrong and this trait made more likely that her depression had paranoid features. Nothing happened to help Jess until presumably her madness, her neglected state and the squalor in which she lived became a concern to others in the town and she was removed to an institution. She would have been regarded as senile and left there till death.

Elderly people with illnesses like those of Eddie and Jess are not uncommon today. But there is a service for care of old people with mental illness. The key insight that led to its foundation in the 1960s was that many older people, formerly regarded as senile and discarded into institutions without much further thought, have treatable conditions, whether depression or an underlying undiagnosed physical illnesses. Now Jess and Eddie would be assessed. Physical conditions such as Eddie's heart disease are treated; disabilities caused by poor sight and teeth corrected as far as possible. Treatment of depression usually with medication would follow with an expectation of recovery. A crucial part of this help would be dealing with their circumstances - their home situation, shortage of money and poor diet.The aim would be to get Eddie and Jess functioning as a couple again at home but Jess on her own might be better offered some assisted residential care.

What if Jess had been recognised as a co-author of Danny Boy? There would have been a regular income for her from royalties, but more importantly her name would have been known as the song was being sung all over the States. She would have been a local celebrity in Ouray and surely not allowed by the citizens to deteriorate and die in an institution.

12. HERBERT, ETHEL AND DAUGHTERS

One of the few things that I was told by my mother about her life before marriage was that she had visited Richmond, Virginia to see her mother who was staying there and that she was away there when Fred died in 1929. She gave me the impression of a holiday visit - no hint that she had been in America for four years with the intention to settle there. When I asked her about Richmond, she told me about the hot weather and the racial segregation on buses. After I started visiting the States regularly myself, I wanted to compare impressions. I probed her about Washington and New York to get her to give a bit more away, but she denied seeing either city and, as I never went to Richmond, that approach led nowhere. She did tell me that about Herbert's fox farm in New York State that she had visited, but couldn't recall where it was – other than it was somewhere very cold. A friend once got out of her a story about being an extra in a film for which part she was dressed in evening gown and fur and had to enter a ballroom as part of group of guests. When I later tackled her on this, she denied ever saying it. I found it very frustrating that she wouldn't tell me her story of a young Englishwoman in the States in the 1920s, particularly as I knew it would have been an exciting time to be there. She kept all the details secret using her usual line that it was all a long time ago and she couldn't remember.

Ethel and her daughters arrived in 1926. They are not mentioned in any of the letters from Herbert to Eddie until 3 years later, other than a remark in1928 that he hadn't heard anything from them that he had anyway done enough for Ethel, who must look to Fred. The three appear in the Richmond telephone directory in1928 and 1929 and the US census as living there in 1930. Why Richmond and where they were for the intervening two years are unknowns - they could have been living without a telephone in Richmond. They didn't visit Herbert, Eddie or Luke for surely that would have been mentioned in the correspondence between them.

Before Ethel left for England in 1925 to claim the girls with a plan to bring them back, Herbert was as usual full of optimistic ambition. "They will live near where we keep the foxes and Fred will see they both go to Vassar or Skidmore College in Saratoga." The reality, one year later, was very different as Herbert exclaims in disgust: 'They land in the US with £10 each and no allowance for 6 months after their arrival.' It was worse still, for Fred wrote to Herbert giving him troubling news about Betty after her departure from England. It was a letter consigning them to Herbert's supervision. Fred wrote that 'Betty has the body of a beautiful woman but the mind of a child.' Herbert was understandably displeased at Fred sending a 21 year old to America with a 'poor mental condition', which was hidden from him until she was on her way. Fred also wrote to Ethel a bit later, 'You must struggle with Betty - remember that though she is 21, she is really not older than 12,' and again in 1927, 'In time Betty will grow up, at present she is not mentally grown up,' and in March 1929, 'I have left you something for your very own which on your death you can pass on to the girls.' This was the codicil of his will bequeathing £400 to her..

They rented accommodation at 2415 Lamb Street and then 2600 Barton Avenue, one block away. Both houses, built around 1910 of timber frame with white painted board exterior, are alike and are still standing. They are on the north side of Richmond in what is now a historic district known as North Barton Heights, but it is less salubrious than it was in the 1920s. A tram runs down the centre of Lamb Street into the centre of town. Marjory is noted on the census a being employed as an office worker in an insurance company. She was happily photographed with a group of friends from work outside the old City Hall.

Dance in Musical Show—Students of the Hutchinson-Drinard Studio, who will appear in the "A. I. B. Revue," to be given following the annual banquet of the Richmond Chapter, American Institute of Banking, at the Commonwealth Club Friday night. The production is under the direction of William L. Pierce and several of Mr. Pierce's latest song numbers, including the "Shag Step," will be given in the program. Left to right, are: Marjorie Weatherly, Lucille Rosenbloom, Aileen Bowles, Dot Rosenbloom and Mary Patten Bruden.
—Photo by Foster.

Marjory performing, Richmond Va 1929.

She also became a student at the Hutchinson Drinard dance studio, possibly Ethel taught there. The Hutchinson School was a family run venture and the students were hired out to put on dance routines at local functions. Betty was unemployed and a source of great worry to Ethel, as she would disappear from home without explanation.

On April 2 1930, Herbert writes to Eddie:

'It's about poor little Betty. They are in Richmond. Betty has gone temporarily insane. The doctor was called, but two nurses refused the case. She was sent to the Westbrook Sanatorium, $30 examination fee, $40 room and board, $30 night nurse - $90weekly.'

Westbrook Sanatorium was established in 1911 in Richmond for the treatment of nervous and mental diseases and of addictions to alcohol and drugs. Like most mental hospitals built in the twentieth century, it followed a core and cluster design. Instead of consisting of one giant building, the old asylum, there is a central administrative block which is surrounded by numerous pavilions, containing single rooms and wards in extensive grounds. The psychiatrist responsible for Betty's care was a Dr Alderman.

Herbert hurried down to Richmond, but first he asked his contacts locally about the care in Westbrook. He was not impressed as shown by the following stories that he repeats in his letter to Eddie. A Dr Royston of the University of North Carolina had attempted suicide by throwing himself out of the window at a London hotel. He had recently committed suicide successfully a week ago while a patient at Westbrook.

'Being allowed out in the grounds alone and, while a grounds man had a large bonfire of leaves and dead shrubs, he threw himself into it and burned himself alive. On top of this, the wife of the owner of the Richmond News Leader had been sent to Westbrook - insane - and placed in the ward Betty was first put. He found her there and, being rich, he had a cottage built for her in the grounds there with supposedly day and night nursing. Later when in his study at home, he heard the front door open and going into the hall, found his wife there, unattended. He called his housekeeper and they called the sanatorium to ask where and how his wife was. He was told that she was resting comfortably in the cottage with a night nurse there. Of course he took her away at once.'

With these stories in mind, Herbert would be in the mood to be critical of the place when he arrived seven days after Betty's admission. He describes his first visit to the ward:

'They had recently moved her to another building (from her admission unit) in daily contact with very insane cases, all much older than Betty. Her condition was terrible. Ethel was with me and I warned her that if Betty were kept there under such conditions, she'd go hopelessly mad. The poor child threw her arms around my neck, cried bitterly, telling me, "I'm so unhappy here; they treat me so badly; they put me in a room down in the basement. Do let me come home."'

Herbert was annoyed that Ethel was being charged $40 per might for a night nurse when Betty was asleep all night. He arranged a transfer with only a day nurse for less money, $80 per week, but told Ethel that her legacy would not last more than a couple of months at that rate. Together they found her a lodging with a widow near the hospital for $25 per week. Marjory wrote to Ricketts, the family solicitor in Bath, explaining what had happened while Herbert wrote to Miriam, as he said pleasantly, explaining to her that it was an opportunity to carry out Fred's wishes with a view to Betty. He recited these events in a long letter to Eddie, but then returned to the sore issue of Fred's will of which he now had a copy. He laboriously hand copied the will twice for each of his brothers so that they could see the points he was making about it. He reiterated how Miriam had 'stolen money through the will, over which she had had a malign influence that was rightly belonging to Betty and Marjory'- £8-10000 each in his view.

He followed that letter to Miriam with one to Ricketts, catching the next mail ship, indicating that if Ethel got no help, then the state lunatic asylum is the only alternative in a pauper's bed –

'An awful fate for a grandchild of Fred. Once the State authorities found out she was an alien, she would be deported and the trustee and next of kin would be compelled by the English authorities to meet her at the docks and receive her..'

This was told to Herbert by the British Consul in Baltimore. Herbert clearly believed that it would shock the pair into doing something. Fortunately Ethel had enough money to meet immediate needs at the lower rate and they could await a reply from England.

One week later, Herbert writes to Eddie again, saying that Betty's condition had deteriorated and she was back in Westbrook at a cost of $100 per week which neither Ethel nor Herbert could meet. Betty was out of control in her lodgings and had taken a violent attitude to Ethel and Marjory. She was on suicidal and homicidal watch. Betty's long term care, Herbert continued, is too expensive in the US as there are only two alternatives here - a private sanatorium or a pauper's bed. A psychiatrist, Dr Scholl, said that the family should return to England as soon as Betty was fit enough to travel to New York for the boat. Herbert returns again to the subject of Miriam and the will, but now adds that 'Fred is partly to blame for this tragedy for not giving Betty enough attention and then turning her over to her mother when she was 21, having had her since a child in his care.'

The next day he sent a note stating that the Westbrook administration was criticising Ethel and Herbert for moving Betty from the "mad" quarters. Ethel meanwhile had received a mealy-mouthed response from Ricketts, sending £16 owing her from some interest on stocks and continued that by telling her that, if Betty's illness were likely to last a long time, then he would be willing to sell part of her legacy of £400 to the value of £220. He would be willing to do so at once, if Ethel cables him. Ricketts observed that the fees that Ethel was currently paying were very high and would be half that in England. Ethel cabled back asking for the money immediately so that they can get to New York as soon as Betty is able to travel. Herbert offered to drive them from Richmond to New York to save the rail fare and the British Consul was willing to arrange with a steamship company for a nurse to accompany them.

To Herbert's mind, Betty's case was not a hopeless one:

'If she is removed from Ethel and Marjory and lives with a kind-hearted nurse with something to do – music and walks. If on the other hand Betty's condition deteriorates and she cannot sail, Ethel will be broke and Miriam, Ricketts, Muriel and Walter face the disgrace if deportation. Miriam must do what is right - if not Bath will no longer be her residence. There hasn't been a letter from her, not a line.'

Three days later, Herbert received what he called a very pleasant letter from Miriam but in it she refuses any help to Ethel. Unwisely, Herbert said, she showed her hostility to Ethel. Somewhat hypocritically, Herbert replies to Miriam inviting her to visit the fox farm as part of her proposed trip to Canada - it being not far from the border. However he is really angry at what he reads between the lines in Miriam's letter, that Ethel should be able to control her own daughter, expostulating that Ethel has only had Betty for four years. She was in Bath with Fred for thirteen. Herbert now puts the pressure on Muriel's husband Walter, getting him to see Ricketts and he ups the ante. He emphasises to Walter that if Betty is still in the US in August she will be deported as an alien pauper lunatic and that Ethel and Marjory would be deported too, as they are in fact illegally in the country on expired passports. Further, Ethel was thinking of declaring herself a pauper before August to bring the deportation process forward, thus saving both sanatorium fees and fares. Herbert says that this will be a story for the local press in Richmond but, as soon as they find out that Betty is Fred's granddaughter, the English papers will copy it. He goes on to blame Fred for using the children to cover up his life with Maude, cutting Ethel adrift and leaving money due to Betty and Marjory to the 'housekeeper'.

Miriam softened enough to allow Ricketts to write to Marjory in late April saying that she, Miriam would help financially once Ethel's legacy was exhausted. Herbert saw this as a trap to make Ethel broke in the US and thus be completely dependent on Miriam for subsistence and any fares home. He advised Ethel to go immediately. To this end, he arranged a report on Betty's condition to be sent from Dr Alderman at Westbrook to Lionel Weatherly with a copy to Ricketts. Herbert received a copy and he cites the conclusion in a letter to Eddie:

'She has a history of manic and depressive episodes extending over the past two years with pronounced homicidal and suicidal tendencies. She is mentally defective – manic depressive psychosis with mental deficiency. Recently her reaction has been more characteristic of dementia praecox and we fear she is going to require indefinite institutional care.'

This opinion confirms that Betty was indeed severely mentally ill, on top of pre-existing intellectual impairment. The latter had been evident to Fred and family when they had to deal with her difficulties at school and in Fred's word to Herbert about having the mind of a 12 year old in the body of a woman. But saying that she was 12 suggests that she had developed enough to care for herself, could read and write and seemingly she could play the piano. The problem was her maturation into adulthood. Betty would have been impulsive, moody and, one would guess have temper tantrums if thwarted. She probably didn't 'learn', in that certain behaviours went on regardless despite correction or attempts to teach her otherwise. The Stanford- Binet Scale, to measure IQ, was then in wide use in the US, though a score was not given in the report. The cause of her retardation could have been brain damage sustained at birth, or could have been be genetic. A range of genes determines intelligence level. From time to time a combination of these genes leads to lower than usual intelligence in the individual - a bad throw of the dice. There is a possibility that she wasn't impaired at all but her education was disrupted and her difficult behaviour caused by early onset manic-depressive disorder. But the psychiatrist's report is definite about her being mentally defective.

The major mental illnesses – the psychoses – are states in which a person's reality changes, when he or she holds as true beliefs (delusions) or experiences (hallucinations) that are false. There is no insight. Psychoses were classified at the beginning of the twentieth century by the German psychiatrist - and father of European psychiatry - Emil Kraepelin. His two broad descriptive categories are manic-depressive psychosis and dementia praecox, later renamed schizophrenia. The former begins with and is characterised by marked changes of mood ranging between depression and elation. In schizophrenia, the psychosis starts with and is dominated by delusions and hallucinations. Mood changes occur but they are not marked and not necessarily congruent with what the individual is experiencing. Distinction between the two in the early stages of psychosis can be difficult, as the individual can be very agitated, terrified or threatening and violent. Even in the days before modern treatments, it became clearer which form of psychosis was present - manic depressive psychosis has a relapsing and remitting course, the person affected having periods of normality in between episodes of mood change . In schizophrenia, the outcome is much worse, the psychotic symptoms become permanent and, without supervision, life out of a hospital is difficult. Dr Alderman showed diagnostic uncertainty between the two categories in this early stage of Betty's illness. His use of the word, reaction indicates the influence of Adolf Mayer, head of psychiatry at Johns Hopkins. While accepting the two broad descriptive categories of psychosis, Mayer understood their onset as a response to adverse circumstances, its form moulded by a patient's own psychological make- up. The Mayerian view leads to a psychiatrist gathering a detailed history in order to understand the interplay of events that led up to the onset and basis of treatment is likely to be a psychological approach. The European view contrasted to that - the onset of psychosis is not understandable through such deduction and treatment should be aimed at reducing symptoms, developing physical approaches to affect the function of the brain.

Manic depressive disorder, called bipolar more usually today, has a strong inherited component in its causation. In Betty's case the underlying intellectual impairment probably is not linked but would impact on how the disorder was manifest and how she responded to help when disturbed. The elated period is now called hypomania rather than mania. Betty would then be overactive, over talkative and sleeping little. She would be full of ideas and schemes, grandiose in nature. A common one is of the possession of vast wealth and thus giving away money or buying extravagantly. Another is of special powers, being chosen to save the world or to communicate with other planets. Sex drive is increased, leading to promiscuity or a public display of sexual organs. If stopped in their plans, the hypomanic person becomes rapidly angry and can be aggressive. Paranoid delusions can follow in which those seen to be thwarting the plans become part of a hostile plot.Hypomania is a nightmare for family who become exhausted by the talkativeness and over- activity, afraid to intervene because of the violence and have to sort out, often with the police, the chaos caused outside the home. Betty going missing from home would be in keeping with hypomania. Ethel would be right to worry. An attractive young woman with the mind of a 12 year old, now sexually disinhibited by hypomania, would be easy prey. A swing into depression can occur suddenly, the patient withdraws, slows up and may refuse to eat. Thoughts are taken up with guilt and self- blame. The person feels hopeless and can contemplate suicide and attempt it if the depressive ideas are sudden and overwhelming. The depressive swing is easier on the relatives although suicide talk is naturally alarming.It is usually easier to get help and to persuade the patient to accept it than the hypomanic phase.

It sounds as if Betty was admitted in a hypomanic phase and rapidly developed paranoid ideas about her mother and sister, frightening them by threats of violence. She also had sudden depressive swings with impulsive suicidal attempts. Nowadays the hypomanic and depressive phases of manic-depressive psychosis can be controlled by medication and a mood stabiliser offered to reduce the chances of their return. These medications weren't developed until the 1950s. Before then, physical treatments aimed at restoring brain function through inducing an epileptic seizure were developed - by using a toxic chemical or through electricity (ECT) or by inducing a coma using insulin, depriving the brain of sugar. Another assault was frontal lobe leucotomy (lobotomy) which was first tried in the late 1930s to reduce excitement and violence in psychotic patients and became widespread practice during the 1940s and 1950s. 1930 was before any of these treatments were in use – perhaps fortunately for Betty as their efficacy was never proved. The approach then was sedation and the use of restraint to control excited and violent psychotic patents. Sedation was by opiate or barbiturate, which had a temporary effect but usually the patients were made worse as they were confused when the medication wore off. Restraints were necessary for staff to cope with violent, hostile and excited patients – in a padded cell, in handcuffs or in a straightjacket. Another practice was to seal the patient in a bath for hours on end – cold water if the patent was over excited and warm water if the patient was depressed.

Patients sat it out in hospital until remission occurred, which with manic depression was likely as the condition is episodic but much less likely with dementia praecox. It seemed that Betty had sufficiently calmed to travel to New York supervised by two nurses to stay in a hotel before boarding ship. The nurses would undoubtedly have some restraints with them plus doses of sedative medication.

Herbert arranged a passage on the SS Minnekahdi sailing on May 31st. A senior nurse from Westbrook would accompany Betty on the journey to England, a second from Westbrook to be with the first for the journey by train to New York. The condition set by Westbrook was that the senior nurse was to be in full charge with no interference from Ethel and Marjory. On the boat, two stewardesses would be there to help the nurse, one by day and one by night as under no circumstances could Betty be left in the charge of just one person. Ethel had enough money left to meet these costs. On arrival in England, Herbert said that it would be up to Lionel to find a suitable place for Betty to go to straight away, that Ethel and the nurse should inspect it and if it wasn't suitable, then they should find a better place and send the bill to Ricketts.

Herbert continued his calls in the region to sell books while based in Richmond. He tells Luke that he went into the Johns Hopkins Medical School in Baltimore. There, he bumped into Dr Welch, one of America's most distinguished physicians, whose life work Herbert had seen written up at length in the New York Times. He described Welch as' friendly for a man as old as he is and who doesn't look his age by several years.' Seizing the opportunity, he described Betty's case to Dr Welch, who Herbert said wanted the whole history. He 'immediately blamed Fred for not giving proper care to Betty, saying that it was a very serious case of neglect, sending her over here (to US). Going into the details of Fred's marriage to Miriam, her age and his, he then said, "Was your brother a virile man?" I told him that I thought he was, to which he replied – "Her carnal influence over him must have been strong."'

Dr William Welch, then in his eightieth year, began his career as a bacteriologist, discovering the organism that caused wound gangrene. He was one of the founders of the medical school, became its Dean, during which time he set up the still renowned school of public health. After retirement, he was given the title as professor of medical history. He died in 1934 and is commemorated by the Welch memorial library at Johns Hopkins.It would have been a strange meeting to watch between the untidy, assertive English book salesman now aged 65 (probably looking older than his age and with bad teeth) who had buttonholed this distinguished and, by the sounds of it,well polished man. Welch chose to listen to Herbert, perhaps to humour him. From Herbert's account, Welch seems to have formulated the cause of Betty's problem exactly as Herbert believed it. One wonders whether, in order to keep the encounter brief, he agreed with everything Herbert said. Herbert would have been incapable of giving an objective account of Fred and Miriam without inserting his own views. Carnal influence doesn't sound like a phrase such a man as Dr Welch would use in a passing conversation.

At the beginning of May 1930, Ethel and Marjory moved to New York, staying in a hotel in Washington Square, while arranging details of the journey home on the 31st.$1250 was to be sent to Marjory by Ricketts from the girl's own money for the fares. Marjory seems to have taken over negotiations with Miriam and Ricketts. Perhaps by now Ethel had had enough and was no longer coping or that it became clear that Marjory would be dealt with as a member of the family, in contrast to Ethel who was regarded as an unwanted dependant? Herbert asked Marjory to stay on the farm, which she did, returning to New York for the 24th when Betty arrived with Miss Moss the head nurse from Westbrook. When they sailed, Betty was in a cabin with her two escorts while Ethel and Marjory shared an adjoining cabin. The journey home was eventful. Betty escaped from her cabin and, without clothes, ran into the ship's dining room during dinner and made a disturbance. This would be quite in keeping with hypomania-. Betty, suddenly announcing that she wanted dinner with her family, being discouraged by the nurse, then becoming angry at being thwarted and running out to do what she wanted.

They docked in London to be met by Elsie Weatherly the surviving sister of Fred's who lived there. Lionel had found a place for Betty at the Royal Holloway Asylum in Virginia Water to which she was transferred. The Royal Holloway Sanatorium was a huge one building institution built in high Victorian style which opened in 1885. It was furnished grandly with drawing rooms, dining room, concert hall, chapel, all set in large grounds. It was designed to give patients the feeling that they were in a place like their home. The clinical ethos was to provide a regular life, attention to physical exercise health and exercise. Occupational therapy was pioneered here. Patients were to feel as free as possible but in fact were under constant if unobtrusive surveillance by the large numbers of resident staff. Patients paid according to how much accommodation they occupied. In1901, there were 400 patients and 200 resident staff. By 1930 the numbers of patients had increased to the extent that a separate residence for nurses was built in the grounds. Each patient had his or her own care book with photograph. The only problem for Betty might have been that the sanatorium officially took patients likely to recover.

This may have been why she was soon transferred to Camberwell House, a reputed private sanatorium in South London where long stay was possible and by all accounts treatment was equally patient-centred. An article in the South London Observer, December 1937, describes some positive features of life there:

'A TWENTY-ACRE ESTATE IN CENTRE OF CAMBERWELL

Where Patients Have:
Books, Dancing, Squash
Films, Croquet, Putting
Plays, Bowls, Tennis

Few Camberwellians realise that Peckham Road runs through a twenty acre pleasure ground laid out in tennis courts, putting and bowling greens with croquet and squash racquets as well. This unsuspected estate belongs to Camberwell House, a home for mental patients established in 1846 and its two sections of fourteen and six acres respectively face each other across the main road. The larger building is on the Town Hall side and here men and women are housed amidst complete and wonderful surroundings of health and medicine. Perhaps nowhere else is the healing crusade of the modern medicine so tireless and indomitable as within walls such as these. Minds that have lost their grip on everyday realities are given simple sports and hobbies, and so led by light, carefully arranged training, back into the channel of sanity, often to successfully cope with the dreaded problems of business and private life that unhinged them before.

Gathering Disarranged Thoughts-Some begin to marshal their faculties by making raffia baskets. Then there are books, for just as reading broadens the mind, so it gently gathers the disarranged thoughts and compels concentration. Adventure stories are the most popular. Dance lessons are given and dances are held in the gracefully pillared and parquet-floored ballroom. Even a 'tuck-shop' is provided as being another link with the normal, sweets, tobacco and other luxuries add an everyday touch. An average of a hundred and twenty people attend the services held at the private chapel, whose walls are decorated with plaster panels traced with designs in coloured powdered glass, the handiwork of an artist who afterwards helped to renovate the shattered cathedral of Rheims. There is a small theatre, too, and professional travelling companies entertain the patients with 'happy ending' plays. Amateurs have offered their services but the audience is quite as critical as any outside and expects really finished performances. Many of the patients are keen filmgoers and regularly visit local cinemas, sometimes in the company of an attendant, sometimes alone.

Their health is looked after by the provision of X-ray and Actiño-therapy, prolonged immersion baths, a pathological laboratory, dental surgery, ophthalmic department, and an operating theatre.

Among the accomplishments of the staff of fifteen gardeners are pineapples grown in the hothouse, a lemon tree with an orange slip grafted on and four hundred bunches of black grapes, also home grown - ideal invalid fare. In a corner of one of the conservatories stand two young banana trees. They are dwarfs, grown from a couple of shilling seeds. These usually attain a height of six feet but apparently they have been pampered- so far they reach eight feet and are pressing against the ceiling above.

Escape Attempts Rare - Everything is done to make the patients feel at home. Most of the patients can appreciate the benefits, and attempted escapes are very rare, in spite of the fact that, as the medical superintendent says, 'So many people seem to have the idea that mental patients are always thirsting to get out.'

In the House operating theatre is the modern hospital marvel -- the 'shadow less' lamp, which, though directly above the operating table, throws only the faintest of shadows under the surgeon's hands so that he cannot get in his own light.

The building for women only on the other side of the main road, with its grounds covering about a third of the complete estate has among its garden wonders a Hulme oak tree, said to be four hundred years old, and a wonderful rose and wisteria pergola.

Though everywhere is the faint sadness inseparable from the mysterious diseases of the brain it is comforting to realise that a steady third of those admitted are able to return to the 'outside' world completely recovered. Many figures famous in the theatrical and literary world have been treated here for nervous breakdowns and other mental disorders.'

The hospital placed an emphasis on tranquil surroundings, supervised activities and attention to the physical health of the residents. Immersion was part of the treatment repertoire but no mention is made of the new shock therapies being introduced.

Ethel and Marjory moved to London, renting rooms in Montague Street off Russell Square; Marjory immediately began work as a wrapper at Selfridges for £1 per week. Herbert, on hearing this, wrote that Walter and Muriel must have hearts of stone to allow it when Marjory could be set up with a proper job, given the office skills she had learnt in America. There was a letter to him from Ethel and Marjory in 1931 asking what to do about money for Betty. All Herbert could advise was that that they should go and see Ricketts and tell him the whole story. After they had left, Herbert wrote to Eddie that he had done his best, as Fred would have wanted, and that Marjory and Ethel would have been lost without him.

He writes to Jess after Eddie's death in 1934 advising her to hang on to the property as things could only get better and again in 1935 after Luke's death. He was upset that he didn't know where Luke, who died a declared pauper, was buried, and furious with Alfred who wrote saying that it was probably better that Luke 'was no longer with us'. Herbert died in Florida in 1940.

Herbert is probably right about his necessary role in dealing with Betty's admission and eventual departure from the US. His assertiveness, strong sense of what was right, together with contacts made on his travels over the years rescued them. Both Ethel and Marjory would have been shell shocked by Betty's illness, by her hostility and, by the sounds of it, verbal and physical assaults on them. Like many family members, they would not yet realise that something irrevocable had happened to Betty and because there are always better days, they would hope that the awfulness would go away. Most patients dislike being in a ward and blame their depression or outbursts on the hospital environment or the staff. As Herbert said, Betty was miserable and being made worse by being with insane patients. Understandably the family wants to do what their relative wants and collude with an idea that it would be better out of hospital. Herbert and Ethel did just that, but the boarding out arrangement broke down in a week. Such anxious relatives can be seen as interfering by staff. But it is really an obligation of the staff to provide information and support for relatives, listen to their concerns and make adjustments so that sudden, risky discharges don't occur.

Ethel and Marjory had to deal with lack of money with consequent potential deportation in the face of a distinct lack of understanding from England. Miriam seems to have hidden behind the solicitor Ricketts who insisted on a strict interpretation of Fred's will. Herbert's obsession with Miriam and her influence over Fred's will must have been less than helpful in dealing with Ricketts, Miriam and Muriel and by his urging the girls on to claim what he regarded as their rights, when it was clear that Fred's will was valid. It was likely to have irked those he was writing to and they would then see the stories about deportation as typical Herbert exaggeration. Money was forthcoming when Marjory did the asking. For Ethel, Betty's illness was yet another loss of a loved one and, in her mind, another thing for which the Weatherlys could blame her.

Marjory had seen her older sister, to whom she had looked as her leader in childhood, change into a disturbed, angry and violent other person. She on the other hand had settled in Richmond with a job, friends and her dancing. Now she was to return to England with nothing and at 23 was taking over arrangements. Betty would be a long-term responsibility and she didn't have her grandfather, the most stable influence in her life, anymore. Miriam, her aunt Muriel and cousins would be her family, but they didn't accept her mother.. This must have been a bleak time for her.

The Royal Holloway Sanatorium was taken over by the NHS in 1948 and closed in the1980s after a fire destroyed much of the building. There are no casebooks extant of Betty's admission, so a source of a photograph of Betty is lost. Camberwell house closed in 1955 because of rising costs and competition from the NHS, all recent records were destroyed then, as the hospital had remained outside the NHS where records are always maintained. An interview with the secretary at the time of closure of Camberwell House does suggest that a humane approach was always maintained there. He said that the place:

'Stood as the epitome of the enlightened approach to mental disorders when public asylums were busy creating, through brutality and ignorance, the mistrust that still lingers in the public mind about mental disorders. There used to be 420 beds with a staff of 227, fees were 25 shillings a week in 1909 rising to £10 in 1955. Now, they were making no profit, many remaining patients couldn't afford it and he wasn't going to turn them out. They'd been with us for years; they were friends.'

The contents were auctioned. Apart from furniture, there were clocks, tables, chairs and pianos. The headline, announcing the sale in the local paper, the South London Press, January 21 1955 was:

'CAMBERWELL'S MENTAL HOSPITAL SELLS UP AFTER 109 YEARS

PADDED CELLS FOR AUCTION

Anyone want a padded cell? Or a straitjacket or two? Those who pass the auction sale notice outside Camberwell House, Peckham Rd, once one of the largest and best known private mental hospitals in the country might speculate, with a macabre kind of humour, how best to use such unexpected bargains.'

The buildings of Camberwell House still stand a part of Southwark council offices. There were two legacies of this time in my mother's life that I can now see. She was always an expert dancer - quickstep, foxtrot and particularly the Charleston. I remember her demonstrating this dance at a party for my twenty-first birthday, when some dance tunes of the period were being played, to my surprise and that of my friends. She was also an expert at wrapping parcels. Neither skill has been handed on.

Ethel and Marjory spent the next years in London. They rented a flat in Highbury and then in Sutherland Avenue in Maida Vale. Money would have been short, as Ethel's family legacy and that from Fred were used up in Richmond and in getting them home from New York. Both Betty and Marjory were now of an age to inherit the money left in trust for them under the terms of Minnie's and Fred's will. Betty's share must have been swallowed up in paying for her sanatorium fees. Judging from their plea for advice in the letter to Herbert in 1931, covering these was a worry. Marjory's income would be required to pay the rent and to support her mother.

Some kind of career was necessary. In 1933 Marjory began training as a physiotherapist at the Middlesex Hospital, qualifying in 1936 with a special diploma in electrical stimulation therapy. Walter James, her Aunt Muriel's husband, provided financial support for her studies. In keeping with her work and her interest in dancing, Marjory was an enthusiastic member of the Women's League for Health and Beauty, which in the mid 1930s was flourishing. This movement aimed to encourage all women to become fit and improve their posture through supervised graded exercises that involved stretching and working muscles against gravity. It was to be a mass movement for all classes; participants were encouraged to exercise together in open spaces; for example office workers would exercise in London parks. Standard blouses and skirts with the Health and Beauty logo were worn. There was a mass rally in Hyde Park in 1935 demonstrating synchronised exercising in which Marjory participated.

Marjory became good friends with Peggy Weatherly, Alfred's daughter, now living in London. Together they would visit Miriam in Bath, Muriel and Walter in Bristol and Lionel Weatherly in Bournemouth. Miriam had moved from Bathwick Lodge after Fred's death to a smaller Georgian terraced house nearby in Durnsford

Marjory after return from USA 1930.

Place. She took her responsibility as copyright holder of Fred's work seriously. She obtained a copy of every published song to have bound into thirty five volumes, which she then catalogued. However her life was now limited by her asthma which was making her continuously breathless and necessitated days in bed with admissions to a local nursing home. Marjory and Miriam became close, although it doesn't seem that Ethel was ever invited to Bath. Miriam Ford, Maude Frankfurt's great niece, remained a close friend, having known Marjory and Betty since childhood.

In1936, Marjory was seeking work as a physiotherapist. She replied to an advertisement for a locum post for a rehabilitative clinic in Nottingham and was appointed. She set off for Nottingham, a completely unknown town to her.. One of her first patients was Alfred Mann, coming for treatment after an injury playing squash. Alfred was established in business, had his own flat, enjoyed sports at which he excelled, had a wide circle of friends and loved attending dinner dances with a group of them at weekends. His pride and joy was a 1934 Lagonda Coupe. The Mann family was respectable – generations of parsons, doctors and bank managers, who were originally from Yorkshire, but Alfred's parents had moved to Nottingham where his father had been manager of the largest bank in the town. Alfred's father was dead and his mother, sister and younger brother had moved to the Lincolnshire coast for better air to help the chest of the younger brother.. Alfred had stayed behind in Nottingham free to enjoy himself, escaping the confines of the family home in Lincolnshire where his mother determined that the atmosphere was both pious and frugal. Alfred and Marjory became engaged in 1937. She and Ethel visited the Manns in Seacroft (outside Skegness). Alfred's sister recalled her first impression of Marjory as being very glamorous but very thin, with black hair and flashing dark eyes. Ethel, she said, was very London, by which she meant smart and amusing. Marjory put her foot in it on her first visit by leaving a hot tap running in the bathroom which soon drained the small hot water tank, meaning no further hot water for the family that day after she had left. The Manns tended to plumpness and dowdiness, perhaps explaining the exoticism that Marjory and Ethel conveyed.

Alfred now 34 and Marjory 31 married in May 1938 at All Souls, Langham Place. The invitations were sent out by Ethel as Mrs Alec Weatherly. Ricketts gave Marjory away, indicating further rapprochement in Bath. Miriam Weatherly was very evident in the photographs and may well have subsided the wedding. Alfred Weatherly officiated; 'Roses of Picardy' was sung during the service as a commemoration of Fred. However Muriel and Walter did not attend, nor any of the cousins, maybe hostility to Ethel still lingered or maybe they weren't invited. The wedding photographs though do confirm how thin Ethel and Marjory were. The honeymoon was spent in the South of France, travelling in the Lagonda. They returned to Nottingham; my mother in effect starting again, making her friends amongst my father's set.

The past returned soon. In October 1938, Ethel died suddenly. She was moving into a new flat in Wembley and, while on a stepladder arranging her books, suffered a cerebral haemorrhage. She was 55. Burial was arranged in a Wembley cemetery. Ethel left no will that required probate, indicating that her estate was less than £500. The responsibility for Betty would now fall on Marjory. Ethel had been the principal visitor to the sanatorium, now it was up to Marjory to see that the bills were paid and that her care was adequate.

Betty was the elephant in the room at the wedding. My father and his family never knew of her existence, so there must have been an agreement between Ethel, Miriam, Ricketts, Alfred Weatherly, Peggy and Miriam Ford to keep silent on the subject. The reason must have been to avoid this family being seen as tainted. The stigma of mental illness was such that my mother for some would be undesirable marriage material. Perhaps she might become affected or, worse, pass it on to her children. There is undoubtedly an increased risk of a similar illness in first-degree relatives – siblings or children. If the rate in the general population of manic-depressive disorder is 1 –2 % for women, the risk in the relative goes up to around 10% - a five-

fold increase but by no means a likely happening. These figures were not known in the 1930s. However popular thinking was influenced by the nineteenth century theory of degeneracy in which mental illness was conceived in affected families (tainted) to pass down the generations getting worse starting with neurotic problems, then evolving into insanity and finally producing imbeciles until the taint died out. Betty who was both insane and intellectually impaired would not sound promising as a future in- law in this respect.

Betty of course did not attend the wedding - in contrast to today when medication would enable her to be calm enough to attend. Similarly she could not have attended her mother's funeral. The only details about Ethel that I was told by my mother were the circumstances of her sudden death and the telling was not accompanied by any emotion. She was remarkably reticent about her otherwise. It is not particularly intrusive for a child to ask about a dead grandmother, yet I was made to feel that she was none of my business. Talking about Ethel probably brought back all the hurts of her earlier life – Ethel disappearing to America, being patronised in Bath, Betty's illness and their struggle in America, shortage of money in London – which she had kept out of mind. Perhaps she found her mother's life so sad and unfair, little ever went right for her,, that talking about her would bring back grief for her. She may have been at the same time angry with her mother, a feeble personality, a dependant woman who needed supporting all her life but then who goes and dies suddenly lumbering her with Betty. An abiding mystery in what I can piece together about Ethel is the absence of any role played by her three sisters in her life or that of her daughters.

Seeing to Betty's welfare after Ethel's death must have been very complicated for my mother, if my father was not to know. After eight years in an asylum, however enlightened, Betty would have changed – long-term patients develop certain common characteristics. Hairstyle and clothes tend to be chosen by staff, initiative goes as the patient becomes used to things done for them and interest in the outside world becomes replaced by the activities in the asylum.

Adding to these changes would be side effects of the treatments she was receiving –sedation from medication, confusion and recent memory loss during the course of shock therapies. These changes together can make a long-term patient seem unattractive, even shaming to some relatives. Out of sight and out of mind is an easy option for families in an era of stigma against the mentally ill and visiting is discontinued. The 'place at table' is no longer there, the patient is not part of the family anymore. The emotional space that Betty had occupied in my mother's mind was likely to have been filled by her marriage and new responsibilities.

On the plus side, Betty was placed in a very humane institution and would likely have settled in. Given her double disadvantage of intellectual impairment and psychosis, some form of supervised residential care might be recommended today even when there is policy to keep patients out hospital and at home as far as possible. A lot would depend even today on family member being willing to take up a carers role .In 1938, there was little available between long term hospital stay and home nursing and payment for the latter would have to be met privately. That option was thus only available for the better off. For Betty, family support was out. My mother had made it clear that she didn't want Betty connected to her new family. With Lionel's supervision and encouragement, Betty must have decided to stay resident; her quality of life anyway would be better than struggling alone in London. The income from Betty's inheritance was enough to cover her fees. Lionel Weatherly who lived on until 1940 kept an eye on things. My mother could therefore have ducked out of visiting before the war in order not to have to deceive my father about a trip to London.

When I first discovered Betty's story, I was outraged that my mother could have ditched her sister and let her live and die in an asylum, knowing how derelict life would be in them at that time. However on reading about Camberwell House, I think a humane solution was found for the care of a very handicapped individual.

13. MARJORY

I was born in Skegness Hospital at the end of 1940. My father had enlisted at the beginning of that year and was stationed in mid Lincolnshire awaiting an overseas posting. When my mother became pregnant she moved to Seacroft to a rented house next to her in-laws, where she was to spend the rest of the war until my father's return. Miriam Weatherly became my godmother in absentia – her heath and the difficulties of travel across England from Bath prevented her attending the christening. My father left early in 1941 for war service in India and Burma, not returning until 1946.

Miriam Weatherly was by now incapacitated by breathlessness, living more in a nursing home than at home. My mother made a trip, mid 1941, by car to take me to see her. She was courageous to drive such a distance during the early years of the war with a six-month-old baby to look after in the car. There was petrol rationing; complete black out at night and all signposts had been removed to confuse the Germans, as a landing was anticipated. Miriam died suddenly in hospital from a complication of her asthma on December 31st 1941. She was 65. In her will, she left the copyrights of all Fred's works solely to my mother. Her house was to be sold and added to her estate, which was distributed as bequests to her own relatives, some Weatherly nieces, Fred's daughters and my mother. The furniture in the house, some of which had come from Hillside was left exclusively to Fred's daughters Muriel and Christine. Betty was not mentioned in the will.

The furniture was later sold at auction, so my mother made a second trip to Bath for that. Unfortunately, she arrived in April 1942 on the day before the city was bombed in a revenge raid for an attack by the RAF on Lubeck. She spent 24 hours in the hotel cellars with me; the auction was postponed. Miriam Ford bid for her at a later date for some small pieces – she was always sad that she didn't have more from 'the Bath house.'

Becoming copyright holder for Fred's works with royalties to be paid for fifty years after Fred's death was a sizeable legacy. My mother said that she was surprised to be the sole beneficiary from them as her aunts, Fred's daughters were still alive. She may have gained some pleasure to have this advantage over her disliked first cousins, who weren't mentioned in Miriam's will. An affectionate relationship had developed between her and Miriam since the return from America, as shown by the visits to Bath, Miriam's high profile at the wedding and the invitation to be my godmother. With Betty to look after, Miriam might also have thought that my mother needed the money more than the James children. My mother who was raised in Fred's house was also probably closer to him in Miriam's view than his other grandchildren.

My father returned in January 1946. I remember being taken to meet him at Boston station – a tiny, very thin man with an officer's hat that seemed far too big for him. We soon moved from Skegness to a rented house in Nottingham, where my parents would have had to go through the enormous adjustments after a five year separation. A few years after his return, he developed diabetes. He was a more difficult person than before the war because of this -my mother would tell me of his irritability and short temper. Like all the wives left without husbands during the war, my mother had become used to independence, making her own decisions. Now she had to discuss them with my father. Fortunately my father (unlike some in the far-eastern theatre) could keep up a correspondence with her during the war, so he had some idea of what had been happening to his wife and son during the time he was away. I undoubtedly added to the difficulties of my father's readjustment. I had until then been brought up with my mother, aunt and grandmother, presumably the centre of their attention. He had to learn to adjust to a five-year-old boy who had nothing but fantasies about what a father was or what a father was supposed to do. It didn't work at all well.

A recent book, 'Stranger in the House', describes, through a series of first hand accounts, the adjustments that many wives and children had to make in order to resume normal life after the return of the man of the family to the straightened circumstances of 1946. It was reassuring that my parents' and my experiences fitted into patterns that emerge in this book. The norm was for the children to settle down with the new situation but in our case it all got much worse.

Betty died on 28 March 1946 in Camberwell House. She was 40. The death certificate reported bronchopneumonia based upon myocardial degeneration (weakness of the heart muscle) as the cause. My mother arranged her burial in the same plot as Ethel in Alperton Cemetery in Wembley on 2 April. My father however spotted the papers arriving in the post concerning Betty's death and estate and demanded to know who they were all about. He was told now about Betty. He became very angry with my mother and said later to Peggy that she, my mother, had been 'mad' to hide Betty from him. Nevertheless my mother was still absolutely insistent that I was never to know about her, which meant his keeping silent on the subject with his relatives and all their friends. Betty died intestate but had an estate approved for probate of £3152, which my mother received as next of kin.

Myocardial degeneration implies diffuse damage of the heart muscle leading to heart failure. The commonest cause is arteriosclerosis in the coronary blood vessels supplying the heart. Betty at 40 was young for that and the condition also is much rarer in women than men. However, if she were a chain smoker, then her risk that would be increased. Alcoholism is another cause, but Betty would have to have had a high intake for many years - possible but never mentioned. No post mortem was carried out which is surprising in a woman of this age, unless her heart failure had been of long standing. Sadly suicide is always a possibility for patients with a long standing mental illness, particularly if Betty had become depressed as part of her manic depressive disorder. The death certificate could have been made innocuous to protect the family and the institution.

Her estate was not insignificant, presumably her share of Fred's and Minnie's trust for their granddaughters. £3000 would have bought a comfortable house in 1946 and, invested, would have provided enough income to cover the fees for Camberwell House.

In May, my mother was admitted to a nursing home in Nottingham where she spent the next two months. In a letter concerning her royalties my father wrote that his wife was not well and that she was likely to be so for some time. I was taken to see my mother once in the nursing home and remember her being in tears with blood running from her mouth - she had just had some teeth extracted. I ran out of the room. It was the last time I saw her for eighteen months as she was transferred to Ruthin Castle in North Wales, then a private hospital specialising in diagnosis, treatment and recovery for medical conditions. Some distinguished physicians who consulted there as well as in London staffed it. I went back to Skegness to live with my aunt and grandmother in the summer of 1946 after term ended. However my grandmother was becoming unwell, indeed died at the beginning of 1947. Looking after her and me full time was too much for my aunt so I was sent to a boarding school about an hour away, so that I would only be living with her in holiday times.

My mother's physical health must have been the cause of concern - I would suspect that low weight and difficulty eating must have resurfaced. The tooth extraction in the nursing home could have been because of a tooth problem but, at that time, there was the 'chronic sepsis' theory of debility - unexplained tiredness, malaise, weakness for example were thought to be associated with a hidden source of infection in the body. Teeth were often blamed and extractions undertaken to improve general health. In fact she was having a nervous breakdown – depression.

1946 was thus a terrible year for all three of us. My father, not in the best of health returned to difficult economic circumstances, had to find a job and a house for his family. Presumably he was hoping for more love and support from his wife and son than he received on return. Three months later, his discovery of Betty showed him that his wife, his mother-in- law and others in her family had been dissembling to him. I can imagine that he was both hurt and angry;

he was always straight forward himself. However my mother's emotional state was such that he had to agree to continue the secrecy over Betty. A few weeks later, his wife was in a nursing home and, after a couple of months there, it was decided that she needed much longer to recover in quiet surroundings away from stresses. He must have wondered if those included him. Her illness landed him with his son with whom he had had no time to establish a relationship. He wouldn't be able to do his job and look after him, so temporary arrangements had to be made until his sister could take charge. By the autumn he was on his own, but having to drive at weekends long distances to see either his wife or son. For someone struggling to adapt himself after the army and war, it must have been a nightmare.

My mother had to meet her husband again after five years to find that, as most wives in these circumstances did, that it was not quite the same person who returned as who left. Adjustment was necessary. Practically, this involved moving from the seaside town where she had been living comfortably watching her son grow, to set up house in a depressing suburb of Nottingham, while her husband restarted work. Any coming to terms with him and her new situation was then disrupted by the news of Betty's death. This must have impacted on her. There was the loss of her last close relative - she had lost her mother, Miriam Weatherly and now Betty in fairly quick succession and each at a much younger age than she might have expected. She must have experienced a surge of grief. In addition, she had hidden Betty away, wiping her out of her day-to-day life since her marriage. Now Betty had died in a mental hospital without family present - guilt makes grief worse. However, she had justified to herself her decision to keep Betty secret because it protected her new family from the stigma of mental illness. Her cover was blown so far as her husband was concerned. Instead of supporting her for what she had done, he was critical, angry, hurt. She had abandoned Betty to no advantage, compounding her guilt. The only way she could salvage something was to demand that her son should not know of Betty's existence. The grief, her guilt and her husband's criticism of her for something she had done to protect him must have been overwhelming and led onto the breakdown.

For me, it was a year that scarred me and shaped my views of my parents through childhood and adolescence. First I had, like many children that year, to discover a father and realise that this person took mother's attention away. In my case, we had little immediate rapport, as he wanted to talk sport to me as something that should interest a boy. Unfortunately I had no interest or aptitude for sports. The sudden disappearance of my mother and her distress in the nursing home was not explained to me by my father, other than she had gone away to get better. Her disappearance meant a complete loss of my security as I was passed to friends, to my aunt and then on to boarding school. The last seemed punishment. There were three other boys who, for whatever reason, entered the school before the minimum age of starting there of six. We were kept away from the main school and slept in a separate room in the headmasters quarters. One or all of us would start crying when the curtains were drawn. After a while, the headmaster's wife would come in and take the most tearful into her bedroom. The only communications from my mother were postcards of Ruthin Castle – a grey crenulated, mediaeval building reconstructed by the Victorians - in which she told me about the ponies in the grounds but saying nothing about herself. It seemed a very frightening looking place. I would print a message for her in return 'hoping that she was better'.

The plus of this separation meant that I got close to my aunt, a mutual affection that lasted into adult life. I could always turn to her. The bad outcome was that I made a connection between my father's return from India, my mother's crying and bleeding mouth in the nursing home, followed by her disappearance. It must have been his fault, I decided. Without information to the contrary at the time - indeed any information at all - about what had happened to her and why, I held on to this belief and it contaminated any chance of a close relationship with him during my childhood and adolescence. My mother came to collect me with my father from the school at the end of the summer term in 1947. In handicraft, I had made a pair of slippers as a present for her, which I could now give her in person. In the car on the way home, she put them on and all the stitches burst. She burst into tears as I did. After a few days, she had gone again and I was back with my aunt. I now blamed myself for causing her going away again.

My parents acquired their first house in a better area of Nottingham, maybe paid for with Betty's money. My mother was there when I finished the winter term in 1947 and went home for the Christmas holidays. Both my father and aunt drummed into me that my mother was not to be upset. I soon realised that telling her anything that suggested that I was anything other than fine did upset her. Telling her how much I hated the school was not possible.

The marriage settled into a pattern, which lasted until my father's early death. My father prospered at work and relaxed with his pre-war friends playing golf or billiards. However at home, he had a wife who was rarely without a complaint – acid on her stomach, constant nausea, sometimes accompanied by vomiting - being the most common. On bad days these symptoms made her agitated; she would pace about, clutching a hot water bottle to her stomach. She would spend days largely in bed and the general practitioner called to prescribe sedation, usually amylobarbitone tablets. There were frequent consultations and investigations of her stomach at the local hospital; but nothing amiss was ever discovered. She was always complaining of feeling cold - I used to find her ,when I returned home, sitting immobile by the large log fire in the sitting room staring into the distance. She sat so close to the fire that she developed permanent heat discoloration of the skin on her shins. It was her only way to get warm, she explained to me.

Though never having any enthusiasm for food or eating, she was obliged to prepare a meal every evening for my father as well as a cooked breakfast. My father was a gourmet but was restricted to a low carbohydrate diet because of his diabetes, limiting what could be prepared for him. He had to put up with his wife's regular complaints about the effort of food preparation. Dinner was often eaten in silence. My mother never laughed and seemed unable to respond to my father's real wit. His jokes, she usually took as criticism and was very upset if I laughed at them. They had to be explained as being nothing personal about her and my father would say that she was being over sensitive. He began to fortify himself with gins on getting home from work; these gave him a jolly heartiness with which he began conversations with me. I was usually too embarrassed to think of a reply. Yet despite all this, on social occasions together at cocktail parties, dinner dances or Sundays at the golf club, my parents would be beautifully turned out and show themselves as a bright, lively sociable couple, much as they must have appeared before the war. My mother's dolling up seemed brittle and artificial to me, knowing that all the brightness would be gone the next day.

But I was a visitor to the home as I stayed at boarding school moving from prep to public school. I had a few friends locally but my centre of gravity was the public school and the friends I made there. Fortunately I was fairly academic and caused little anxiety about my progress. When I determined on medicine as a career, it was a source of great pleasure to both parents as they both had doctors in their own families. I always remained distant with my father, answering his questions but never spontaneously telling him anything. The days at home with my mother during holidays could be taken up with me comforting her about her symptoms when she wasn't well or talking about day to day events or her friends when she was better. There was never any depth to these conversations for I was screening out potentially upsetting content and she had cut off from me all her early life. They were exchanges between two part people.

I saw the marriage the way she did - my father being difficult because of his diabetes and inclination to drink too much. Placating him, thus defusing potential altercations when he came home from work, was a regular talking point between us around teatime. I continued to think of her as the put upon party in her difficult times with my father at home and worried about her even when I was away at school. As I got older, I decided that she was 'neurotic' and was irritated that she couldn't enjoy life more.

The royalties from Fred's works made a huge difference to our lives. My father took charge of the tax affairs and, in the days of surtaxes, was always preoccupied by schemes to reduce payments. Despite the taxes, this money meant that they could educate me expensively and we could have holidays away, as well as live comfortably, including hiring a cook at times to remove my mother's worst burden. Occasionally Danny Boy or Roses of Picardy would be sung on the variety shows on television. My mother would always say that it was one of Grand-papa's. It was the only time, unless I probed her for something to talk about when were alone, that Fred and the Weatherlys ever came up.

When I started doing my psychiatry as a medical student, it became clearer to me that my mother was more than a neurotic woman but that she had appeared that because of a persisting agitated depression. I still thought that it started with my father's return and maintained by their unsupportive marriage. But now on discovering about Betty and the year of her death, it dawned on me that the trigger in M\ay 1946 wasn't my father's return or an unhappy marriage but must have been Betty's death some two months earlier.

Normal grieving, is a process, with recognisable stages along the way, that most people who have lost someone close to them undergo and can last up to a year. For that time, theperson shows the symptoms of a depression. Resolution is most likely if the person can display grief and others accept that and are prepared to talk about the death. The process can be prolonged if there is an element of guilt in the bereaved or the process is suppressed. A protracted grief reaction merges into an agitated depression with sadness, tearfulness, anxiety and often many physical symptoms. Grief can be suppressed for many reasons ranging from a coping style of a stiff upper lip to the social necessity of having to carry on as normal, perhaps at work or for the sake of the children.

My mother would have had no one in whom to confide her grief to because of her continued wish for secrecy about Betty and my father's hostility on that subject. But Betty's death may not have been that shocking for her; Betty after all had been out of her life for sixteen years. Her death may have triggered her grief for Fred, her mother or Miriam and a realisation that she had lost everyone in her family that had mattered to her. When each of these important figures died, my mother was in no position to mourn for them. She was busy in America when Fred died, had just married when Ethel died and was separated by the war when Miriam died.

The diagnosis of a delayed grief reaction can be easily missed if consultations concern anxiety and physical symptoms and the patient's loss is not recent. My mother's treatment was for a putative physical illness with attendant anxiety both at Ruthin Castle, which specifically didn't admit psychiatric cases, and in subsequent years in Nottingham. If she hid her grieving and believed her symptoms to have a physical basis, she would have had to encounter a skilled doctor who probed for the typical thoughts of a person still grieving. Today, if patients can be brought to understand that unresolved grief is still causing them problems, then counselling in which the patient is taken through 'guided mourning' to complete the process is effective. Sometimes this has to be accompanied by a course of antidepressant medication to counteract symptoms of depression. My mother never received the latter, though these drugs were then becoming available, nor any psychological help - only sedation which at the best is a temporary palliative.

My parent's marriage was damaged for years after Betty's death through my mother's continued episodes of anxiety, depression dominated by symptoms relating to her eating or bowel function. While my father knew of Betty's death, he probably would not have connected this behaviour to it and must have found the home situation very wearying. The difficulties between my parents, which I had always thought causative of my mother's illness, were probably secondary to it. My mother's relationship with me was also affected because of her need for me to be her 'antidepressant', the son who was doing well, in whom she could feel pride thereby offset an inner world haunted by guilt and sadness. Even when I was grown up and studying medicine, I never knew the cause of her illness, so couldn't help to get her more appropriate treatment.

As my father approached retirement, his diabetes had become more troublesome. Thus he planned to retire as soon as he could at 60 and together my parents planned to settle in the South of France. By 1960, my mother seemed much calmer and my parents' relationship a happier one. I began to get to know my father, as he and I would have dinner together when he came to London, where I was studying, for business. I discovered his expertise in food and wine, something that I was happy to learn and share but which had been wasted on my mother. I relished his teasing sense of humour. As I had learnt bridge, I could now ask him to join me and friends for a game in the flat we shared. I was lucky to have had this brief positive time with him, for he died suddenly of a heart attack at the age of 60 in 1963.

My mother mourned him, but before long decided to leave Nottingham to settle in Malta where her cousin Peggy was now living. She blossomed there in the heat and with the social life. Her symptoms disappeared and, for the first time in my life, I didn't have to worry about her. She found a sense of humour and could join in laughter. She generously entertained my friends and me for dinner when she came to London. We ate out a lot – her dislike of cooking continued. The acid stomach could still rear its head when dissecting a menu to find something to eat that wouldn't upset her. Still anxious about upsetting her, I never challenged this. Thus I was always keen for other people to join us, as she was usually at her best- interested in their background, marriages and children, jobs and friends. Furthermore she would remember all their details for next time. Not surprisingly most found her to be attractive, well dressed, good company and generous.

This happiness continued for several more years after her return to England after eight years in Malta until, following surgery for bowel cancer, her memory began to fail so this period of mutual independence was over. I returned to my responsibility of looking after her. Worsening short-term memory loss made independent living impossible and it became necessary to settle her in a residential home nearby. There, she soon became inseparable from another resident, also with moderate dementia, which she referred to as her sister. I was surprised at this, as my mother's impairment of short-term memory did not make her misidentify or forget whom people are, as can occur with many dementias. I was very pleased that this friendship made her so happy, enabling her to settle in the home and relieve my anxiety over her. Only now, can I see the importance for her of having a sister in her life; a relationship she recreated to sustain her in her old age and frailty. My mother died in 1989 at the age of 82.

CLOSURE - FRED PLAGIARIST AND WOMANISER?

Was Fred Weatherly a plagiarist?

Jess went to her death twenty-five years after Danny Boy's publication believing that Fred had stolen her birthright, the melody of the Londonderry Air that her father had taught her along with other Irish music. While she couldn't claim the melody as hers, she had written words beginning 'O Kerry Boy', as a tribute to her father Dennis from that county, which she had hoped one day to publish. She left the account, written after Fred's death, of a meeting in Fred's drawing room in Bath in 1912 in which she sang the melody to him, while Fred learnt it on the piano by accompanying her. She didn't specify that she sang any words –there were several alternatives in existence then- nor her own. She may have only vocalised the tune. Her complaint was not that Fred stole her words but that her personal contribution to the song was never acknowledged and that, after the success of Danny Boy, she would never get any words of hers published.

Fred's account failed to acknowledge any personal contact with Jess, when he wrote that a sister-in-law in America sent the melody to him. Both his and her accounts do though share two statements, which were that Fred had never come across the tune until he received or heard it and that he immediately described it as one of the most beautiful melodies that he had ever heard.

There is evident conflict between these accounts. One way of resolving it would be to dismiss Jess as a fantasist. Jess was writing hers in 1930 as part of a long diatribe against Fred. She was hurting as, by now, Eddie and she were on the bread line and dependant on what money would be sent to them from England. Fred's death had meant their allowance had dried up so that Eddie and she had to turn without much hope to Miriam for help. On the day she wrote, Jess was just back from Ouray and had seen a new version of the sheet music of Danny Boy on sale, which she couldn't afford to buy. She turned to 'Piano and Gown' and read Fred's account again saying that he was sent the music. She was angry that she was now in the position of desperate supplicant when she was due some part of the royalties now going to Miriam. The melody of the Londonderry Air was one that she identified with her father, which gave her a strong personal attachment to it. Rather than facing that she had let go of something precious and with it, her chance of commemorating her father, was it easier to comfort herself with an image of singing to Fred with her father in mind and thus believing that Danny Boy was partly from her and for her father? If she made that step, then she could believe that Fred owed her something and that she or Eddie should have been recognised in the will. Better again thinking that, than facing a reality that she and Eddie were too optimistic in expecting to be left money by Fred, who had recently remarried before his death and was devoted to his new wife.

In favour of Jess's exaggerating her claim to Danny Boy and to some part of the royalties is that neither she nor Eddie confronted Fred directly on the subject. The couple accepted money from Maude and, later from Fred, an income until his death. Both remarked that Fred never made any connection between these payments and Danny Boy, but over the years they didn't bring that subject up in letters as it might have implied that they didn't trust him. They preferred not to risk upsetting Fred and thus endanger the money that they were getting. But in my view, if Jess had long felt that Fred had stolen her father's song and never acknowledged her contribution, which is what she was writing in 1930, it would have been in her character for moral indignation to override caution and to let Fred know what she thought. Instead she accepted the payments and handouts that Fred never linked to Danny Boy. The 1930 story could thus be her fabrication built out of a long grievance about Fred when his will had left them high and dry. If she only did what Fred wrote, namely send sheet music across to England, then she would have no claim on the song and not be owed anything by Fred because of it.

There is evidence to suggest that Jess was recalling a true event. I was told in Ouray that someone had read a piece from the 1920s about her in the local paper, in which she made the same claim of authorship of Danny Boy as she wrote in 1930. I have been unable to locate this article. If true, then her story was one with which she had gone public some years earlier; it wasn't something that she imagined when feeling angry about Fred's will. She was being consistent. Then there are some circumstantial facts to support Jess. The transatlantic passengers' register of the period showed them on a boat to England in 191, returning early 1913. Fred's drawing room did contain his piano in front of the bay window and he himself wrote that he would accompany singers on it. But most important for me, having read plenty that Jess wrote, is that she was honest in her account of things, including her own failings. Her language could be highly coloured and her imagery affected by her Catholic upbringing, her views of Eddie were distorted by her passion for him, but she never covered up the depressing reality of their lives with any other wishful stories.

If we accept that Jess was recounting what happened in Bath in1912, then Fred's account is untrue. He wrote that 'a sister-in-law sent me the Londonderry Air with a suggestion that he set some words to it'. What does it mean by 'sending the Londonderry Air'? In the days before recordings were commercially available, Jess would have to have sent sheet music. A theory doing the rounds, since Jess came into the picture through the 1997 broadcast, is that she could have annotated the tune as she heard it played by Irish migrants, of which there were many, working the mines around Ouray. But there is no evidence that she had the musical training to do this. Jess's story of the meeting in Bath with its conversational details seems more convincing than Fred's summary statement. But the telling fact is that Jess and Eddie were in England when they were supposed to be sending the music from America.

Fred when writing his memoirs in 1925 did two things, He called Jess 'a sister-in-law' when referring to her by name and he omitted any personal contact between them over the music. His memory wasn't at fault. 'Piano and Gown' is full of details of people and events that he recalled since his childhood, so it's extremely unlikely he would have forgotten her singing to him only thirteen years earlier. He deliberately suppressed any personal musical contribution by her to the song and anonymised her. 'A' sister-in-law suggests that he had several in America. As Luke never married and Herbert had had no contact with his wife for years, it was a deliberate snub to leave Jess out when writing the book. He did this despite corresponding with Eddie and Jess up to and after publication of 'Piano and Gown'. As Jess wrote, it was a cruel thing that he did.

Some successful people find it hard to acknowledge the help of others. Jess after all did not compose the Londonderry Air; she brought it to his attention - she was a messenger, and writing that she sent the music rather than interpreted it for him makes it easier for him to ignore her part. Fred, like everyone then, was class conscious. Though Jess was his brother Eddie's wife, she was from a completely different drawer to the Weatherly family – a poor Irish-American background and not well educated - spelling mistakes are noticeable in her writings. It could be that he didn't believe that someone such as her should expect public acknowledgement for a Fred Weatherly song. A kinder possibility is that he didn't deliberately cut her out because of vanity or snobbishness, but that it was carelessness and a cover up. By 1913 when the song was published, Eddie and Jess were back in the States. At that stage, Fred wouldn't have known that Danny Boy was going to be such a best seller and it may not have seemed important to have her name recognised alongside his in what, publishing yet another song, was for him a routine event. When the song was proving so popular and therefore profitable, he may have had some conscience about this omission. It was around 1916 that he sent £500 and a few years later started the allowance of £10 per month to Eddie, the only one of his brother to be so helped. He made no connection between this money and Danny Boy, but he could have seen it himself as compensation. If he admitted a role for Jess in the song once it was known worldwide, she could have demanded that that he go to the publisher to get her name put on the song sheets and arrange for her to have a share of the royalties. Fred would have found that very embarrassing. Hence his silence on the subject and, fortunately for him, Eddie and Jess chose not to confront him, allowing his strategy to succeed.

Fred didn't plagiarise her verses. Those of Danny Boy do not resemble at all those written by Jess, but the title 'Oh Danny Boy' does seem derivative of 'Oh Kerry Boy' . There's no reason to doubt Fred's account of modifying his own 1910 words to fit the melody when he heard it. Unless earlier versions come to light showing how he changed the verses, we can't know how much the final version of Danny Boy was influenced by his grief at the death of his son and then by hearing Jess sing to him. Jess must have had an influence on the final version of the song. She interpreted that melody for him as an Irishwoman full of feeling for her family's country' s folk tradition and remembering her dead father as she did so. She would transmit something through her singing that Fred captured, thus enabling someone who had never been to Ireland to create such an' Irish' song. Here is an explanation for that mystery. An Irish American lady brought up with sounds of Irish folk music, mourning her father, was his regrettably unacknowledged muse. The Irish American community as well as loving the song can now know that Danny Boy wasn't just a another song churned out by a successful English songwriter but that one of their own gave it its special resonance.

Fred's relationships with women – could he be called a womaniser?

Fred has for me until now been the old man of the photographs of his late years, very much the grandfather figure. I imagined a life of comfort, order and propriety as befitted a lawyer of the period. My mother transmitted this view to me. So tracing his life from childhood has been an eye-opener. My account concentrates on his personality development and behaviour as family man. I have touched only on his renown in the world of the ballad and later in life as a lawyer. As an outsider to the former, it is hard not to be impressed by Fred's innate ability to turn out myriads of verses, having so many set to music by distinguished composers and published. Included are two or three that can be listed among the best known songs of all time. I hope he will merit a proper biography one day, written by someone with an understanding of the world of late nineteenth and early twentieth century song so that Fred's contribution can be put into its context.

Fred recognised as he wrote his memoirs the two drives inside him - for song writing associated with an appetite for the arts in general and theatre in particular and for the law, bringing with it the intellectual challenge of being a defence counsel but also membership of the establishment. They can be seen as the mother side and father side of him. He was fortunate that at home as a child he had license to express and develop his interest in the arts and verse writing through the example of his mother and the patient, Owen Cole. Otherwise, growing up with his father, a man of duty and hard work, he might have felt it necessary to suppress them in favour of a serious career from school onwards. But the mother/arts side of him was allowed precedence, enabling him at Oxford to mix with people of whom his father would have disapproved. His song-writing career blossomed and for a young man he earned well and his published volumes gained him recognition. Tutoring took second place and became a chore.

Then at 39, he suddenly decides he had better start at the Bar if he was ever to make any thing of it. Thirty-nine was and is late to do this. The other part of him, the father in him that had been dormant, started to influence his thinking. When writing his memoirs later, he dated his interest in the law from his time at school in Hereford but it was never mentioned when describing his life over the next twenty years. His father was of course still much alive and may have in reality repeatedly put to Fred that he was frittering his life away in Oxford but as likely is that Fred had internalised his father's attitude towards a career and this change was in response to internal disquiet. During the years in London, he juggled the demands of his pupillage and commitments to writing for the musical world and its concomitant social life. In his memoirs he tells the reader, as though to fend off criticism, that song-writing could fit round the timetable of his legal career. What may have pushed him further towards the law was his failure to make it in the world of serious music; he found the criticisms of his libretti translations wounding. He must have felt that he was doomed to turning out popular songs and that didn't satisfy his ambition. Many, knowing that they could make a comfortable living from such an innate ability, would be content with that. But Fred was driven to start a new career.

After London, being a lawyer was the dominant role in his life. He seemed to become lawyerly in his dealings with others – judgemental and pernickety, like a headmaster at times as my mother said. In his memoirs it is his legal cases that he describes in detail. It wasn't until old age that he relished again his song writing and the royalties from them. The public paid to listen to his lectures and recitals of his songs. Then came the jubilee dinners offered by colleagues in the music publishing business, the broadcasts and the appellation of Grand Old Man of Song. He now accepted that his talent was to please the ordinary person playing on a tin trumpet, as he called it, to an audience of millions rather than be part of the musical establishment. In old age, he became a King's Counsel, an accolade from the establishment for his career at the Bar, so he knew that both parts of him were valued; any conflict in him was over. His obituaries pick up on his contentedness as an old man.

This tension within between his two career drives is not what makes Fred Weatherly's life so interesting. Relationships with women were vital to him. He had three long ones with very different types without a break between them and his partners were devoted to him. He must have had something. I have always been impressed by that initial exclamation by my mother on coming across a photo – 'Oh the darling man'.

He idealised his mother, as did all his brothers. He kept her in his memory as his inspiration for his creative activity and her goodness was such for him that she was the vehicle through which he perceived the apparition of Christ. The marriage to an older, quiet, serious and dutiful woman when just down from Oxford, may have been an attempt to recreate her. She was the sort of wife that his father would understand, able to run a home, be a hostess, bring up children but not challenge his authority. Maybe he even found her for Fred – the daughter of a surgeon in a neighbouring village or Fred had decided rather prosaically that, as he was going to set himself up tutoring, he needed a wife who could support him in that. Minnie fulfilled this role, producing three children as well during the Oxford years. In the memoirs, Minnie is recalled for her devotion and her housekeeping abilities but not given a name.

But it was during these Oxford years that he wrote many songs with young French girls as the subject. For example, there is little Yvette, which has as its refrain:

'Little Yvette, I'm thinking of you; afar by the silver sea

Just as of old I'm dreaming of you and the kiss you gave to me

Little Yvette I'm longing for you with love that will never wane

Oh flower of my heart; I' m coming to you to make you my own again'.

He must have fantasised about beautiful young women as an escape from the sober life with his wife. The short story of the Commemoration Ball that I quoted in which his wife was invalided out and he, for a while, finding a lost love also gives this game away. Minnie Weatherly didn't still his romantic longings. The emotional gap between him and Minnie must have widened in London, as Fred enjoyed a social life on the town while Minnie stayed at home. He had plenty of opportunities to pursue glamorous young women, intelligent and independent as well, so could move from fantasy to reality. Maybe it was about this period in his life that Herbert describes Fred as sowing 'so many seeds in his life that bad crops must come out'. Herbert implied several times that Fred was sexually very active and easily charmed.

By the time the couple moved to Clifton, the marriage was over. Fred was aware that Minnie's depression was a response to the loss of his affection but nevertheless it enabled him to separate and set her up in another place for health reasons. He had met a new partner, the sophisticated, wealthy and attractive Maude, who had already left her husband – a much more interesting prospect than Minnie now. By bringing Maude to live with him as Mrs Weatherly when moving to Bath from Bristol, he stepped outside the normal rules. To some extent, he got away with it because Minnie was ill and anyway an unassertive character, even feeble as described to me. Perhaps if she had fought her corner for the marriage or demanded a divorce, Fred would have found it harder to leave her and might have carried on an affair with Maude discreetly as was the custom. The cost of this upheaval was loss of contact with his son and distance between him and his daughters, who remained close to their mother. Further, his family helped ,as they must have preferred the fiction of Maude as Mrs Weatherly in Bath, only known to be untrue to a few, to their father living openly with a Mrs Francfort. What suggests that it wasn't Minnie's illness that caused the separation, but that the marriage was over, is that Fred made no provision for her to return to the home should she get better. Maude took over her role and Minnie was not mentioned. The granddaughters thus never knew Minnie, Maude was the de facto grandmother. One outcome of the separation was that Muriel, Fred's elder daughter, must have seen where her mother's meekness got her and grew into a dominating woman.

Fred was happy with Maude who is described by all as charming. Today he would not be seen as doing anything exceptional in starting a new relationship; his children were grown up and he made financial provision for the wife he was leaving. Both Fred and Maude would get divorced and marry each other. Even if Minnie and Alfred Francfort were unwilling, today the divorces would be granted after a passage of time. There would be no great scandal. One hundred years ago, both their reputations would have been publicly shattered by an acrimonious divorce. But Minnie did not cooperate in a divorce; she was devout and would always be Fred's wife. She referred right to the end of her life to Fred as her dear husband, keeping her dignity, in the style of Katharine of Aragon, by not relinquishing her status as his wife. Anyone can understand Fred seeking happiness with Maude to whom he was now much better matched, but there is something heartless in the way that the faithful Minnie was put permanently out of his way.

He demonstrated heartlessness too in his dealings with his daughter- in-law Ethel. He regarded her as of the wrong social class and thus decided that she was not able to handle her affairs or bring up the children in the way he would like. This gave him the right, as he saw it, to take over the upbringing of her children and, instead of supporting her, insist that she worked to keep herself, something that he wouldn't have done if she were regarded as a social equal. When Herbert was setting up his fox farm in New York, Fred decided that Ethel could be 'shipped off 'there, once again out of the way. He took charge of her financial affairs, so that he administered her grandfather's legacy. Ethel like Minnie was not a fighter. Depressed after her husband's death, with no money of her own to make alternative plans for herself and children, she had little option than to comply. I think there was specific antipathy from Fred to her, maybe because he blamed her for his son's death, maybe her voice or mannerisms were 'wrong' and irritated him.

There was no evidence that she was an unfit mother, so Fred's removal of her children was a heartless act towards her and, in the light of today's knowledge, damaging for the children. If Herbert is to be believed, he and Maude wanted to give the girls a good life, better than Ethel could have done, but they also wanted to enhance their image in Bath of a couple doing good by taking in his near destitute grandchildren. Ethel would have to be absent for that to succeed or people could ask why the children weren't with their mother –hence her exile. Antipathy to Ethel lasted through to 1925 when Ethel returned from America to join her daughters, as shown by Fred offering no welcome and telling her that she would have to accommodate herself in Bath. Only at the very end of his life did he relent with a last codicil to his will, leaving her a small, personal legacy. The same dismissive attitude to the rights of a woman he regarded as a social inferior applied to Ethel as to Jess after the Danny Boy encounter.

Fred was happy with Maude, so far as one can tell from what his brothers wrote; a state that survived the irregularity and deception required in their relationship. I believe that this was more than because of the usefulness of her wealth at an awkward financial time in Fred's life and the assets that she transferred to him. It's frustrating not to have a photograph, for, without it, it's hard to develop a sense of Maude. Fred's family liked her as shown by their visits to them as a couple.

Unfortunately, Maude's illness gradually changed her from being his independent partner to a frail dependant, less able to give Fred the companionship he needed from women. Fred was anxious and upset about her decline but nevertheless his eyes turned to the companion /helper, Miriam. Herbert was sure that Miriam ensnared Fred with a view to getting the old man's wealth. Certainly Miriam's quiet skills of listening, soothing and helping would be very appealing to a stressed old man. It seems that they did start an affair before Maude died and married pretty soon afterwards, Miriam continuing to live in the house with him in the interim. This time, Miriam's background didn't seem to matter – the daughter of a Welsh stationmaster, but her musical training must have helped overcome that to enable her to pass comfortably in Fred's social circle. That this affair was going on around Maude's sick bed outraged Herbert, but maybe Maude knew and encouraged them, happy to think that Fred would be looked after when she was dead. She did make Miriam her executor. From photographs of them together, and from what he wrote, Miriam's company made Fred extremely happy, particularly if, as Herbert hints, there was an active physical relationship too. Marriage to Miriam made him socially respectable again so that must have made life with her even more pleasant.

His preoccupation with attractive women and interest in possible sexual activity never left him. In old age, perhaps a bit disinhibited, he was seen as an old goat, telling risqué jokes and making overtures to young women. Muriel kept her children and grandchildren away from him, for fear of what he might say. However Fred in his remark about love conquering all seemed to recognise that his irregular but happy life with his women and his pleasant fantasies about them were more important to him than honours and respectability. He knew that he had stepped out of line but it was worth it.

15. CLOSURE - MENTAL ILLNESS, THE FAMILY SECRET

As I researched the Weatherly family, the numbers who were reported to have suffered a mental illness, four of which I have described earlier, struck me. Is there a gene at work? There is a possibility that the depressions evident in my mother and aunt were part of an inheritance from their grandmother Minnie, in which case it was a Hardwick inheritance. Christine, Fred's younger daughter was also described to me as depressed as she got older – if so, part of the same tree. What is handed down is a predisposition to depression which becomes manifest in conjunction with adverse external events or stresses. The genes underlying this predisposition are likely to be several, the more of which are inherited, the more strong the predisposition or likelihood of reacting that way. The fact that the depressions I have described were different in their form and age of onset and in how understandable they were in the context of current circumstances- yes (Minnie and my mother) or no (Betty) - doesn't rule out an inherited component. However, other routes into depression are also illustrated; for Jess and Eddie it was physical illness and the privations of their life including malnutrition; for Minnie, Jess and Marjory loss and grief.

At the same time, there seems to be an unusual number of doctors or health professionals in the family. Among the 83 members of the family descending from and including Fred's sibship, I have discovered 5 general physicians,1 surgeon, 4 psychiatrists, 1 psychotherapist and 2 nurses. The family has remained pretty middle class over the generations, so medicine along with law, accountancy etc would be considered a suitable career option. Doctoring runs in families, as children will model themselves on relatives. Most doctors encourage their younger relatives and offer advice on medical school and can arrange work experience in a hospital for someone trying to make up their mind. All the general doctors and the surgeon shown in the list were descendants of Arthur Weatherly, through three generations, suggesting a strong family tradition. Three psychiatrists and a psychotherapist seem noteworthy however. They were/are from different branches of the family and didn't know of each other's existence until now. None seemed influenced by having Lionel Weatherly as antecedent - his own daughters carried on running nursing homes for the mentally ill, but none became doctors. The choice of psychiatry was not following a tradition, as the parents of the four were not doctors or involved in health care. A possibility is that it relates to the experience of mental illness in the family.

My mother and her secrets.

All parents will keep part of their lives secret from their children. Past affairs, for example, are not relevant to their child's future. I think my mother did more than keep some personal peccadilloes secret. She withheld a huge amount of information about herself that her husband should have known when marrying her and she told lies in order to do so. When I was older, I became bored and frustrated in conversations with her, which always were about the same rather superficial things. I realised that there wasn't much emotional matter, save her anxieties about her health and at times my welfare. She never discussed deaths, sadness or pain at losses whether of my father or anyone else. Of course I had no idea, and I doubt my father did either, that her early life was characterised by so much emotional pain, that she had decided to amputate her past from her life after marriage. Filling her thinking time and conversation with others with chatter about day-to-day events and interest in others must have been part of that strategy. Awkward questions about herself could be avoided. I have now followed the events that she had to cope with earlier in her life and have an understanding as to why she wanted to leave them behind.

From early in life, she wanted for emotional security. She lost her father when she was three and after a year or so living with her mother and aunt, she and Betty were uprooted and moved to Bath. Then she effectively lost her mother who went to London, presumably seeing her children infrequently because she was not made welcome at her grandfather's house. Then Ethel was sent to America staying for six or seven years, which must have effectively removed her out of the existence of a small child. Loss of a parent in childhood is a known risk factor for later depression. Children do adjust to a parents' death. Young children need stable adult figures to whom to attach and will find someone else to replace a dead parent. Ethel though wasn't dead. She was there, but not there for her children. My mother later attached to Fred and Maude and was well looked after by them. But without adequate explanation about her mother's absence, which Fred would be unlikely to have given her, Ethel's disappearance would be bewildering and damaging to my mother developing a core sense of her worth. 'I loved my mother but she's gone – was it my fault? Will people you love always abandon you? Better not trust people who claim to love you?' Both these beliefs lead to an insecure attachment style which makes it difficult to form intimate relationships later in life.

While adjusting to life without Ethel, my mother would also have had to contend with her sister. Betty was the dominant one. Because of her 'wild behaviour' but also because of her attractiveness, Betty must have received more adult attention than my mother. In addition, Betty, despite educational difficulties, could sing and play the piano, presumably talents appreciated by Fred. My mother couldn't do either. She was practical and sporty, good at tennis and athletics, if anything. It must have been galling for her that Betty was sent off on a cultural trip to Italy with Fred's friends, while my mother was put to work at her aunt's house in order to study.

It would have seemed quite appropriate to Fred and Maude to arrange for my mother, and presumably Betty, to spend time at their aunts with their first cousins of the same sort of age. She told me, as an explanation as to why she never saw her first cousins, of a Christmas when her aunt Muriel handed out presents - jewellery for her daughters and a sewing box for my mother with the words, 'You are always going to have to work for a living'. There was still anger in her voice when recounting that to me even forty years later. If she didn't like it there, it would have been impossible to tell Fred about it or to refuse to go, given that they were also his family. She would often get embarrassingly indignant if she felt ignored or pushed aside. Queue barging would enrage; shop assistants who didn't give her undivided attention would be ticked off. This over-reaction perhaps dated from this childhood experience of feeling in the background. But there are usually two sides of the story. My mother was probably already sensitive and anxious and must have had difficulty in fitting with a boisterous group of cousins - the more she showed any upset with them, the more she was likely to be disparaged.

Her lifelong eating problems developed during this childhood. These were complaints of a small appetite, easily feeling bloated and being fussy about foods to eat. Discomfort with food persisted all her life and was eventually, in her mind, blamed on an acid stomach. Eating problems can be the characteristic response of the conscientious, good child (usually a girl) who is uncomplaining in the background while much more attention is given to a more assertive sibling. Weight loss gets the adults' attention. I think my mother was showing her stress.

The arrival of Ethel in 1925 must have been a godsend; it was as a rescue from Muriel's household. Fred and Miriam were by now happily married and wanted to be free of the girls, so a return to their house was not going to be welcome. I can't help but think that my mother must have been excited to leave Bath behind and set off for a new life in America. She was carrying baggage from her childhood. Despite this, she found a happy time in Richmond - new friends, a job and dance lessons.

I still think of my mother as an only child and have to remember that Betty was there too and would have featured prominently in my mother and Ethel's daily concerns. Ethel sounded worried about Betty even before her return to England in 1925. By then, now aged 19, Betty's over activity, impulsiveness and childishness would make her noticeable socially and thus constitute a problem for her mother and sister. If Ethel and she had come to some modus vivendi in

Richmond, it would have been shattered when Betty became psychotic. It must have been terrifying to see her become violent and angry with irrational ideas, out of reach of their normal way of dealing with her. The admission ward in Westbrook Hospital gave them their first view of the disturbed en masse. The ward would have been very noisy, patients in restraint shouting to be released, others wandering around shouting in response to their hallucinations. No wonder Ethel responded to Herbert's suggestion that Betty would be better off elsewhere. However her readmission a week later in an even more disturbed state, threatening to kill both Ethel and my mother, showed them how bad it was. Soon they knew that their attempt at a new life in America was over. My mother must have been resentful, even if, as dutiful daughter, she couldn't ever show that to her mother.

The journey home exposed my mother to many of the stigma of being associated with someone with a severe mental illness. There was the attitude of Miriam and Ricketts - it is Ethel's fault for not controlling her; they were paying too much money on care. My mother would be well aware that the illness was nothing to do with Ethel and that caring for someone so disturbed is impossible without cost. But, I suspect it was the journey home that was shaming for her. Betty, probably in restraint being escorted by two nurses, accompanied them on the boat. People would stare and turn away or ask loudly why someone like her had to travel with them - a certain amount of pity, a lot of embarrassment. Then the dining room incident would have been mortifying. Thinking Betty out of the way in her cabin, my mother would have dressed to go into dinner with her mother, presenting a smart and respectable appearance. Betty burst in to shatter that image and cause consternation in the dining room.

Insane people were regarded as frightening, dangerous, to be locked up. Families did not mention any such illness amongst them. It would be a source of malevolent gossip. Lionel's humanitarian, domestic care was not widespread and only concerned what he called early cases and not people as disturbed as Betty. My mother had now experienced insanity at first hand and that must have been enough for her. She did not have the temperament to be a pioneer for the rights of the mentally ill, rather she would have been afraid of being tarred by association with Betty with consequent social rejection. In the background was the treatment of her grandmother, Minnie, who was kept out of sight. When Betty was safely placed in an institution, I believe my mother chose to live her life without further involvement with her.

As a relationship with my father developed, she must have been afraid that he or his family might find out about Betty. The Mann family were generally warm and tolerant but exuded middle class respectability. Silence on the subject was arranged with any family and friends who were likely to come into contact with my father. There was a short interval after the wedding in 1938 and the upheaval of the war, then pregnancy. The only lie that she would have to put out was that she was an only child if any of her new friends asked if she had brothers or sisters. The deaths of Ethel and then Miriam made this denial harder as she became next of kin for Betty and received Fred's royalties. The former would mean that the staff of Camberwell House would want to know where my mother lived and could theoretically contact her at any time. The latter could excite interest in Fred and the Weatherlys in anyone she told about receiving them.

My arrival must have reinforced her determination to keep Betty out of the family. She would be well aware of the idea of mental illness running in families and therefore she could pass it on to me. 'If I didn't know about it, then it wouldn't happen to me'- a mantra to protect me? Maybe it was after Betty's death, when very overwrought, that she tore out Betty's photographs. That they were roughly torn out rather than cut out of the album indicates some emotion at the time of doing it. It was a final cleansing of the mad sister.

She had to keep her guard up with me as I asked her about her family. She followed a rule of keeping her evasions simple - I don't know, I can't remember, it's a long time ago. I never challenged her, even though I knew that Fred brought her up and it was thus inconceivable that she didn't know the names of his brothers and sisters. The strength of her defence was shown when, having so diligently hidden her experience of mental illness from me, she had to take on board my career choice and that I was training in Camberwell, where Betty had died some twenty years earlier. I mentioned once the problems about being sent to boarding school at 5. She immediately burst into tears and said it wasn't her fault. I never pursued that topic. My mother had done what she thought best to protect me from her family taint, as she saw it. My well-being and success were proof that she had succeeded. The cost to her in anxiety was substantial, having to live a lie, bottle up her own emotions and never let slip much about her own past. It was a feat of will and determination.

I was certainly wrong to blame my father for what happened to me and realise that he was a victim of the circumstances as well. My mother found her own way to survive her emotionally deprived and disrupted upbringing, of the horror watching her sister becoming insane and determined, to the detriment of her marriage, that it was her duty to shield me at all costs. It was courageous. Today people are freer to be open about such things. She must never have believed that she could be. At a time of losses and stresses, depression overwhelmed her. My 'abandonment' in a boarding school resulted. It wasn't her fault any more than my father's. A decision had to be made about me - it wasn't malevolent. I understand that now.

Thus I have gained much through this quest. It was a search for the story behind Danny Boy. I have discovered a new story, but there are many other stories about this very interesting family of which I now can feel a part. I have also found a piece of my own story and with that a greater sense of closeness to my parents as I discover what they were about. Without Danny Boy, it wouldn't have happened.

Made in the USA
San Bernardino, CA
09 April 2014